STAR WARS™
BATTLES
THAT CHANGED THE
GALAXY

  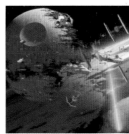 

STAR WARS
BATTLES
THAT CHANGED THE
GALAXY

Written by
JASON FRY, COLE HORTON,
CHRIS KEMPSHALL, and AMY RATCLIFFE

DK

Contents

Foreword

The battles in *Star Wars* are some of the most iconic in film history, from the rebels' brave attack on the first Death Star, to the elephantine AT-ATs marching across the snow plains of Hoth, to the frenzied Battle of Starkiller Base, to the visually stunning Battle of Crait, the "wars" part of *Star Wars* has always filled fans with a jaw-dropping sense of awe. The stakes for each battle are enormously high, the situations complicated, and the battles themselves leave a lasting impression, both within a galaxy far, far away, and in the real world.

As a visual effects supervisor, I've been fortunate enough to have helped craft some of these battles. When ILM created the opening sequence of *Revenge of the Sith*, the Battle of Coruscant, the fate of the galaxy was on the line—it was epic in scope and yet very personal. While the audience needed to experience the scale of the battle with an intensity that we hadn't yet seen in *Star Wars*, their attention needed to be squarely centered on Obi-Wan and Anakin. That same balance can also be seen in the Battle of Starkiller Base from *The Force Awakens*. The underdog band of Resistance starships must stop a planet-destroying superweapon, but we must counter that with the heroes' lives on the line—including Poe Dameron's—so that the audience sees the spectacle of the battle alongside the very personal, human story. Crafting the visual effects takes an army, and the completion of each sequence is our own internal battle—a battle against time. We bring technology and artistry to bear

as we battle against our own thoughts and concepts that we leverage to create sequences that resonate in the imaginations of our fans around the world. And as we craft each blaster bolt, roaring TIE fighter, plume of smoke, and explosion, we work through each sequence in minute detail.

And that's the beauty of the book you hold before you—it shows the scale and scope of each battle, both from within the films and beyond, encompassing Lucasfilm animation, publishing, and games. It provides details that fans may have missed the first time around, and rounds up every major battle from a chronological standpoint. It's an objective and comprehensive look at the "wars" that have made-up the Skywalker saga.

So prepare yourselves to experience the battles of *Star Wars* in an entirely new way—a way that will allow you to relive classic battles yet see them in an entirely new light at the same time.

Enjoy the book, and may the Force be with you!

Roger Guyett

Roger Guyett
Visual Effect Supervisor, ILM

Introduction

After centuries of relative peace and prosperity, recent galactic history has been marked by widespread and destructive conflicts. The Galactic Republic had stood for a millennium and yet, in a little over 50 years, three major wars consumed much of the galaxy. In their wake they left toppled regimes and countless devastated worlds. This volume, compiled by some of the finest historians of our time, seeks to explain the nature of these conflicts to present and future generations of the galaxy.

Battles of the Republic

At the time, few could comprehend the wide-ranging implications of the conflict that eventually destroyed the Galactic Republic, or recognize the cynical nature of its orchestration. We know now that Darth Sidious, in the guise of Supreme Chancellor Palpatine, and his apprentice Count Dooku had planned the Clone Wars in tandem to seize power and destroy the Jedi Order. But these two figures only manipulated the grievances that caused this conflict; they did not create them. The bureaucracy and corruption of the Galactic Republic marked a government that was already degrading rapidly. The emergence of the Separatists split the galaxy in two, and the scale and spread of the Clone Wars was unlike anything the galaxy had seen in centuries. Worlds were ravaged, factions were radicalized, and a military industrial complex was created by the

Galactic Republic that would endure for decades. By the conflict's sudden and shocking end, many of the cornerstones of galactic society were gone. The Jedi Order was exterminated, and the Republic was reorganized by Palpatine into the Galactic Empire.

Sparks of Rebellion

The emergence of the Galactic Empire saw the galaxy enter a new era of totalitarianism and military expansion. Whereas the Galactic Republic had expanded slowly over time as new worlds and systems sought to join peacefully, the Empire ruthlessly expanded its borders by conquest and annexation. Emperor Palpatine had envisioned a regime that would last for a thousand years and draw all star systems under its control. Worlds that fell to the Empire had their natural resources and assets stripped to feed the ever-growing Imperial war machine. Star Destroyers and TIE fighters became ubiquitous across the galaxy while, in secret, the Empire pushed forward with the construction of the Death Star battle station that would finally crush all resistance. However, the more the Empire exerted its control, the more a spirit of rebellion began to stir. The earliest actions undertaken by what would become the Rebel Alliance ranged from minor acts of resistance to the wider organization of isolated cells designed to disrupt Imperial activity. Whereas the Clone Wars had been marked by pitched battles both in space and on planetary surfaces by technologically advanced

opponents, the first actions undertaken by the Rebel Alliance were notable for their guerrilla tactics and the Alliance's continued unwillingness to engage in open war against the Empire. This burgeoning asymmetric conflict spread across the Outer Rim and undermined the Empire's attempts to maintain rule simply through the use of fear and force. All-out warfare became inevitable.

Galactic Civil War
If the Clone Wars split the galaxy between rival systems, then the Galactic Civil War divided families. Those loyal to the Empire were prepared to turn a blind eye to its worst military atrocities, such as the destruction of Alderaan, in favor of a society that seemed safe and secure. Supporters of the Rebel Alliance revolted against a regime that oppressed and enslaved whole worlds, and rallied in support of a return to the Republic. Set in opposition, these two ideologies could not suffer each other to exist. The Empire possessed all of the technological and military advantages over the Rebel Alliance save for the latter's dispersed command style and ability to operate in secret. Battles spread across key spacelanes and ranged from isolated systems such as Hoth to the surface of key manufacturing bases such as Sullust. The Galactic Civil War was an escalating conflict. With every victory the Rebel Alliance utilized propaganda to broadcast the limits of Imperial rule. In response, the Empire stepped up their

oppression of dissent and their military output. Front lines such as had existed in the Clone Wars became a relative thing of the past. The rebels used their flexibility to strike in as many places as possible. Any world could conceivably shelter a rebel cell or be selected as a viable target for a rebel assault. As a result, the Empire sought to crush them all. Given the stakes for both sides, the outcome of this conflict could only ever have been the defeat and decapitation of one command structure or another. The rebel victory at Endor resulted in the toppling of the most militaristic and powerful regime the galaxy had ever seen. Though the war continued, the New Republic's ultimate victory was no longer in question; in the aftermath of the Battle of Jakku and the Imperial surrender, many hoped that the age of galactic-scale warfare was finally at an end.

First Order-Resistance War
The study of military history can be difficult in close proximity to the events themselves. The resurgence of Imperial ideology through the First Order now appears to have been an obvious threat, but the New Republic either did not recognize it or was unwilling to confront it. Their reluctance cost them dearly. The destruction of the New Republic and the resulting First Order-Resistance war pitched the galaxy back into another destructive conflict orchestrated by Palpatine. The lessons outlined within this volume may help the galaxy avoid another.

BATTLES OF THE REPUBLIC

- **NABOO**
  Droid Invasion

- **1ST GEONOSIS**
  Dawn of the Clone Wars

- **CHRISTOPHSIS**
  Breaking the Blockade

- **TETH**
  Clifftop Conflict

- **RYLOTH**
  Freedom-Fighter
  Collaboration

- ***MALEVOLENCE*** **CAMPAIGN**
  Hunting the Fleet Killer

- **RISHI MOON**
  Sounding the All-Clear

- **BOTHAWUI**
  Holding the Line

- **QUELL**
  Sky Battle

- **1ST FELUCIA**
  Fighting in Fungus

- **MALASTARE**
  Shadow of the Bomb

- **2ND GEONOSIS**
  Return to the Hive

- **KAMINO**
  Attack on the Clones

- **LOLA SAYU**
  Rescue Operation

- **2ND FELUCIA**
  Triple Threat

- **MON CALA**
  Water War

- **UMBARA**
  Night Battle

- **DATHOMIR**
  Massacre of the
  Nightsisters

- **ONDERON**
  Guerrilla Warfare

- **ANAXES**
  Desperate Counterstrike

- **MANDALORE**
  Uncivil War

- **CORUSCANT**
  Attack on the Capital

- **KASHYYYK**
  Twilight of the Wookiees

- **UTAPAU**
  Downfall of
  General Grievous

- **MYGEETO**
  Long-Sought Prize

- **SALEUCAMI**
  Death on the Rim

- **CATO NEIMOIDIA**
  Battle Interrupted

- **3RD FELUCIA**
  Outer Rim Siege

CHAPTER 1

Battles of the Republic: Introduction

GALAXY MAP

Tides of War While early battles were concentrated in the galaxy's outlying regions, the war spread across the galaxy and Core-Worlders had their confidence shaken by Separatist attacks on systems as central as Coruscant. Many of its final battles played out in the same region in which it had started, the Outer Rim.

KEY
1 Naboo
2 Geonosis
3 Christophsis
4 Teth
5 Ryloth
6 *Malevolence* Campaign
7 Rishi Moon
8 Bothawui
9 Quell
10 1st Felucia
11 Malastare
12 2nd Geonosis
13 Kamino
14 Lola Sayu
15 2nd Felucia
16 Mon Cala
17 Umbara
18 Dathomir
19 Onderon
20 Anaxes
21 Mandalore
22 Coruscant
23 Kashyyyk
24 Utapau
25 Mygeeto
26 Saleucami
27 Cato Neimoidia
28 3rd Felucia

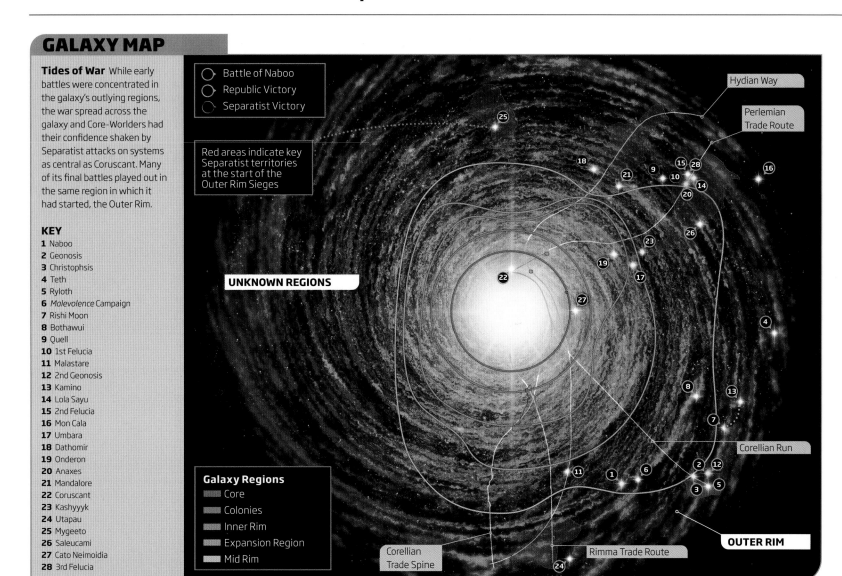

Battle of Naboo
Republic Victory
Separatist Victory

Red areas indicate key Separatist territories at the start of the Outer Rim Sieges

Hydian Way
Perlemian Trade Route
UNKNOWN REGIONS
Corellian Run
OUTER RIM
Corellian Trade Spine
Rimma Trade Route

Galaxy Regions
- Core
- Colonies
- Inner Rim
- Expansion Region
- Mid Rim

TIMELINE

BFE: Before Formation of Empire

1 Naboo
This precursor to the Clone Wars put Senator Palpatine in a position of power to instigate future conflicts.

2 Geonosis
The discovery of factories producing a Separatist droid army led to all-out war between the Republic and Confederacy of Independent Systems.

5 Ryloth
A brutal Separatist occupation led to an uneasy alliance between the Republic and local freedom fighters.

6 *Malevolence* Campaign
Using a secret naval superweapon, General Grievous conducted a series of sneak attacks against the Republic fleet that demanded a counterassault.

9 Quell
A Republic fleet fell to the overwhelming force of the Separatist navy in this high-altitude engagement.

12 2nd Geonosis
The Republic launched a second invasion of the Geonosian homeworld after a new droid factory was built.

13 Kamino
General Grievous attempted to cripple the production of clones with a risky assault at the heart of the Republic army.

13 BFE

3 BFE

2 BFE

3 Christophsis
Jedi ingenuity helped the Republic repel the first Separatist invasion of this crystalline planet.

4 Teth
The Grand Army mounted an armored invasion of Teth to rescue the son of Jabba the Hutt, swaying this powerful ally to the Republic's side.

7 Rishi Moon
A covert Separatist strike on a key communications station attempted to clear the nearby planet of Kamino for an attack.

8 Bothawui
The planet's asteroid ring served as a battleground between Separatist and Republic fleets. These floating rocks provided a strategic advantage to the Jedi.

10 1st Felucia
The Separatist army won a decisive victory among the exotic flora of Felucia, leaving the Republic to retreat from their position.

11 Malastare
This prolonged campaign would have ended in Separatist victory had it not been for a Republic superweapon.

14 Lola Sayu
An infiltration operation was followed by a fleet battle as the Republic rescued high-value prisoners.

After standing for a thousand years, decades of decline in the Galactic Republic culminated in a crisis known as the Clone Wars. Calls for galactic unity and the government's slogan, "We are all the Republic," had long since faded by the time Sheev Palpatine began sowing seeds of conflict under the guise of a trade dispute between the Naboo and Trade Federation. The battle for Naboo simply underscored the ineffectual nature of the Galactic Republic and allowed Palpatine to take political control of the Senate.

Crisis and the Clone Wars

Under the secret influence of Palpatine, Count Dooku of Serenno merely stoked the long-simmering tensions between the Core Worlds and far-flung territories in order to form the Confederacy of Independent Systems, a collection of Separatist-minded star systems that broke from Republic rule. The Separatist Crisis saw Palpatine given emergency powers and the creation of the Republic's first Grand Army to combat the Confederacy. Composed primarily of clone soldiers purchased from Kamino, they were led in battle by the Knights of the Jedi Order, powerful wielders of the mystical energy known as the Force. For a thousand generations, the Jedi acted as peacekeepers, but the Order was ill-prepared for their new role as wartime generals. Facing the Jedi and their clones, the Separatists were a collection of star systems covertly backed by corporate entities including the Trade Federation, Commerce Guild, Corporate Alliance, and

Techno Union. With seemingly infinite capital at their disposal, the Separatists manufactured a colossal droid army of their own. Following the outbreak of war, the opening phases became a frantic exercise in securing territory by both sides. Both sought to ally themselves with neutral systems, leaving planets who did not align themselves at risk of invasion. Points along hyperspace lanes and trade routes, so vital for military supply and reinforcements, often served as key battlegrounds.

War-Torn Regions

The Outer Rim region of the galaxy was particularly war-torn as it was home to many Confederate systems. The Separatists used this to their advantage in the early stages of the war, attacking the newly formed Grand Army across countless worlds. This strategy gave them an early upper hand, and although the path to it was still far from certain, Separatist victory seemed like a possibility. Yet as the war ground on, the Republic recovered from its early missteps. The ever-growing clone army gained valuable battlefield experience and was further bolstered by growing naval forces. The Republic Senate approved increased military spending and any attempts toward a cease-fire were undermined from within by Palpatine. As the galaxy grew weary from prolonged war, Palpatine was finally in a position to overthrow the Republic. With his enemies weakened and the public desperate for peace at any cost, Palpatine ended the Clone Wars and declared himself Galactic Emperor.

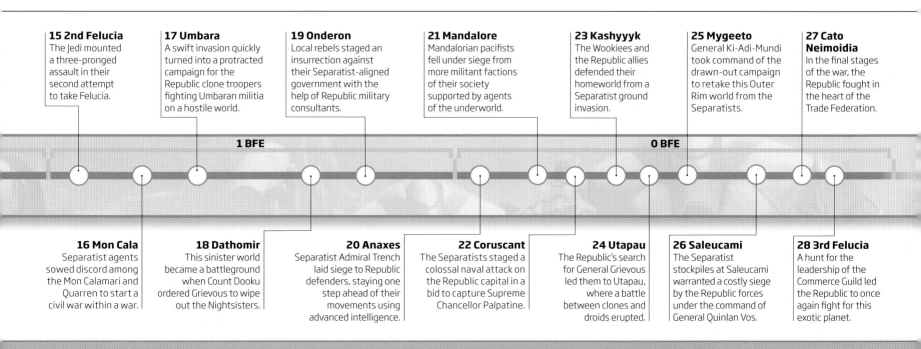

15 2nd Felucia
The Jedi mounted a three-pronged assault in their second attempt to take Felucia.

17 Umbara
A swift invasion quickly turned into a protracted campaign for the Republic clone troopers fighting Umbaran militia on a hostile world.

19 Onderon
Local rebels staged an insurrection against their Separatist-aligned government with the help of Republic military consultants.

21 Mandalore
Mandalorian pacifists fell under siege from more militant factions of their society supported by agents of the underworld.

23 Kashyyyk
The Wookiees and the Republic allies defended their homeworld from a Separatist ground invasion.

25 Mygeeto
General Ki-Adi-Mundi took command of the drawn-out campaign to retake this Outer Rim world from the Separatists.

27 Cato Neimoidia
In the final stages of the war, the Republic fought in the heart of the Trade Federation.

1 BFE   0 BFE

16 Mon Cala
Separatist agents sowed discord among the Mon Calamari and Quarren to start a civil war within a war.

18 Dathomir
This sinister world became a battleground when Count Dooku ordered Grievous to wipe out the Nightsisters.

20 Anaxes
Separatist Admiral Trench laid siege to Republic defenders, staying one step ahead of their movements using advanced intelligence.

22 Coruscant
The Separatists staged a colossal naval attack on the Republic capital in a bid to capture Supreme Chancellor Palpatine.

24 Utapau
The Republic's search for General Grievous led them to Utapau, where a battle between clones and droids erupted.

26 Saleucami
The Separatist stockpiles at Saleucami warranted a costly siege by the Republic forces under the command of General Quinlan Vos.

28 3rd Felucia
A hunt for the leadership of the Commerce Guild led the Republic to once again fight for this exotic planet.

Naboo

DATE: 13 BFE ▪ **LOCATION:** NABOO, MID RIM ▪ **COMBATANTS:** NABOO/ GUNGANS VS. TRADE FEDERATION ▪ **OUTCOME:** NABOO/GUNGAN VICTORY

DROID INVASION

The unlikely battle of Naboo began not on the temperate battlefields of the planet's grasslands, but in the chambers of the Galactic Senate on Coruscant. Free Trade Zones in the Mid Rim, territory that corporations relied on for maximum profits, were now subject to Republic taxes. The outraged viceroy of the Trade Federation sought to draw attention to the matter by making a show of strength against the unassuming planet of Naboo.

The conflict began with a full blockade of the planet. Naboo's recent political decisions left it particularly susceptible to such a tactic. The previous monarch's policy of isolationism left it with few nearby allies, and a labor shortage in more recent months meant Naboo had planned to source much of its food from offworld imports. When shipping was halted, Naboo had few reserves and its own crops had been left to rot in the fields. After seven days, food stores ran low, but Naboo's Queen Amidala refused to cede to the Trade Federation's demands. Surprised by the young monarch's resolve and fearful of Republic intrusion, Viceroy Nute Gunray ordered a military invasion of the planet.

While the blockade might have had some legal footing, the Trade Federation's invasion did not. They counted on a swift capture of Queen Amidala to force her to sign a treaty that would legalize their occupation. They believed that Naboo's suffering would persuade her to ratify their

Commanders

QUEEN PADMÉ AMIDALA
The 14-year-old queen of Naboo displayed wisdom beyond her years upon taking office. Her predisposition toward coalition building, a strategy she employed in the earliest days of her reign, proved to be vital when forging an alliance with the Gungans. United under her leadership, the two peoples of Naboo repelled the invasion.

VICEROY NUTE GUNRAY (CAPTURED)
Driven by greed and coaxed by the sinister Darth Sidious, the viceroy of the Trade Federation was ill-suited for his role as a wartime leader. Always hiding behind his droid soldiers, the corporate pawn underestimated the stubborn resolve of the Naboo, who refused to surrender during his blockade, or the subsequent invasion and occupation.

▲ **Mechanical Blitz** The Trade Federation's formidable mechanized army employed transports, tanks, and other vehicles to quickly reposition their troops. The fast and maneuverable Single Troop Armored Platform (STAP) provided advanced scouting, while the heavily armed Armored Assault Tank (AAT) defended infantry transports on the move.

▲ **A Regal Reward** The Trade Federation quickly established air superiority after meeting only light resistance from Naboo pilots. Their ground forces rapidly captured the capital of Naboo, Theed. The city's swift capitulation meant that it went largely undamaged.

treaty, no matter how harsh it was. As queen, Amidala was the only official authorized to sign such a treaty and her escape off planet delayed the accord, but extended her peoples' suffering.

While the queen made her way to Coruscant to plead to the Senate for assistance, the situation on Naboo became increasingly dire. Most of Theed's citizens were placed in prison camps under armed guard. While open insurrection was futile, a small group of security volunteers began organizing a resistance while they awaited the queen's return.

KEY COMBATANT: INVASION FORCES

While it was not uncommon for galactic corporations to maintain their own security forces, the Trade Federation required a substantial military to complete a full-scale planetary invasion. In the weeks leading up to the conflict, they had increased the size of their standing army by ordering additional battle droids from the foundries on Geonosis.

▶ **Landing Zones** The Trade Federation safely deployed their invasion army away from population centers, shielded under forest cover.

Naboo (continued)

▲ **Field Commander** The droid commander OOM-9 surveyed the battlefield from atop his tank.

Unable to secure assistance from the Galactic Senate, defense of Naboo fell to its inhabitants. The loyalty of Naboo's limited all-volunteer security force was unquestioned, but they lacked the numbers and materiel to mount a decisive strike on their own. Even the addition of the Naboo Palace Guard and two Jedi ambassadors would not sway the fight in their favor. Though the two had had limited political relations for generations, the surface-dwelling Naboo would need the help of their underwater neighbors, the

Gungans. Queen Amidala herself made the plea for their support, and following a string of droid attacks on their underwater settlements, the Gungan leadership, headed by Boss Nass, pledged its Grand Army to the allied cause.

While the Naboo attempted to retake the Royal Palace and strike in space, it fell to the Gungan Grand Army to lead a diversionary attack 65 kilometers (40 miles) south of Theed in a region known as the Great Grass Plain. In response, the Trade Federation repositioned most of their forces for a direct assault. Their initial artillery barrage could not penetrate the Gungans' mobile energy shields, but this was only a temporary setback. The droid army needed only to press the attack and disable the shields, then unleash the full fury of their mechanized force.

▲ **Closing Ranks** Under a hail of enemy fire, the Trade Federation's droid forces breached the energy shroud protecting the Gungan Grand Army from long-range attacks. The battle droids methodically marched through the Gungan barrage with no regard for their personal wellbeing.

KEY COMBATANT: GUNGAN GRAND ARMY

The Gungan military had changed little since their conflicts with the Naboo generations before. They continued to rely on organic mounts to carry their equipment into battle, they wielded polearms, and their primary weapons were energy balls hurled by catapult or by hand. They did not utilize blasters, but did employ energy shields of various sizes to protect their army from direct fire. Though the Gungans were universally proud of their army, their forces were considered technologically crude by the standards of the Trade Federation.

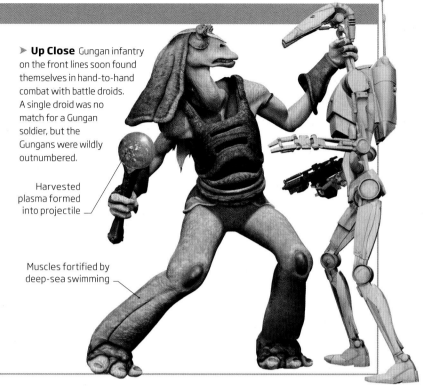

▶ **Up Close** Gungan infantry on the front lines soon found themselves in hand-to-hand combat with battle droids. A single droid was no match for a Gungan soldier, but the Gungans were wildly outnumbered.

Harvested plasma formed into projectile

Muscles fortified by deep-sea swimming

▲ **On the March** Gungan cavalry flanked the slow-moving Grand Army as they took position on the plain.

▶ **Deadly Destroyer**
A Gungan cavalry charge was met by the rapid fire of droidekas. These heavily armed droids made up only a small portion of the Trade Federation's army, but they were responsible for bringing down the Gungans' shield generators and inflicted a disproportionately high number of casualties on the Gungan troops.

▼ **Energy Artillery** Gungan catapults were an effective weapon against tight formations of battle droids. Despite a slow rate of fire, their oversized plasma boomas exploded on contact dealing splash damage over a wide area.

Naboo: Decisive Moment

With the Naboo capital conquered, its people in camps, and wishing to soften the appearance of the occupation should the Republic send emissaries to evaluate the situation, the Trade Federation disbanded their blockade. They left only one command ship in orbit to control the mechanical army on the planet's surface. If the modest Naboo starfighter corps could destroy the Control Ship's communications array in space, they could disable the entire droid army below, relieving the Gungans in their diversionary attack and making the capture of the Trade Federation viceroy assured.

The first objective of Queen Amidala's infiltration of the Royal Palace was the recapture of the palace starship hangar. From there, the seasoned pilot Ric Olié led Bravo Squadron in formation toward the Control Ship in orbit. The Trade Federation

◀ **Art of War** The sleek design of the N-1 starfighter was a reflection of Naboo culture. The Naboo's love of the arts, architecture, and design was clear in their starship design, as the fighter balanced function and elegance. There simply weren't enough of these hand-crafted fighters—nor enough volunteer pilots—to inflict meaningful damage on the heavily shielded hull of the Droid Control Ship.

▲ **Rapid Infiltration** In a flash, a single Naboo starfighter rocketed through the crescent-shaped hangar of the droid control ship, catching traffic control crews off guard. They were unable to report the situation to the command bridge in time.

◀ ▲ **Devastating Loss** Although the *Lucrehulk*-class cargo freighter was nearly impervious to starfighter assault on the outside, a direct hit on its main reactor from the inside caused a destructive chain reaction that rippled through the ship. All Trade Federation personnel on board were killed in the blast.

defenses were formidable and the all-volunteer squadron was quickly overwhelmed. With their numbers decreasing and hope of victory dwindling, a lone Naboo starfighter made an errant attack run inside the control ship's hangar. From this surprise position, a volley of proton torpedoes destroyed the battleship's reactor from within. This unlikely victory in space single-handedly turned the tide of the battle, allowing the Naboo and their Gungan allies to snatch victory from the jaws of defeat.

Naboo (continued)

The ground battle on the plain was steadily turning against the outnumbered and outgunned Grand Army. When the Gungans' shield generators were destroyed, the Trade Federation tanks were cleared to press their attack. Gungan General Tobler Ceel and his officers signaled the retreat, ordering the Gungans to flee for their lives. The infantry, cavalry, and artillery forces were unable to outpace their mechanical pursuers and the Grand Army was forced to surrender. At this point, the ground battle was a decisive victory for the Trade Federation. Their losses were marginal and with the Gungans contained, the army would have turned its attention back to Theed and the rescue of the Trade Federation viceroy. But this counterattack never came to be.

▲ **Sudden End** The Gungans were shocked to find their droid captors suddenly powering down around them.

The sudden destruction of the Trade Federation Control Ship in orbit dealt a critical blow to the droid army. By design, all droids in the company's security force were controlled by a single central computer, and its obliteration left the entire army inoperable. Against all odds, Queen Amidala's bold attack strategy had worked. The Gungans stood victorious on the Great Grass Plain, Bravo Squadron had struck a killing blow in space, and Amidala herself had captured Viceroy Gunray.

A new treaty was signed, ending the occupation and barring the Trade Federation from meddling with Naboo. The planet celebrated its victory, largely unaware that the Battle for Naboo

CASUALTIES

NABOO/GUNGANS: While the pilots of Bravo Squadron suffered heavy losses, the Naboo security forces who assaulted the Royal Palace fared relatively well. The Gungans bore the brunt of the casualties in the fight against the Trade Federation. Hundreds of Gungans sacrificed their lives on the Great Grass Plains.
TRADE FEDERATION: Forced to capitulate and surrender the whole of their army on the ground, the Trade Federation's neutralized battle droids and destroyed vehicles were melted down and repurposed for the civic beautification of Naboo.

▶ **Temporary Surrender** The Gungans were briefly captured before the victorious droid army was deactivated.

▲ **Tide Turned** Though they were surrounded by the enemy and their militia was in shambles, the Gungan Grand Army's fortunes changed in an instant. Instead of throwing their hands up in surrender, they found themselves cheering in jubilation.

was to have a lasting impact on galactic politics and would serve as a prelude to an even larger conflict. While the Naboo went back to a peaceful existence, the Trade Federation learned from their mistakes on the battlefield and began rebuilding their private droid army. Naboo's Senator Palpatine seized on invasion sympathies in the Galactic Senate and was elected as Chancellor of the Republic. Despite their new leadership, the ineffectual Senate allowed the Trade Federation to continue operating, and the wider galaxy returned to the political quarreling that would eventually lead to the Separatist movement and the outbreak of the Clone Wars.

▲ **Victory Parade** For the first time in generations, the Naboo hosted their planetary neighbors in Theed. The two peoples celebrated their joint victory, exchanging a symbolic emblem of peace to commemorate the start of a long-standing alliance.

Strategic Worlds

▲ **Jedha** The site of ancient Jedi ruins, Jedha did not appear to be of crucial importance to the Galactic Empire. But the kyber mines provided essential components for the Death Star.

The conflicts that have gripped the galaxy have differed in their forms and focus; from secession to conquest, and rebellion to resurgence. However, while the nature of warfare may change, the general principles behind it remain, and foremost among these is the identification of key strategic objectives. An understanding of the aims of the different warring factions allows us to understand how vital trade routes, the production of rare resources, major industrial centers, or seats of government dictated military operations. Control of these strategic points would have a decisive impact on the ability of a military force to achieve their objectives and then secure overall victory.

RARE RESOURCES

The Galactic Empire exerted a great deal of energy in securing planets, such as Mimban, which held key resources. The expansion of the Imperial military required huge amounts of raw materials, even before the emerging policy of superweapon construction. At first glance, the world of Jedha would not appear to be of any strategic importance. But its kyber crystal mines were vital for the construction of the Death Star's superlaser. Without knowing exactly what these crystals were intended for, but recognizing the Empire's invested interest, Saw Gerrera's

Partisans sought to disrupt Imperial operations on Jedha. Following repeated breaches of security and the completion of mining operations, the Empire destroyed Jedha City.

MILITARY PRODUCTION

The ability to produce military equipment in significant numbers could be the difference between winning or losing a war. Therefore control, or disruption, of industrial worlds had important strategic implications. When the Republic captured Geonosis at the beginning of the Clone Wars it appeared that they would severely damage the Separatist war effort. But the machinery on the world could not be converted to Republic usage, and a Separatist counterattack later retook the planet. Even after the Battle of Endor, the New Republic recognized that final victory over the Empire depended on their ability to capture or destroy the shipyards at Kuat. The resulting New Republic victory there cost the Empire a sizeable defensive fleet and the ability to rapidly produce warships. Both played a significant role in their subsequent downfall.

◄ **Kashyyyk** The Wookiee homeworld of Kashyyyk lay at an important hyperspace checkpoint and, as a result, became a target for the Separatist forces.

HYPERSPACE LANES

▲ **Sullust** Rebel operations ensured that this planet would become a "safe world" for the Alliance.

Waging war across the galaxy required access to key hyperspace lanes and trade routes. The Separatists aimed to capture the Wookiee homeworld of Kashyyyk not simply to rob the Republic of their support, but also because the world lay at a crucial hyperspace checkpoint. Similarly, the Galactic Empire maintained tight control of Corellia partially as a shipyard but also because of its placement on the eponymous Corellian Trade Spine that led to the Outer Rim.

KEY INFO

GALACTIC CAPITALS

Seats of government have varied in their strategic importance in the galactic wars. The Separatists nearly won the Clone Wars by raiding Coruscant to kidnap Supreme Chancellor Palpatine. However, the Rebel Alliance avoided the Imperial capital before the Battle of Endor and afterward elected to isolate the world rather than fight over it. Supreme Leader Snoke (presumably at Palpatine's direction) placed the First Order capital on board the Star Dreadnought *Supremacy* to avoid it becoming a target. The wisdom of having such a mobile capital was demonstrated when the First Order effectively decapitated the New Republic by destroying its capital on Hosnian Prime.

▶ **Hosnian Prime** The New Republic capital was the first target of Starkiller Base, and its destruction shocked the galaxy.

▲ **Corellia** This Core World was both a major production center for the Empire and an access point for hyperspace lanes leading to the Outer Rim.

SAFE WORLDS

The Rebel Alliance survived the duration of the Galactic Civil War because of its ability to hide, either on unpopulated worlds or secretly under the Empire's nose. It was Yavin 4 and Hoth's apparent lack of strategic significance that made them so attractive to the Alliance as potential bases. Such isolated worlds kept the rebels safe for a time but also almost led to disaster; the rebels felt secure enough to concentrate their forces, giving the Empire the opportunity

to launch near Rebellion-ending attacks on both worlds. Following the evacuation from Hoth, "Operation Ringbreaker" aimed to sow chaos on Imperial worlds and stirred an uprising into effect on Sullust, a key production facility for the Empire. Even though Alliance forces were eventually driven off the world, the Alliance had sowed the seeds for a rebel-backed insurgency that ousted the Imperial forces and made it a "safe world." So successful was this that the rebels used Sullust as their staging point to attack Endor.

▲ **Battle is Joined** As the Grand Army of the Republic landed on Geonosis and began to advance on the Separatist staging areas, thousand of battle droids marched out to meet them.

KEY WEAPON: AT-TE COMBAT WALKER

The AT-TE was the precursor of many variants of all terrain assault walkers that would stomp across the galaxy's battlefields for decades to come. The six legs of this weapon platform enabled it to make steady progress across the rocky Geonosian surface. Six anti-personnel laser cannons ensured that enemy infantry could not come close enough to disable the walker, and a large mass-driver cannon mounted on its back was powerful enough to damage or destroy enemy armor pieces. First seeing action in the Battle of Geonosis, the AT-TE became a mainstay in the Republic army for the duration of the Clone Wars, and continued to serve in the early years of the Galactic Empire.

◄ **Armored Warfare** The Republic's AT-TEs marched inexorably across the Geonosian battlefield under heavy fire, providing a degree of protection for the clones who were exposed on the desert surface with minimal cover.

1st Geonosis

DATE: 3 BFE ▪ **LOCATION:** GEONOSIS, OUTER RIM TERRITORIES ▪
COMBATANTS: REPUBLIC VS. SEPARATISTS ▪ **OUTCOME:** REPUBLIC VICTORY

DAWN OF THE CLONE WARS

The opening battle of the Clone Wars was a chaotic and confused engagement on Geonosis. The former Jedi Count Dooku had become the leader of the nascent Confederacy of Independent Systems, aiming to break from the perceived bureaucratic and corrupt rule of the Galactic Republic and Coruscant.

Having discovered a secret clone army being created on Kamino, ostensibly for the Republic, the Jedi Knight Obi-Wan Kenobi tracked the original genetic donor to Geonosis, where he witnessed a convention between Dooku and the leaders of the various galactic companies and conglomerates that were making plans to secede from the Republic. Beneath Geonosis' surface huge factories were building thousands of battle droids for use against the Republic. Kenobi relayed this information back to the Jedi Temple on Coruscant shortly before his capture.

In response, the Republic Senate voted for Supreme Chancellor Palpatine to be given emergency powers to convert the clone army into a Grand Army of the Republic. Jedi Grand Master Yoda moved to requisition the clones while Master Mace Windu gathered a Jedi strike force to rescue Kenobi.

As the Separatist leadership watched the attempted execution of Kenobi and his fellow prisoners Anakin Skywalker and Senator Padmé Amidala, the Jedi infiltrated the main arena. Master Windu's arrest of Dooku was interrupted by the arrival of dozens of battle droids, and the two sides entered combat. The Jedi were on the verge of being overwhelmed when Master Yoda arrived with the clone army to evacuate them from the arena and swing the battle in the Republic's favor.

Commanders

GRAND MASTER YODA
Grand Master of the Jedi Order, Yoda was an immensely wise and powerful Force user. However, he, like most of the Jedi, was unaccustomed to military command. Though he orchestrated a Republic victory, Yoda allowed key Separatist leaders and materiel to escape the battle.

ARCHDUKE POGGLE THE LESSER
When Republic forces arrived, Poggle the Lesser realized that for the Separatist cause to survive its leaders and the bulk of its armies must escape. Knowing that the battle droids not yet loaded onto ships could be sacrificed, he sent them into the fray to buy time for an evacuation.

▲ **Loyal but Limited** Though lacking the ability to form complicated tactics and strategies, battle droids were unerringly loyal to their commanders. They would march into any conflict and attempt to overwhelm the opposition with sheer weight of numbers and constant blaster fire.

1st Geonosis: Decisive Moment

The arrival of Jedi at the arena on Geonosis proved to be the opening move in the Clone Wars. While some of the more than 200 Jedi to arrive on the planet secured their landing site, the majority snuck into the arena during the attempted execution of Senator Amidala, Obi-Wan Kenobi, and Anakin Skywalker, where they waited for the perfect moment to intervene.

Master Mace Windu's move to arrest Count Dooku was the signal for the Jedi to act and by igniting their lightsabers in the arena stands they caused chaos among the watching Geonosians. However, the arrival of super battle droids forced the two sides into conflict.

The Jedi Order had not fought a battle in such numbers since the days of the High Republic, and the short-ranged nature of their lightsabers proved prohibitive against blaster-wielding battle droids. While the droids were not

▲ **Arena Execution** The leaders of the Trade Federation would not agree to a treaty with the Confederacy of Independent Systems until Senator Padmé Amidala was dead. In response the Geonosians organized an elaborate, but failed, execution by wild animal for Amidala, Obi-Wan Kenobi, and Anakin Skywalker.

▼ **Advanced Droids** A significant upgrade on the original designs, super battle droids had strong armor and powerful wrist blasters. These droids also had a sense of superiority over basic droids and would knock them aside in battle.

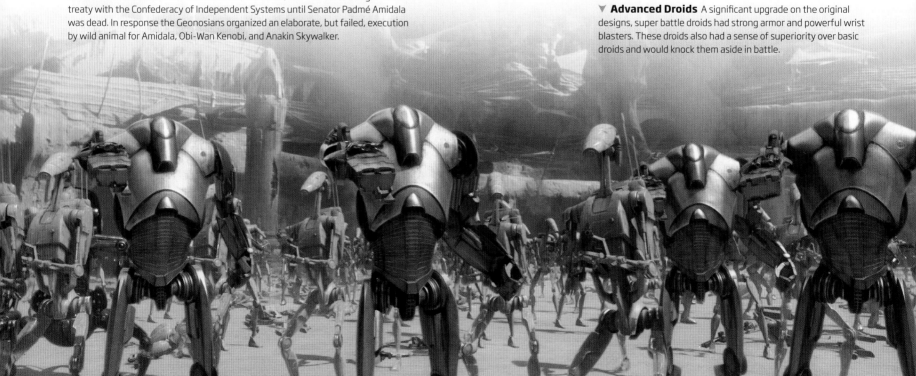

▼ **Last Stand** Surrounded by battle droids, the remaining Jedi were on the verge of being overwhelmed. Though they could deflect away many blaster shots, any missed blocks could prove fatal.

programmed with any great tactical ability, the sheer numbers of them and the rate at which they could fire acted as a potentially decisive force multiplier. Though the Jedi could redirect shots back against their opponents, the volume of incoming fire made such precision difficult.

The Jedi were forced to abandon their positions within the stands and descend to the arena floor to close the distance with the attacking droids. As a result, they were rapidly surrounded and suffered heavy casualties. The droid assault was paused so Count Dooku could offer the chance for a surrender, an offer that was refused.

However, the sudden arrival of Grand Master Yoda and the first waves of the clone army allowed the surviving Jedi to be rescued, initiating the next phase of the battle.

▲ **Republic Arrival** Moments after having offered the surviving Jedi the chance to surrender, Count Dooku watched on as Republic gunships arrived to rescue them. Though many had been killed, the survivors included several members of the Jedi Council who would lead clones in the battles to come.

1st Geonosis (continued)

As the battle moved beyond the arena it became clear that there were significant command and tactical issues facing both forces. For the Republic, the clone army had been well trained but never tested in battle. The surviving Jedi had previously identified themselves as "keepers of the peace, not soldiers," and though the clone troopers deferred to them, the lack of tactical and military training in the Jedi Order showed.

For the Separatists, the appearance of the Republic forces caused the leaders of the Trade Federation to attempt an immediate evacuation of their Command Spheres from the planet's surface. While there were many battle droids available to combat the Republic, the majority of the Separatist military resources had already been loaded aboard these vessels and were now liable to be destroyed if they could not escape.

Neither side was able to fully deploy in time for a pitched battle, and the main forces engaged each other around the Trade Federation landing zones. The Republic held a clear advantage in air support and were able to use Low Altitude Assault Transport/infantry (LAAT/i) gunships to deploy clones and Jedi directly into battle while also undertaking aerial attacks on Separatist ships. The Separatists sent columns of battle droids into action against the Republic to slow down their forward offensives.

▼ **Separatist Armor** The DSD1 dwarf spider droid was an anti-personnel armored weapon in the Separatist army. Its blaster cannon could wreak havoc on clone trooper formations.

▲ **Republic Advance** In an attempt to prevent Separatist ships from leaving the planet, clone troopers and their Jedi commanders advanced quickly after deployment. The outskirts of the Trade Federation landing zones were first reached by the Mirialan Jedi siblings Sidn-ee and Till-ee, but they could not prevent the huge Command Spheres escaping.

While lacking the autonomy or inventiveness of the clone troopers, the Separatist battle droids were a known military technology and could be largely relied upon to follow orders without question and use massed fire against the enemy. The deployment of OG-9 spider droids and hailfire droids to the front lines also provided the Separatists with heavy firepower. Though the clones could outfight the Separatists, every Jedi that was killed in the process caused further disruption to the Republic command structure and restricted their operations.

▲ **Mobile Warfare** The hailfire droid fulfilled the role of a mobile ordnance platform for the Separatists. Its heat-seeking missiles could punch clean through the frontal armor of an AT-TE.

KEY WEAPON: REPUBLIC GUNSHIP

Throughout the Battle of Geonosis the Republic had almost complete air superiority. The highly versatile LAAT/i and LAAT/c gunships were able to deploy clone troopers in advance of the front lines, then use missiles and anti-personnel lasers to disrupt droid formations and destroy cargo transports filled with war materiel. Though some Geonosian fighters made it into the air they were often overwhelmed by the Republic gunships. However, the LAATs were vulnerable during landing and takeoff, and a number were brought down while attempting to deploy new ground forces.

▶ **Air Power** Armed with laser turrets and homing missiles, the LAAT could deploy soldiers across the battlefield and then engage and destroy enemy armored units.

1st Geonosis (continued)

Once the prisoners had been rescued from the arena, the main objective of the Republic forces became unclear. Jedi leading from the front began to cut through battle droids, but to no obvious end. These small units were unable to overwhelm the opposition or prevent the ongoing evacuation. Additionally, the further forward they pressed the harder it became for Republic artillery to provide support without risking losses to friendly fire.

There still existed two routes to a war-ending victory for the Republic: the destruction of the Separatist battle force either on the ground or while fleeing, or the capture of the main Separatist leaders such as Dooku and Poggle the Lesser. However, neither of these were achieved. Concentrated fire from hastily deployed artillery turbolasers brought down some

▲ **Heavy Hitter** The SPHA-T weapons platform fired a concentrated turbolaser beam capable of punching through heavy durasteel armor plating. However, the cumbersome weapons took time to move into position. The chaotic nature of the First Battle of Geonosis meant that many could not be used effectively.

▼ **Concentrated Firepower** When the Trade Federation Command Spheres began to evacuate, Republic Self-Propelled Heavy Artillery Turbolasers (SPHA-Ts) were quickly deployed to open fire. Working together they were able to bring down one vessel, but the others continued to escape.

DOOKU'S ESCAPE

While the main battle raged elsewhere, Count Dooku took the plans for the Death Star and made his way to a private hangar via speeder bike. He was intercepted en route by an LAAT/i carrying the Jedi Obi-Wan Kenobi and Anakin Skywalker. However, in the absence of reinforcements they were not able to divert his journey and Dooku's fighter escort came to his defense. The Jedi were off-loaded on a landing pad but their transport was shot down moments later. A furious lightsaber duel ensued, but the Jedi were unable to prevent Dooku from escaping.

▶ **Separatist Leader** Count Dooku publicly led the Confederacy of Independent Systems but, secretly, was a Sith Lord serving his master, Darth Sidious.

of the spheres but most escaped the surface. The Republic's failure to establish a tangible orbital blockade allowed for a full Separatist retreat.

While Obi-Wan Kenobi, Anakin Skywalker, and Yoda would attempt to capture Count Dooku, the lack of a concerted effort meant he was able to defeat or distract the Jedi. He escaped the planet, taking with him the initial plans for the superweapon that would one day become the Death Star, without the Republic ever knowing those plans had been there. Similarly, the cyborg Separatist leader General Grievous escaped through the hive tunnels beneath Geonosis, leaving no survivors to speak of his existence.

Though the Republic gained control of Geonosis, its perceived strategic significance soon waned. The factories could not be converted to produce materiel for the clone army. The Republic had achieved an initial victory of sorts in this first battle, but had missed their only opportunity to end the war at a single stroke.

▼ **Droid Cargo** Techno Union starships carrying thousands of battle droids were stationed on Geonosis' surface. In the early stages of the battle they were highly vulnerable to attack from Republic air units, and many were destroyed on the ground.

Christophsis

DATE: 3 BFE ▪ **LOCATION:** CHRISTOPHSIS, OUTER RIM ▪
COMBATANTS: REPUBLIC VS. SEPARATISTS ▪ **OUTCOME:** REPUBLIC VICTORY

BREAKING THE BLOCKADE

With an eye toward using Christophsis' resources for their own purposes, the Separatists invaded and captured the planet. General Whorm Loathsom led the ground forces and besieged the capital city while Admiral Trench used Separatist warships to create a blockade, preventing the Republic from freeing the planet or even delivering relief supplies to refugees. General Anakin Skywalker and Admiral Wullf Yularen attempted to use Republic Star Destroyers to burst through Trench's line of ships to no avail. When Skywalker and Yularen asked for additional resources, General Obi-Wan Kenobi brought a prototype Republic stealth ship.

◄ **Roger Roger**
Battle droids marched in Christophsis' capital city of Chaleydonia. Comprising the thrust of the Separatist army, battle droids were always available in staggering numbers, which made them a formidable match for Jedi and clone troopers.

▲ **Separatist Blockade** Republic Star Destroyers, commanded by General Anakin Skywalker and Admiral Wullf Yularen, couldn't make headway against the Separatist blockade above Christophsis. Admiral Trench used 30 warships to keep Republic forces at bay.

Commanders

GENERAL OBI-WAN KENOBI
After General Obi-Wan Kenobi brought the stealth ship and the Republic broke the Separatist blockade, he took command of the clone army on the planet's surface. Christophsis was one of Kenobi's earliest campaigns as a commander, and he had to learn the art of military strategy while under fire—lessons that he would utilize in many future conflicts.

GENERAL WHORM LOATHSOM (CAPTURED)
General Whorm Loathsom led the Separatist ground assault on Christophsis. The tactically astute Kerkoiden used an energy shield to protect his forces during the siege of Chaleydonia. He fell for Kenobi's false offer of surrender, allowing Anakin Skywalker and Ahsoka Tano to destroy the shield generator.

▲ **Trooper Delivery** As one of the early battles of the Clone Wars, the Battle of Christophsis illustrated how the clone troopers and Jedi could function together. Republic gunships delivered clone troopers to the planet's surface to provide necessary reinforcements against the Separatists and their battle droids.

Kenobi ordered Skywalker and Yularen to use the stealth ship to sneak past Trench's blockade and get the crucial supplies on board to Senator Bail Organa on the surface. Skywalker disobeyed those orders. Instead, the Jedi plotted to use the cloaked ship to conduct a sneak attack. He decloaked the stealth ship to use its weapons, but Trench prevented any damage with his vessel's shields, and was now aware of his adversary's presence.

In searching Trench's military records, Kenobi learned that the Separatist leader had defeated cloaked ships before. The veteran tactician knew to track any such vessels using the ship's magnetic signature. Skywalker cloaked again and waited for the enemy to detect the stealth ship and launch tracking torpedoes. Then he navigated the craft toward Trench's dreadnought, the *Invincible*. Skywalker's maneuver turned the torpedoes back on the admiral's ship; Anakin moved his vessel to safety and the weapons hit the *Invincible*. The trick broke the blockade and allowed the stealth ship and Republic army to get to the surface.

KEY WEAPON: REPUBLIC STEALTH SHIP

Obi-Wan Kenobi brought a IPV-2C stealth corvette prototype to Christophsis to deliver relief supplies to the surface. The uniquely shaped ship had 28 cloak projectors and was equipped with anti-ship laser cannons and proton torpedoes. However, the ship had to decloak to fire. Though Admiral Trench could track the stealth ship's movements, Anakin Skywalker used those tactics against him.

Cloak projectors cover central hull

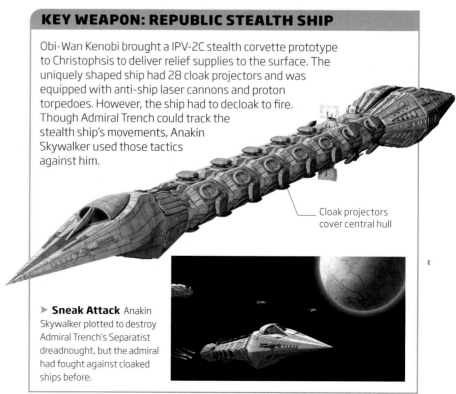

▶ **Sneak Attack** Anakin Skywalker plotted to destroy Admiral Trench's Separatist dreadnought, but the admiral had fought against cloaked ships before.

Christophsis (continued)

▲ **Front Lines** The Republic established a base on the ground in Chaleydonia after they broke the enemy blockade. Commander Cody and Captain Rex led the clone troopers into urban combat in the streets of the city.

After the Republic set up their base on the surface, they strove to gain ground against the Separatists in Christophsis' capital city, Chaleydonia. They experimented with various tactics to wrest control from the Separatists. But with the blockade re-forming above the planet, the Separatists possessed far larger numbers and used them to press the Republic. The Separatists also had the advantage of a clone spy feeding them intelligence about the Republic's position and strategies.

General Loathsom rose to the challenge of crushing the Republic forces. Well-timed use of a deflector shield kept the Separatist armies protected while the Jedi generals struggled with obtaining reinforcements. This was a frustration throughout the Clone Wars: the Separatists often had a far simpler task

transporting additional droid reinforcements to a location. Republic reinforcements ultimately arrived, but the army only gained the upper hand when Kenobi tricked Loathsom, offering to negotiate a Republic surrender, then ambushing the Separatist general. Kenobi's falsehood turned what would have likely been a Separatist victory into a Republic one, but the lie also meant the Separatists wouldn't believe any such offer again.

The Battle of Christophsis highlighted an important issue for the Republic army: the clones' free will. Clone Sergeant Slick believed the Jedi Order was exploiting him and his brothers, and divulged secret information to the enemy in exchange for promised freedom. Concerned that others would follow Slick's path, the Republic chose to keep his duplicity a secret.

▲ **Climbing Attack** While B2-series super battle droids were more advanced than B1 droids, their thicker armor casing was no match for Jedi and their lightsabers. Kenobi focused on eliminating the B2 battle droids first.

▶ **Crystal Battlefield** Chaleydonia was known as Crystal City because of the towering green formations dotting its landscape. Republic veterans of this battle would later refer to it as "cracking the crystal."

KEY WEAPON: REPUBLIC ARTILLERY

The Republic army went on the offensive against Loathsom's Separatist droid soldiers with heavy artillery. They utilized AV-7 anti-vehicle cannons for their long-range offensive, and expected that the barrage of cannon blasts would decimate the droids. The assault temporarily worked. Recognizing their disadvantage, Loathsom eventually pulled the droids back behind a portable deflector shield that protected them from the heavy guns. The clone troopers successfully defended the heavy cannons from Separatist counterattack, then annihilated the droids after the Jedi disabled the shield generator.

▶ **AV-7 Cannons** One clone trooper could operate each cannon, maximizing the Republic's resources.

Teth

DATE: 3 BFE ▪ **LOCATION:** TETH, WILD SPACE ▪ **COMBATANTS:** REPUBLIC VS. SEPARATISTS ▪ **OUTCOME:** REPUBLIC VICTORY

CLIFFTOP CONFLICT

The Battle of Teth was part of an intricate plan to bring the Hutt clans into the Separatist Confederacy and thus gain control of the Hutts' hyperspace routes in the Outer Rim Territories. Darth Sidious continually looked at the wider war to formulate strategies, and concocted plans several steps ahead of his foes. So with Generals Anakin Skywalker and Obi-Wan Kenobi distracted on Christophsis, Count Dooku's assassin Asajj Ventress kidnapped Jabba the Hutt's son, Rotta, from Tatooine. She took the child to Teth along with battalions of battle droids and

waited for the Republic to walk into her trap.

Even though the Separatists were sequestered in a clifftop monastery, the Republic was able to storm their location. Skywalker and his Padawan, Ahsoka Tano, led Captain Rex and Torrent Company in a precarious climb up the cliff utilizing AT-TE walkers and ascension cables. Though they had to ascend under heavy Separatist fire from the clifftop, they quickly dispatched the Separatists' outer defenses and found a droid willing to divulge Rotta's location. That droid was a decoy planted by Ventress, and

▲ **Monastery Shelter** Facing overwhelming Separatist reinforcements, Captain Rex and the clone troopers stood between the Jedi and the battle droids. Though ultimately overrun, they sealed the monastery doors and laid down fire to keep the battle droids at bay.

when Skywalker and Tano found the Huttlet she used their rescue to try to frame the Republic for the kidnapping and infuriate Jabba to the point that he would join the Separatists.

Ventress toyed with her prey. She held back Separatist reinforcements, allowing Skywalker and Tano to believe they had won. But when they attempted to leave with Rotta, Ventress sent in her reserves and trapped Rex and his clones inside the monastery. Still, Skywalker and Tano successfully escaped from the planet. Learning of the troubles on Teth, General Kenobi arrived with Commander Cody and additional clones, who managed to turn the tide against the Separatists. Ventress fled the battle after a duel with Kenobi.

Skywalker and Tano successfully returned Rotta to his father. As a result of the battle, the Republic negotiated a treaty with Jabba the Hutt and gained access to the supply routes in the Outer Rim. This meant the clone armies could move through Jabba's territories unimpeded. Despite this, the gears of the war were starting to turn in the Separatists' favor.

Commanders

GENERAL OBI-WAN KENOBI
As Skywalker and Tano attempted to return Jabba's son, General Kenobi ordered his clone trooper reserves to assist Captain Rex and Torrent Company. He kept Ventress occupied with a duel through the monastery. After she escaped, Kenobi joined the fray against the battle droids.

COMMANDER ASAJJ VENTRESS
Loyal to her master, Count Dooku, Asajj Ventress kidnapped Rotta to serve his overarching plan. Ventress commanded her forces to stop the Jedi from rescuing the Huttlet, using her particular talents for close combat and deceit. She dueled with the three Jedi and employed a Force mind trick on Captain Rex.

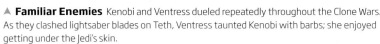

▲ **Familiar Enemies** Kenobi and Ventress dueled repeatedly throughout the Clone Wars. As they clashed lightsaber blades on Teth, Ventress taunted Kenobi with barbs; she enjoyed getting under the Jedi's skin.

KEY LOCATION: B'OMARR MONASTERY

The monastery on Teth was just one of the B'omarr Order's homes. The monks in this cult removed their own brains in order to eliminate all physical sensation and use solely their minds to contemplate the galaxy and enlightenment. The brains were placed in life-sustaining jars that were carried around in droid walkers. It is said that this allowed the monks to live multiple lifetimes.

▲ **Ancient and Abandoned** Its remote, inaccessible location made the deserted B'omarr Monastery on Teth an ideal fortress. Ventress took it over and used it to hide Rotta.

Ryloth

DATE: 3 BFE ▪ **LOCATION:** RYLOTH, OUTER RIM TERRITORIES ▪
COMBATANTS: REPUBLIC VS. SEPARATISTS ▪ **OUTCOME:** REPUBLIC VICTORY

FREEDOM-FIGHTER COLLABORATION

The war affected every planet it played out upon. Both the Republic and the Separatists left behind casualties, broken local governments, damaged land, and uncertainty. The ripples of the Clone Wars were particularly visible on Ryloth, a planet much contested because of its hyperspace location. Its Twi'lek citizens had tried to avoid getting involved in the war, telling both sides that they wanted to remain neutral and free, despite technically being part of the Republic with representation in the Senate.

The Separatists did not consider the wishes of Rylothians; Wat Tambor commanded an invasion of the planet and established an orbital blockade. The small Republic garrison on the planet was quickly overrun, but one group of Twi'leks believed in freedom with such devotion that they formed a resistance organization under the leadership of Cham Syndulla. The invasion forced the Republic's hand: they dispatched reinforcements to Ryloth to reclaim the territory from Tambor.

As with numerous other battles in the Clone Wars, the Republic had to crush the Separatist blockade before engaging on the planet's surface. Allocating the correct military resources for each

▶ **Taking Fire** B1-series battle droids were manufactured to operate any kind of standardized weapon, which added flexibility.

TWI'LEK RESISTANCE

Born from the Separatist invasion of Ryloth and a belief that they'd been abandoned by the Republic, the Twi'lek Resistance wanted their homeworld to be free. Cham Syndulla oversaw the group, organizing the freedom fighters to execute guerrilla attacks against the droid army. After they liberated Ryloth, Syndulla continued to command the organization. They became known as the Free Ryloth Movement when the Empire later occupied the planet.

◀ **Two-Legged Transport** Capable of carrying heavy loads, blurrgs were used as battle mounts by the Twi'lek Resistance.

theater of war was a constant exercise in strategy for the Jedi, and a difficult one for what had previously been a peacekeeping organization.

With repeat heroes Generals Kenobi, Skywalker, and Windu, along with Commander Tano and a number of seasoned clone troopers, the Republic forces were able to claim victory and liberate Ryloth. They could not have done so without Syndulla's Twi'lek resistance forces fighting alongside them. The partnership between the two groups, made on the condition that the Republic would not replace the Separatists on Ryloth, proved to be a model for the Republic as they worked with local populations on other Separatist-occupied worlds.

▼ **Last Stand** Cut off from Republic supplies and reinforcements, Jedi General Ima-Gun Di and Clone Captain Keeli sacrificed themselves to give Twi'lek resistance fighters and their families the opportunity to escape the droid army.

▲ **Blockade Stalwart** Captain Mar Tuuk commanded the Confederacy *Lucrehulk*-class battleship at the center of the Separatist's blockade of Ryloth. The Republic broke through by ramming the Star Destroyer *Defender* into Tuuk's flagship.

Commanders

GENERAL MACE WINDU
To eradicate the Separatists, Windu knew the Republic needed to take the capital, Lessu. He allied with the resistance fighters to charge the city's bridge in an attack that would come to be known as "The Hammer of Ryloth."

EMIR WAT TAMBOR (CAPTURED)
Foreman of the Techno Union, Wat Tambor was appointed emir of Ryloth by Count Dooku. He clung to the planet with the aid of the tactical droid TA-175, but his greed ultimately cost him. He surrendered unconditionally to General Windu.

❝ Let the Republic come. Our ship is unstoppable! ❞

GENERAL GRIEVOUS, COMMANDER OF THE *MALEVOLENCE*

Commanders

GENERAL PLO KOON
Sent to hunt down the mysterious warship destroying Republic ships in the Core, Plo Koon nearly became a high-profile victim of Grievous' terror weapon. He survived and helped plan the attack that would end the *Malevolence*'s threat.

GENERAL GRIEVOUS
Grievous exulted in the terror the *Malevolence* inspired, but was frustrated by the ship's chronic malfunctions and crew of battle droids. The droids' lack of tactical programming left him unable to unlock the ship's true potential.

▲ **Warlord's Trap** The *Malevolence* destroyed Plo Koon's flagship, the *Triumphant*, at Abregado, forcing the Jedi general and his clone troops to evacuate in escape pods. Grievous sent out boarding ships to hunt down the survivors, but Skywalker and Tano rescued Master Plo and all escaped to warn of the Separatist threat.

Malevolence Campaign

DATE: 3 BFE ▪ **LOCATION:** VARIOUS ▪ **COMBATANTS:** REPUBLIC VS. SEPARATISTS ▪ **OUTCOME:** REPUBLIC VICTORY

▲ **Death of a Giant** When Shadow Squadron overloaded the *Malevolence*'s portside cannon, the ion energy had nowhere to go and boomeranged back into the reactor and battery grid that took up much of the giant ship's cavernous interior.

◀ **Deadly Weapon** Ion pulses normally just disable ships, but the *Malevolence* generated such powerful energies that its ion waves ripped targets into scrap.

HUNTING THE FLEET KILLER

The Separatists built the *Malevolence* in secret at the Pammant Docks, unleashing it under the command of General Grievous. The first of the Separatists' new *Subjugator*-class warships, the massive battleship was four times the size of the Republic's *Venator*-class Star Destroyers and boasted twin ion pulse-cannons capable of laying waste to an entire task force. It was the brainchild of a shipwright who dreamed of recapturing ships' waste heat and other propulsion byproducts and funneling this energy into massive grids of batteries–an ambitious idea that still needed some tinkering. As Grievous discovered, the *Malevolence* was a danger to itself as well as to its enemies, with ion blasts often bleeding back into the ship's other systems and disrupting them.

Count Dooku saw that the *Malevolence* could be a superb terror weapon, forcing the Republic to scramble entire fleets to track it down. It destroyed much of the Republic Fourth Fleet, ambushed General Plo Koon's flagship at Abregado, and then targeted the Kaliida Shoals Medical Center where tens of thousands of injured clones were being treated.

The Republic sent Plo Koon, Anakin Skywalker, and Ahsoka Tano to hunt down the battleship with a squadron of Y-wings. The hastily assembled Shadow Squadron engaged the *Malevolence* at Kaliida Shoals, targeting its bridge in hope of disabling the pulse-cannon controls and killing Grievous. When that failed, the pilots targeted the pulse-cannons directly, overloading the ship's portside weapon and badly damaging the vessel. Grievous fled, hotly pursued by the Republic as his crew frantically tried to repair the *Malevolence*'s hyperdrive. They succeeded, but Skywalker had sabotaged the ship's navicomputer and it plowed into the Dead Moon of Antar.

KEY WEAPON: THE *MALEVOLENCE*

The *Malevolence*'s creator, Sullustan engineer Ruggle Schmong, struggled to find a backer for his theory about a new way to power starships, with shipbuilders concluding that the systems needed to capture propulsion energy required more space than was commercially practical. But he found a warm reception from Separatist war ministers, who offered credits and raw materials to make his dream a reality.

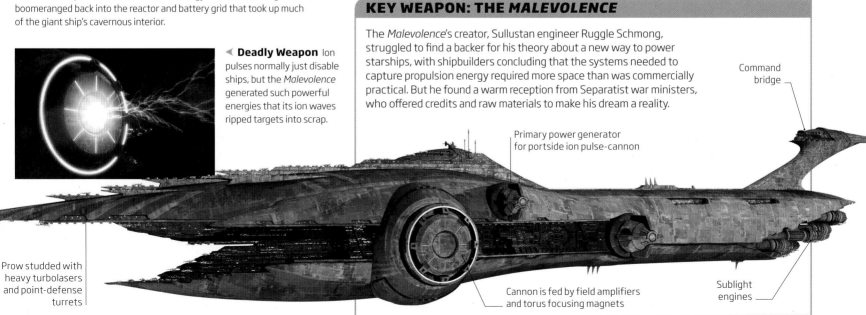

Command bridge

Primary power generator for portside ion pulse-cannon

Prow studded with heavy turbolasers and point-defense turrets

Cannon is fed by field amplifiers and torus focusing magnets

Sublight engines

Capital Ships

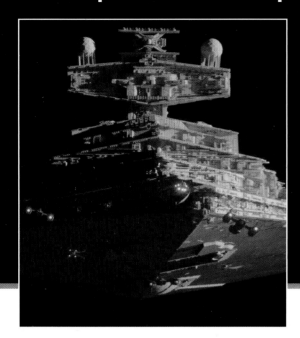

The "shipspotters" who gather in spaceport observation galleries will tell you that starship names and classifications are wildly contradictory, with shipwrights, species, and guilds all championing their own terminology. But all classification systems agree on one thing: a capital ship is a military starship 100 meters or more in length. Such vessels have been mainstays of starfleets for millennia, but larger ships of the line–those with keels 600 meters or longer–have come in and out of fashion in response to technological advances and economic incentives. The Clone Wars kicked off a new era of huge warships, with the Empire, First Order, and Sith acolytes all producing battleships of unprecedented size and power.

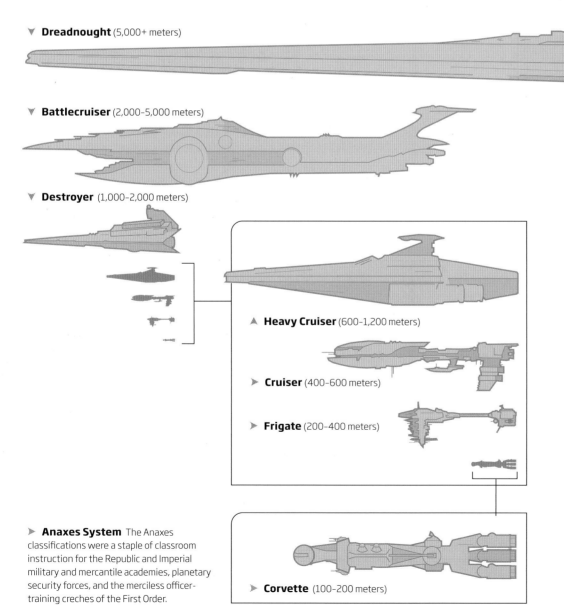

▼ **Dreadnought** (5,000+ meters)

▼ **Battlecruiser** (2,000-5,000 meters)

▼ **Destroyer** (1,000-2,000 meters)

▲ **Heavy Cruiser** (600-1,200 meters)

▶ **Cruiser** (400-600 meters)

▶ **Frigate** (200-400 meters)

▶ **Corvette** (100-200 meters)

▶ **Anaxes System** The Anaxes classifications were a staple of classroom instruction for the Republic and Imperial military and mercantile academies, planetary security forces, and the merciless officer-training creches of the First Order.

A HISTORY OF WARSHIPS

The Anaxes War College System is the galaxy's standard capital ship classification system. First instituted during the Clone Wars, it expanded existing nomenclature with three new classes–destroyer, battlecruiser, and dreadnought–to account for the massive warships built by sector fleets, powerful guilds, and the Republic and Separatist navies. These classifications are flexible, with ships moving up and down a class based on their armament or role. The Anaxes architects also adopted a shorthand for use during military engagements, drilled into cadets at military academies: corvettes, space transports, and starfighters were *gunships*; frigates and lighter cruisers were *cruisers*; and larger ships of the line were *battleships*. Historians argue

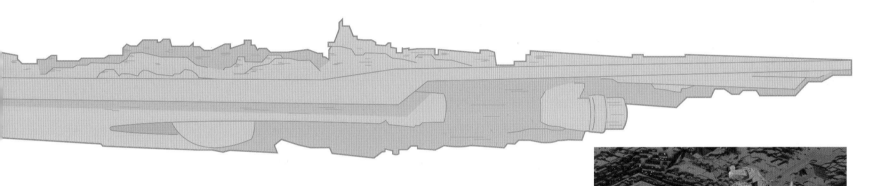

▲ **Dreadnought** The era of superweapons led to the creation of dreadnoughts such as the *Executor*-class. These craft were terror weapons of a heretofore unimaginable size.

endlessly about the exact characteristics of the ships of the line deployed by ancient empires, but generally agree that such warships were dwarfed by their modern descendants. Capital ships as large as the modern galaxy's were first deployed during the Alsakan Conflicts, but the so-called "dreadnought era" ended when cutting-edge turbolasers were developed that could rip apart ray shields, making large warships obsolete. Battleships returned to the spacelanes after Verpine shipbuilders revolutionized shield design, only to fall out of favor once again amid economic strains and Republic restrictions on capital ships larger than modern cruisers. In the last decades of the Republic, peacekeeping was largely the responsibility of sector or planetary defense forces, with Coruscant assembling ad hoc fleets from member

systems in times of trouble. As the Republic rotted, restrictions on ships' size and capabilities were routinely ignored. Trade guilds and powerful planets built battleships for their own protection, egged on by the ambitious, credit-hungry shipwrights of Kuat Drive Yards. This arms race accelerated dramatically during the Clone Wars, as KDY supplied destroyers for the Republic navy–a lucrative business it continued under the Empire. The 1,600-meter *Imperial*-class destroyer formed the backbone of the Imperial navy, bolstered by a handful of larger battlecruisers and dreadnoughts. After the destruction of the first Death Star, the Empire unveiled a new class of 19-kilometer "Super Star Destroyers" intended to be the pinnacle of capital ship power. Thirteen of these *Executor*-class craft were believed built, but only three

apparently survived the war between the New Republic and the Empire's remnants. The New Republic eschewed capital ship construction, but within the Unknown Regions, the First Order and Palpatine's Sith acolytes were creating huge new warships such as the *Resurgent*-class destroyer, the *Mandator IV*-class dreadnought and the *Xyston*-class destroyer, the latter armed with an axial superlaser. Snoke's flagship, the *Supremacy,* was a massive flying wedge more than 60 kilometers wide. Serving as his mobile capital, it was acclaimed as the largest capital ship in galactic history.

▼ **Being Overrun** Separatist B1 battle droids were not known for their intelligence, but their vast numbers made them an overwhelming force on Rishi Station.

Rishi Moon

DATE: 3 BFE ▪ **LOCATION:** RISHI MOON, OUTER RIM TERRITORIES ▪ **COMBATANTS:** REPUBLIC VS. SEPARATISTS ▪ **OUTCOME:** TACTICAL REPUBLIC VICTORY

SOUNDING THE ALL-CLEAR

Being able to launch a surprise attack against Kamino, home of the Republic's cloning facilities, would be a boon for the Separatists, and in the first year of the Clone Wars they attempted such a maneuver by first invading Rishi Station. Their objective: to infiltrate the Republic tracking station and keep the outpost's all-clear signal broadcasting while the Separatist fleet besieged Kamino and destroyed the cloning facilities, effectively ending the war in a single stroke.

The Separatists utilized a meteor shower as cover to send *Droch*-class boarding ships with commando droids to the moon's surface. More sophisticated than standard battle droids, the

commando models were both faster and more threatening. They could even mimic the voices of the clones, a key tactical advantage for the Separatists. The droids successfully infiltrated the station, staffed by mostly rookie clone troopers, including Domino Squad.

The clones at Rishi soon lost control of the base and the all-clear signal. The battle shifted when more experienced

clones, Commander Cody and Captain Rex, stopped at Rishi Station for a routine inspection. But General Grievous arrived with additional Separatist forces too.

With numerous enemies present and the all-clear signal still active, Captain Rex ordered the destruction of the base. The facility was demolished in a tibanna gas explosion, forcing the Separatists to abandon their planned attack on Kamino.

KEY LOCATION: RISHI STATION

Rishi Station was a listening outpost, established as part of a chain to protect Kamino. Though a vitally important posting, clone troopers usually found the assignment tedious as they monitored transmissions and listened for any indication that the Separatists plotted to assail Kamino and its precious clone facilities—facilities that made the Republic war effort possible.

▶ **Remote Base** Rishi Station was the only structure on the barren Rishi moon.

Bothawui

DATE: 3 BFE ■ **LOCATION:** BOTHAWUI, MID RIM ■ **COMBATANTS:** REPUBLIC VS. SEPARATISTS ■
OUTCOME: REPUBLIC VICTORY

HOLDING THE LINE

The Separatists counted multiple victories along the Outer Rim as the Republic lost ground and the support of key planets. To maintain their foothold in the Mid Rim and halt the Separatist advance, the Republic planned to make a stand at Bothawui. Knowing the enemy wanted to claim the strategic planet, General Anakin Skywalker and Commander Ahsoka Tano were sent to defend it with three *Venator*-class Star Destroyers. Skywalker once again ignored the guidance of his master, General Obi-Wan Kenobi, who directed them to retreat. Kenobi did not believe the Republic ships could stand against General Grievous' much larger fleet. Kenobi was wrong.

Grievous didn't approach Bothawui from conventional vectors: the Kaleesh warlord commanded his fleet through Bothawui's planetary ring. This tactic allowed Grievous to damage a Republic cruiser before Skywalker led Gold Squadron into the engagement. While Gold Squadron lured the droid fighters into combat, Tano triggered a Republic ambush. Faced with a sudden and unexpected barrage, Grievous quickly fled in his personal starfighter, *Soulless One*, rather than risk destruction or capture. He left the Separatist fleet behind to be destroyed.

Both actions were indicative of Skywalker and Grievous' respective methods: Skywalker often chose bold, unexpected moves, and Grievous fled as soon as he realized a battle was not in his favor. Though the Republic did not capture Grievous this time, they successfully stopped the Separatists from further establishing their strength in the Mid Rim.

SPRINGING THE AMBUSH

General Grievous had continually eluded the Republic, so Skywalker leaped at the chance to defeat the Separatist leader. He studied previous engagements with the Separatists in order to better understand Grievous' tactics and beat his enemy at his own game. Skywalker allowed Grievous to send his ships into Bothawui's ring, where he fell into Anakin's trap. The Jedi had staged clones in AT-TE walkers atop the asteroids, from which they opened fire on the unshielded rear sections of Grievous' ships after they had passed overhead. This unexpected strategy took the cyborg general unawares.

▲ **Pincer Movement** Captain Rex and his brigade hid among the asteroids, while Skywalker led a frontal assault with the V-19 Torrent starfighters of Gold Squadron.

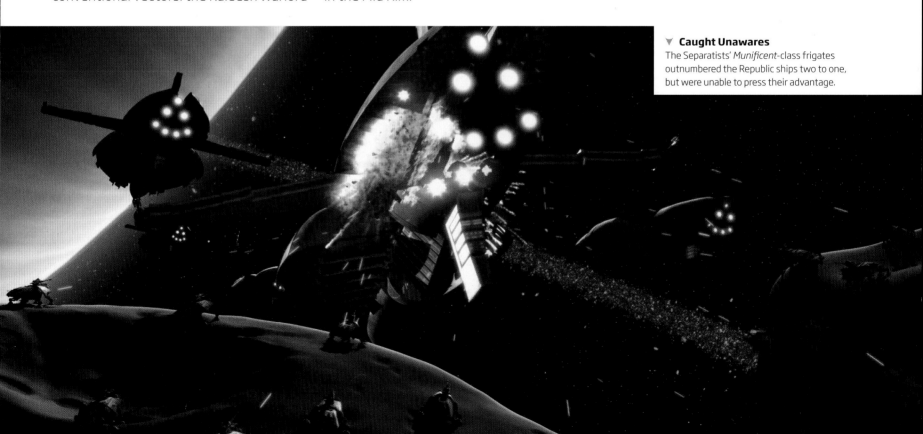

▼ **Caught Unawares**
The Separatists' *Munificent*-class frigates outnumbered the Republic ships two to one, but were unable to press their advantage.

Quell

DATE: 2 BFE ▪ **LOCATION:** QUELL, OUTER RIM TERRITORIES ▪ **COMBATANTS:** REPUBLIC VS. SEPARATISTS ▪ **OUTCOME:** SEPARATIST VICTORY

SKY BATTLE

The Separatist navy regularly used its superior numbers to its advantage, no more so than in the Outer Rim. It was here in the distant reaches of the galaxy that Separatism flourished and the Republic initially struggled to maintain its control. One such campaign took place at Quell, where a Republic fleet commanded by Jedi General Aayla Secura sustained heavy losses while under assault from a squadron of Separatist frigates.

Fellow Jedi General Anakin Skywalker mounted a rescue of Secura from his flagship, the *Resolute*, with little time to spare. With her supporting destroyers defeated, Secura's flagship succumbed to a boarding action undertaken by rocket droids and a persistent battering from the Separatist capital ships. In addition to the loss of three Star Destroyers, the Battle of Quell led to heavy Republic casualties as significant sections of the clone crews and combat detachments were unable to abandon ship before their vessels impacted the surface. This unqualified victory for the Confederacy underscored how the Republic's ultimate triumph in the war appeared far from certain.

▲ **Creative Countermeasures** The Separatists' use of rocket droids called for inventive tactics to counter them. General Anakin Skywalker risked his life to fight them while in mid-flight.

ABANDONING SHIP

General Skywalker ordered a *Consular*-class cruiser to dock with Secura's flagship. As the Star Destroyer plummeted toward the planet's surface, the Jedi generals made their way through the stricken vessel to the rescue ship and escaped. Separatist fighters forced the ship to make an emergency hyperspace jump from the upper atmosphere, an exceedingly rare and dangerous maneuver. While Secura was saved, there were many casualties among her 327th Star Corps of clone soldiers.

▲ **Heated Situation** As they fell through the atmosphere, the ships' hulls experienced an intense heat buildup, adding more risk to an already dangerous rescue operation.

▼ **High Altitude Attack** The overwhelming Separatist assault caused the Republic ships to fall from orbit into Quell's upper atmosphere, where the attacks intensified.

▼ **Final Stand** Generals Kenobi and Skywalker formed a tight defensive perimeter around their remaining armored vehicles in hopes that a rescue would soon arrive.

1st Felucia

DATE: 2 BFE ▪ **LOCATION:** FELUCIA, OUTER RIM TERRITORIES ▪ **COMBATANTS:** REPUBLIC VS. SEPARATISTS ▪ **OUTCOME:** SEPARATIST VICTORY

FIGHTING IN FUNGUS

KEY TERRAIN: FUNGAL FOREST

Felucia was notable for its unique ecosystem of translucent towering plants and fungi. Its colorful jungles teemed with life, though it was sparsely populated by sentient lifeforms. Military forces soon discovered that the towering flora restricted troop movements, leaving them susceptible to being overrun. Without proper reconnaissance, commanders attempting to gain territory risked overextending their lines, unaware what lay just on the other side of the concentrated growth.

▲ **Defensive Perimeter** Stranded in a narrow clearing with enemies closing in, Republic forces formed a defensive circle with their AT-TE armored walkers providing cover.

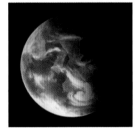

The Republic and Confederacy of Independent Systems fought multiple campaigns for control of Felucia. Its strategic value was driven, in part, by its agricultural production of nysillim, an herb with healing properties. The Republic's first campaign on the planet ended up outnumbered and nearly overrun by the tireless droid army. A hurried rescue effort called for Republic cruisers to blow a hole in the Separatist planetary blockade in orbit and deploy rescue gunships to the surface to airlift the survivors. General Plo Koon personally led the assault, clearing a path through droid starfighter defenses. Upon reaching the surface, Master Plo discovered a dire situation on the ground,

▲ **Air Superiority** Droid starfighters launched from orbit strafed the stranded Republic troops and hampered efforts to deploy rescue craft to the surface.

where Generals Kenobi and Skywalker had made a defensive perimeter around their dwindling armored forces.

Just east of this position, Commander Ahsoka Tano mounted a valiant but foolhardy counterattack, and was forced to retreat to avoid being overrun. Though the battle was lost, the rescue ensured that some of the Republic's most valuable commanders could be redeployed to strategic fronts elsewhere in the galaxy.

Malastare

DATE: 2 BFE ▪ **LOCATION:** MALASTARE, MID RIM ▪
COMBATANTS: REPUBLIC VS. SEPARATISTS ▪
OUTCOME: REPUBLIC VICTORY

SHADOW OF THE BOMB

Both the Republic and Separatists committed significant resources to Malastare in hopes that victory might secure the world's vital fuel resources for their cause. It became one of the longest and fiercest engagements of the Clone Wars, devolving into a prolonged battle of attrition—one that seemed certain to end in victory for the Separatists as the clones retreated to their final holdout at the Dugs' Imperial Palace. There, the leader of the Dugs, Doge Nakha Urus, allied himself with the Republic, fearing enslavement at the hands of the Separatists.

As the Republic grew desperate it turned to a terrifying new superweapon, the electro-proton bomb, whose use was authorized by Supreme Chancellor Palpatine himself. Republic forces lured the droid army near to the palace and then dropped a single bomb at the center of the Separatist formation. Designed to only damage droids, it created an initial concussive shock wave followed by a sphere of ion energy that shut down all mechanical beings.

While the bomb worked as intended against droids, it unexpectedly opened a sinkhole under the detonation site, engulfing many Republic troops. Worse yet, the blast awakened a lone Zillo Beast, a towering lifeform long thought to be extinct, that was resistant to most weapons. As the Dugs looked to ancient tactics in an effort to destroy the beast, the Jedi generals agreed to subdue and relocate the creature offworld before it could do more harm to the natives. Satisfied by the beast's removal, the Dugs ratified a treaty that granted the Republic access to Malastare's fuel supplies.

▲ **Sustained Resistance** Under heavy fire, Republic AT-TEs and local militia marched to meet the Separatists on the bleak plain at the foot of the Dug Imperial Palace.

Commanders

GENERAL MACE WINDU
Even at the end of the grueling campaign the Jedi Master was unwilling to compromise his values and harm an innocent lifeform. Tensions rose between the general and Dug leadership as they threatened to annihilate the Zillo Beast, but Windu found an alternative way of removing the danger.

TN-123 (DESTROYED IN ACTION)
The calculating droid commander on Malastare believed he had the Republic cornered at the Imperial Palace. He knew his combined infantry, cavalry, armor, and fighter units could win a war of attrition, but was powerless against the doomsday weapon that annihilated his army.

▲ **Native Warriors** Dug soldiers joined with the Republic to defend their planet from Separatist invaders. They marched into battle armed with electrostaves, polearms powerful enough to incapacitate living and droid soldiers alike. Their speedy cavalry fought from the saddles of insectomorph mounts.

▲ **Moment of Detonation** The electro-proton bomb created a devastating ion blast meant to deactivate the mechanical droid army while leaving the Republic's clone troopers unscathed. It produced an unintended crater in the planet's surface, with devastating consequences for the Dugs.

SUBDUING THE BEAST

The Dugs attempted to destroy the creature using an age-old method: assailing it with the fuel harvested from Malastare's core. The attack merely provoked the beast out of its cavern where it was met by the Republic's assault tanks. Typically reserved for anti-vehicle roles, the ion blasts from these mobile artillery units were the only offensive weapon in the Republic arsenal that affected the creature. The unit took heavy losses as their numbing attacks slowly wore the creature down. Once subdued, Republic scientists transported the creature to Coruscant for further analysis, hoping to replicate its highly resistant skin for use in their own armor.

▶ **Focused Fire** A battery of RX-200 *Falchion*-class assault tanks was able to temporarily subdue the beast.

2nd Geonosis

DATE: 2 BFE ▪ **LOCATION:** GEONOSIS, OUTER RIM TERRITORIES ▪ **COMBATANTS:** REPUBLIC VS. SEPARATISTS ▪ **OUTCOME:** REPUBLIC VICTORY

RETURN TO THE HIVE

With the Grand Army spread thin by engagements across the galaxy, defeated Separatist planets long thought to be secure began rising up against the Republic. The most notable of these was Geonosis, site of the very first battle of the Clone Wars. The Republic mobilized a second invasion to crush Geonosian resistance once and for all, a move provoked by the discovery of the largest droid factory ever built, financed by the Banking Clan to allow the Geonosians to produce more Separatist war droids than ever before.

Seeking to destroy the new foundries before they were fully operational and capture the Geonosian archduke, the Republic led a planet-wide assault under the command of Generals Obi-Wan Kenobi, Ki-Adi-Mundi, and Anakin Skywalker. The three generals were to mount a three-pronged assault on a landing site known as Point Rain, but the battle plan soon fell apart upon their arrival.

The Republic attempted to use dive bombing against anti-air emplacements, but the well-armed Geonosian flak batteries inflicted heavy casualties on

▲ **Deadly Diversion** Generals Unduli and Skywalker faced 10 garrisons of droid troops, luring them out from the factory into open battle upon a narrow bridge. The Republic troopers faced assaults from all sides, including aerial attacks from winged Geonosian soldiers.

the Republic landing craft. All three generals took fire in the opening moments of the operation, with only General Kenobi's forces arriving at the landing zone as planned. Both Ki-Adi-Mundi and Skywalker faced long marches against staunch static defenses before they arrived at the rendezvous point, where their own shattered armies found Kenobi's troops mounting a dire defense. Though Kenobi and Ki-Adi-Mundi were both injured in the fighting, the combined strength of the surviving clones was enough to continue toward their ultimate target, the shield generator protecting the newly constructed droid factory.

Jedi General Luminara Unduli joined Anakin Skywalker for the final assault, staging a diversionary attack at the foot of the foundry while their Padawans snuck inside to destroy the massive facility from within. With the factory demolished, Unduli led the search for Archduke Poggle the Lesser, not only capturing the warlord but uncovering the identity of the hive's true leader, Karina the Great. In the end, the Geonosian foundries and leadership were silenced.

Commanders

GENERAL OBI-WAN KENOBI
Kenobi's forces were the only ones to reach the landing site at Point Rain. Without the support of the additional armies, his troops set up a defensive perimeter to hold the line against waves of Geonosian counterattacks. He himself was injured, but fought until reinforcements arrived.

ARCHDUKE POGGLE THE LESSER (CAPTURED)
Poggle the Lesser conspired with the Banking Clan to build new foundries on his home planet. He believed that defensive shielding, heavily armored super tanks, and almost limitless production of droids would be enough to defend his new factories from any assault.

▼ **Fiery Offense** The Republic employed specially outfitted flamethrower units against the hordes of Geonosian warriors, neutralizing the Geonosians' natural advantages: mobility and numerical superiority.

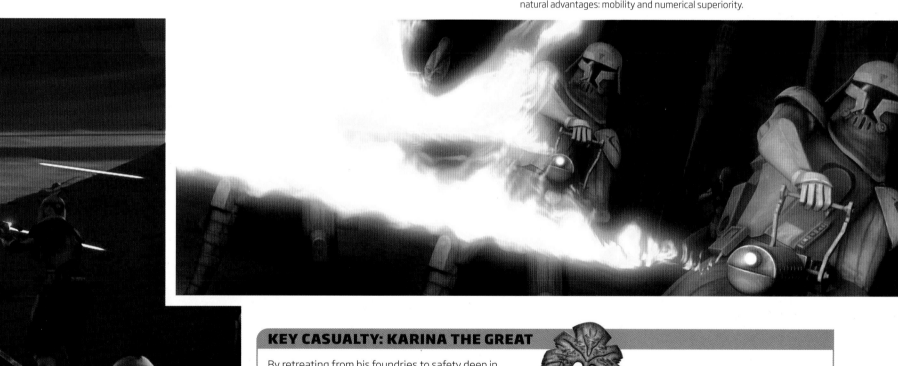

KEY CASUALTY: KARINA THE GREAT

By retreating from his foundries to safety deep in the hive, Archduke Poggle the Lesser led the Republic to the true Geonosian leader: Queen Karina the Great. The mother of all Geonosians in the hive, Karina was hidden deep in the maze of catacombs where she controlled her "empire" of drones through a single hive mind. This mind control was so powerful it could maintain its connection to both living and dead beings, and was even strong enough to control the mind of a Jedi.

▼ **Hive Mother** The Republic had long heard rumors of a hidden Geonosian leader.

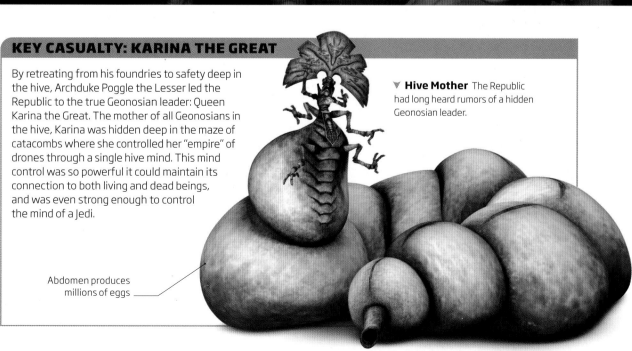

Abdomen produces millions of eggs

➤ **Holding the Line** The Republic defensive blockade around Kamino held throughout the battle thanks to its superior numbers and firepower, but could not prevent small assault craft falling to the surface concealed among the debris.

Kamino

DATE: 2 BFE ▪ **LOCATION:** KAMINO, EXTRAGALACTIC ▪ **COMBATANTS:** REPUBLIC VS. SEPARATISTS ▪ **OUTCOME:** REPUBLIC VICTORY

ATTACK ON THE CLONES

Attacking the aquatic planet of Kamino was one of the most risky and deceptive maneuvers of the Clone Wars. An intercepted message from General Grievous alerted the Republic to the planned invasion of Kamino, which was home to the production facilities for new clones for the Republic army and therefore of vital importance to the war effort. While the Republic fleet prepared to meet the invasion in space, they were unaware that the Separatists had planned a complex, multi-phased attack. Phase one called for the Separatist fleet to engage the Republic blockade around the planet while phase two would consist of a ground assault by aquatic droids. Both would serve as a distraction for the primary goal: crippling clone production by stealing the prime DNA sample from which all of the Republic's clone troops were copied.

At first, the Republic believed they were withstanding the assault in space, unaware that the starship debris falling to the water below disguised Separatist troops. Once assembled beneath the waves, the assault craft sprung into action,

Commanders

ADMIRAL WULLF YULAREN
Armed with advance warning of the Separatist invasion, Admiral Yularen was in a strong position to defend the planet. He inflicted significant damage on the smaller Separatist fleet, but was unaware that the orbital engagement was merely a distraction.

GENERAL GRIEVOUS
Known throughout the war for his ruthless tactics and deceit, the cyborg general's plan to attack Kamino was no exception. He recognized the superiority of clone soldiers over his droids and personally led the surface assault to distract the defending garrison.

KEY WEAPON: TRIDENT ASSAULT VEHICLE

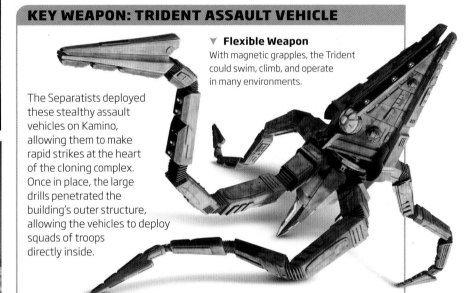

▼ **Flexible Weapon**
With magnetic grapples, the Trident could swim, climb, and operate in many environments.

The Separatists deployed these stealthy assault vehicles on Kamino, allowing them to make rapid strikes at the heart of the cloning complex. Once in place, the large drills penetrated the building's outer structure, allowing the vehicles to deploy squads of troops directly inside.

▲ **Aquatic Assault** Separatist aqua droids maneuvered underwater to gain the element of surprise, then rapidly transitioned to surface operation when engaging the defending clones.

depositing droids throughout the cloning complex in Tipoca City. Jedi Generals Shaak Ti, Obi-Wan Kenobi, and Anakin Skywalker redirected their focus to the surface to repel the assault, backed by the 501st Clone Battalion, the local garrison, and clone cadets. Skywalker discovered a Separatist assassin, Asajj Ventress, in time to foil her attempt to steal the DNA sample.

Ultimately, Grievous' risky attack failed and the damage was contained. Clone production soon resumed, and the Separatists faced an ever-increasing number of clones throughout the remainder of the war.

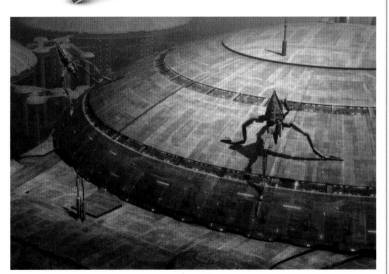

▲ **Destructive Deployment** Trident assault craft embedded their durasteel tentacles into the domed exterior of Tipoca City, causing significant damage to the cloning structures within.

Lola Sayu

DATE: 1 BFE ▪ **LOCATION:** LOLA SAYU, OUTER RIM TERRITORIES ▪
COMBATANTS: REPUBLIC VS. SEPARATISTS ▪
OUTCOME: REPUBLIC VICTORY

RESCUE OPERATION

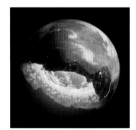

The Republic's strike on Lola Sayu was not to capture territory, but instead to protect secret military intelligence. In order to safeguard the knowledge of a hyperspace lane known as the Nexus Route and prevent it from falling into enemy hands, Jedi Master Even Piell and Captain Wilhuff Tarkin each memorized half of the route before being captured by the Separatists, after which they faced harsh interrogation. Seeking to protect this valuable intelligence and rescue the prisoners, General Obi-Wan Kenobi led a stealth incursion deep into Separatist space to free Master Piell and Captain Tarkin from the most isolated, impenetrable Separatist facility: the Citadel. While General Kenobi successfully infiltrated the enemy base, his team was soon discovered and required evacuation. The Republic sent four Star Destroyers in a final attempt to rescue the rescuers.

As the two fleets clashed, Jedi General Saesee Tinn led a starfighter assault on the blockade, supported by Generals Adi Gallia and Kit Fisto. The nimble Jedi starfighters weaved their way through the asteroids that ringed the planet, piercing the blockade and cutting a path toward the planet for Jedi Master Plo Koon, who commanded the single landing craft tasked with evacuating the ground team. While clone fighter pilots continued the engagement in orbit, the Jedi-led assault

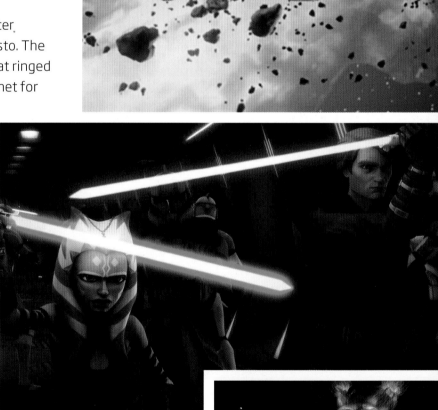

Commanders

GENERAL SAESEE TIIN
From the cockpit of his Jedi starfighter, Jedi Master Saesee Tiin led a squadron of ARC-170 starfighters against the Separatist blockade. The skilled Jedi pilot safely escorted the landing craft to the surface, enabling the rescue of Kenobi and the survivors.

OSI SOBECK (KILLED IN ACTION)
The cruel Phindian warden of the Citadel, Sobeck would stop at nothing to avoid an embarrassing loss of prisoners. He attempted to personally prevent the escape of the Republic prisoner Captain Tarkin, but was killed in the resulting skirmish by the Jedi Padawan Ahsoka Tano.

▲ **Side by Side** Commander Ahsoka Tano joined the rescue effort alongside her master, Anakin Skywalker. Even Piell entrusted her with his half of the knowledge of the Nexus Route before he perished, giving her strict orders to share it only with the Jedi Council.

▲ **Noble Sacrifice** Even Piell survived interrogation but was killed attempting to escape Lola Sayu.

▼ Separatist Blockade
Realizing that a Republic assault was imminent, Separatist leaders positioned their warships amid the asteroid debris, allowing them to mount a formidable defense.

team reached the rendezvous point, rescued the ground team, and quickly made their escape before more Separatist defenders could arrive.

As soon as the Jedi rescuers arrived safely in the ships' hangars, the Republic fleet disengaged and jumped to hyperspace. While the battle itself was but a distraction for the rescue effort, it is notable for the number and caliber of Jedi present for the engagement. That the Republic committed so many Jedi Masters to the rescue was a testament to the value of the information they sought to recover, as the Nexus Route would have given the Confederacy a direct hyperspace lane from their own territory into the heart of Republic space. It is believed that Darth Sidious later provided knowledge of the route to his Separatist pawns in order to facilitate their surprise strike on Coruscant in the closing stages of the Clone Wars.

KEY LOCATION: THE CITADEL

Built long before the Clone Wars by the Republic, the Citadel was purposely designed to imprison rogue Jedi. When the planet was captured early in the conflict by the Separatists, they quickly recognized the value of such a facility for the incarceration and interrogation of their Jedi foes. Heavily guarded, the Citadel was equally as difficult to infiltrate as it was to escape from.

➤ No Reprieve Escapees faced the planet's harsh sulfuric seas.

2nd Felucia

DATE: 1 BFE ▪ **LOCATION:** FELUCIA, OUTER RIM TERRITORIES ▪ **COMBATANTS:** REPUBLIC VS. SEPARATISTS ▪
OUTCOME: REPUBLIC VICTORY

TRIPLE THREAT

While countless worlds hosted battles during the Clone Wars, some planets were deemed too strategic to lose and were fought over again and again. Felucia was such a planet, its natural resources and proximity to a hyperspace lane giving it high value. In an effort to re-establish Republic control over the jungle-covered Outer Rim locale, Jedi Master Plo Koon concocted a plan leveraging the presence of himself and the two Jedi who accompanied him, General Anakin

Skywalker and Skywalker's Padawan, Commander Ahsoka Tano—whom Plo had found as a child and brought to the Jedi Temple. It marked the second battle on Felucia during the war.

To aid their mission, the Republic worked with Felucian scouts native to the planet. Throughout the war the Separatists rarely conducted outreach to locals, thereby losing the opportunity to gain strategic knowledge and insight into worlds they occupied. As many Felucians were farmers, they were acutely familiar with the local geography and the unique adversities of the landscape, dense with fungal formations. Having befriended some Felucian

◀ **Jedi Disappeared** Commander Ahsoka Tano's forces handled one part of the three-pronged attack against the Separatists. They scaled a wall with grappling hooks to gain access to the Separatist outpost and overcome the battle droids. As the fight neared its end, Trandoshan hunters who were on Felucia for sport captured the Padawan.

Commanders

GENERAL PLO KOON
Having fought in the 1st Battle of Felucia, Plo Koon returned to claim the planet for the Republic. Aware that General Grievous was sending reinforcements, Plo knew they must take the enemy base quickly, and decided that dividing the Republic forces was the most sound approach.

TZ-33 (DESTROYED IN ACTION)
Designed for military strategic analysis and tactics, TZ-33 calculated the battle as an inevitable Separatist victory after receiving additional battle droids. He was unaware of the Republic's looming ambush. Though he launched a counterattack, TZ-33 was too late to save the outpost and himself.

◀ **Long Reach** All Terrain Tactical Enforcers (AT-TEs), well suited for Felucia's challenging jungle surface, also possessed the advantage of range. The mass-driver cannons mounted atop the AT-TE walkers allowed the Republic to attack the outpost from an adjacent ridge.

farmers during a previous entanglement on the planet, Skywalker and Tano turned to local scouts for help pinpointing the weaknesses of the main Separatist outpost.

Plo Koon's strategy split the Republic party into three squads: Tano would lead Clone Sergeant Sinker, Clone Corporal Comet, and others up the rear wall of the outpost with grappling hooks; Plo himself would take Commander Wolffe and his squad over the left wall with jetpacks; and Skywalker and Captain Rex would bring the 501st Clone Battalion through the front door.

Though their opponent, the tactical droid TZ-33, was programmed for military strategy, he didn't anticipate this maneuver. The sheer number of droids often strengthened the Separatist position, but their programming only went so far. The Republic captured the Separatist base in short order, gaining control of Felucia and the surrounding region. But it would not be the final battle fought over the world.

FRONTAL ASSAULT

General Anakin Skywalker and Captain Rex had perhaps the most key mission in the Republic attack on the Separatist outpost: storming the front gate. With AT-TE walkers providing cover, they led the 501st Clone Battalion on a frontal approach. Plo Koon knew that once the tank fire made the Separatists aware of the Republic ambush they would form up for a counterattack and lower the front gate. DSD1 dwarf spider droids comprised the first wave of the Separatist defense, but Skywalker destroyed several of them before breaching the outpost's interior and locating TZ-33.

▶ **Droid Destruction** After dismantling numerous BX-series droid commandos, Skywalker sliced TZ-33 in half with his lightsaber.

Mon Cala

DATE: 1 BFE ▪ **LOCATION:** MON CALA, OUTER RIM ▪ **COMBATANTS:** REPUBLIC VS. SEPARATISTS ▪ **OUTCOME:** REPUBLIC VICTORY

WATER WAR

While the Clone Wars raged in the wider galaxy, political tensions ran high on Mon Cala. There, the Quarren and the Mon Calamari struggled to maintain a fragile coexistence. Seeing the strategic value of the planet, both the Republic and the Separatists sent political and military envoys to project their influence. The tensions reached a tipping point when the planet's ruler, Mon Calamari King Yos Kolina, was assassinated and civil war erupted.

Through much of the conflict, the Quarren and their Separatist allies held the upper hand. After the initial invasion, most of the Mon Calamari and clone armies were captured, a fate that befell even the Gungan Grand Army, called from Naboo as reinforcements. Despite the Separatist victories on the battlefield, Prince Lee-Char was an ever-present threat to their plans. Until he could be captured, he served as a symbol of Mon Calamari freedom.

The civil war on Mon Cala took on a brutal character. The Separatists' savage attacks with Karkarodon soldiers, the use of cybernetic superweapons, torture of captured generals, and the internment of combatants and civilians alike made it one of the most vicious campaigns of the war. Ultimately, these heavy-handed tactics led the Quarren leadership to reconsider their

▼ **Undersea Battlefield** The aquatic combat on Mon Cala posed unique challenges not found on the surface. Attacks came from all sides, and the combatants used fast-moving miniature submarines to close on enemy lines.

▲ **Republic Reinforcements** Outfitted with rebreathers and underwater beam rifles, specialized clones reinforced the Mon Calamari in their defense of their capital city. Upon their capture, the Republic was unable to quickly replace such specialist troops.

alliance with the Separatists. Discovering their treacherous intentions for the planet was the final straw, leading to the Quarren rising up against their overlords. The combined forces of the Quarren, Mon Calamari, Republic, and Gungans were enough to push the Separatists off the planet. With peace restored, Prince Lee-Char took the throne and ruled for decades to come.

KEY COMBATANT: THE QUARREN

Before the war, a strained peace had existed between the Mon Calamari and their planetary neighbors, the Quarren. The Mon Calamari had long ruled the shared planet, but the death of King Yos Kolina without an experienced heir led some Quarren to believe it was time for their species to rule their aquatic homeworld. The were caught off guard by the deception they faced from their new Separatist allies.

► **Separatist Pawn** Quarren leader Nossor Ri started the civil war, unaware of his Separatist allies' sinister plans.

Commanders

PRINCE LEE-CHAR
The son of King Yos Kolina was not only heir to the Mon Calamari throne, as incoming king he was also supreme commander of Mon Cala's military. The inexperienced prince turned to a seasoned advisor, Captain Gial Ackbar, for military strategy, but was forced to muster his own courage to rally his people.

COMMANDER RIFF TAMSON (KILLED IN ACTION)
Acting as Separatist ambassador to the Quarren, the militant Karkarodon Riff Tamson infiltrated the Mon Calamari royal palace and assassinated King Yos Kolina. By instigating a civil war, Tamson believed he could secure the planet for the Separatists and appoint himself to the throne.

KEY WEAPON: HYDROID MEDUSA

When their initial assault failed, the Separatists deployed their half-machine, half-creature secret weapons. The giant hydroid medusas moved slowly through the seas, electrocuting anyone in their path. Their cybernetically enhanced bodies were nearly impregnable, allowing the colossal jellyfish to almost singlehandedly turn the tide of the battle in the Separatists' favor. The Quarren simply gathered up the stunned survivors, taking most of the Mon Calamari army and Republic clones prisoner.

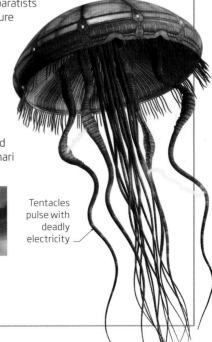

Tentacles pulse with deadly electricity

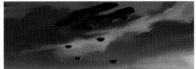

▲ **Rapid Deployment** Safely above water, a single Separatist landing craft airdropped enough hydroid medusas to gain control of an entire underwater city.

Umbara

DATE: 1 BFE ▪ **LOCATION:** UMBARA, EXPANSION REGION ▪
COMBATANTS: REPUBLIC VS. SEPARATISTS ▪
OUTCOME: REPUBLIC VICTORY

NIGHT BATTLE

The remote, perpetually dark planet of Umbara hosted a series of brutal battles as the Separatist-aligned Umbarans defended their homeworld, which lay along a vital supply route. The Republic's invasion strategy called for a rapid strike on the Umbaran capital city, beginning with a blockade-smashing attack on the Separatist fleet protecting the planet. Upon reaching the ground, the 212th Attack Battalion under the leadership of General Obi-Wan Kenobi, supported by Generals Saesee Tiin and Pong Krell, was to quickly take the Umbaran capital along the southern front. General Anakin Skywalker's 501st Clone Battalion was to strike in the north to block native reinforcements as the Republic pushed to quickly capture and hold the capital city. Strong resistance from combat droids and Umbaran soldiers, combined with difficult environmental conditions, foiled the Republic's plan for a swift victory. Kenobi's troops lost momentum and were forced to fight a prolonged battle on the outskirts of the capital. Skywalker's frontal assault and subsequent capture of a defensive ridge was nearly undone by sustained ambushes by Umbaran guerrillas, turned back only by the overwhelming force of Republic low-altitude airstrikes. In addition to advanced weapons technology and sneak attacks, Republic clones faced hostile terrain and aggressive native creatures. With obscured visibility due to the planet's lack of sunlight, friendly fire also took its toll.

After the initial landing, command of the 501st fell to General Pong Krell when Skywalker was recalled to Coruscant. Following a failed attempt to reinforce the capital along the main roads, Krell and the 501st redirected to a nearby enemy airbase with the aim of severing a resupply point.

▲ **Combat in the Shadows** Umbaran militia attacked from the darkness using their knowledge of local flora and fauna to inflict significant casualties on Republic clones. They used mines, boobytraps, and ambushes to wear down the invaders.

KEY WEAPON: UMBARAN TECH

The Republic assault was met with a surprising host of advanced Umbaran military technology. The Impeding Assault Tank bristled with cannons and turrets as it crawled across and under the planet's surface. In the sky, hit-and-run Umbaran starfighter attacks struck in the darkness. Their spherical ray-shielded cockpits, plasma cannons, and flexible airframes were unlike anything found in Republic arsenals. Even their holographic control schemes, requiring precise hand motions by the user, were foreign to the clones who captured them.

▶ **Captured Craft** A wing of captured Zenuas 33 starfighters were key to Republic victory.

▲ **Traitor General** Pong Krell's reputation for following strict protocol and disregarding high clone casualty rates preceded him when he took temporary command of the 501st. Recklessness with his clones' lives and the discovery of his secret allegiance to Count Dooku led to a mutiny, with the combined forces of the 212th and 501st capturing and executing the Besalisk.

▲ **The Third Front** While battles for the capital and airbase raged on the ground, Republic pilots engaged the remnants of the Separatist blockade in orbit. The Z-95 Headhunter fighters struggled to break through the frigates and support ships forming a defensive ring around a central supply vessel.

Heavily guarded by armored units, the base was only captured by a stealth mission that turned the Umbarans' weapons against them.

The 212th remained entrenched around the capital, held back by the threat of long-range missiles and a Separatist supply ship in orbit. Using the newly captured Umbaran starfighters, clones under Krell's command infiltrated the ship in orbit, destroyed its power core from the inside, and created the opening Kenobi needed to secure the city. Republic troops routed the holdouts and the Republic secured the planet after a multi-day campaign.

Commanders

GENERAL ANAKIN SKYWALKER
The Jedi Knight Anakin Skywalker successfully led the initial ground invasion in the north. The brash Skywalker earned the respect of his troops by leading from the front. His leadership style stood in stark contrast to that of Pong Krell, who did not value his clones' abilities, nor their lives.

TM-171 (DESTROYED IN ACTION)
From his command center aboard the DH-Omni Support Vessel in orbit above Umbara, this tactical droid ordered strategic resupply operations that allowed his troops on the ground to withstand the Republic assault, until a highly improbable sneak attack by a trio of clones destroyed his ship.

Dathomir

DATE: 1 BFE ▪ **LOCATION:** DATHOMIR, OUTER RIM TERRITORIES ▪ **COMBATANTS:** SEPARATISTS VS. NIGHTSISTERS ▪ **OUTCOME:** SEPARATIST VICTORY

MASSACRE OF THE NIGHTSISTERS

A remote planet in the Quelli sector, Dathomir didn't offer much strategically in either its location or resources. Neither side in the Clone Wars would claim an advantage by controlling the planet. The Nightsisters and Nightbrothers called the world home and remained neutral. Despite all of those factors, the Separatists attacked Dathomir to annihilate the Nightsisters near the end of the war. Count Dooku targeted the planet because of Asajj Ventress, his one-time personal assassin. Ventress had returned to her home on Dathomir after Dooku

cast her aside and had worked with Clan Mother Talzin to plot revenge against him. Dooku struck back.

Count Dooku assigned General Grievous to lead the attack on Dathomir. He began by ordering an aerial bombardment by *Vulture*-class starfighters and *Hyena*-class bombers, directing their fire at the Nightsisters' fortress to flush them out into the open. The airstrike was only a precursor to Grievous' ground assault, which comprised Armored Assault Tanks (AAT) and a Defoliator Deployment Tank (DDT). The latter burned the tangled forest surrounding the

KEY COMBATANT: THE NIGHTSISTERS

The Witches of Dathomir embraced the dark energies of their home planet and channeled them in their magicks. Led by a Clan Mother, the Nightsisters valued hierarchy and ritual. Elder Nightsisters passed down spellcraft, relying on the clan's lengthy oral history to impart wisdom, while designated members of the coven taught their fellow Nightsisters combat techniques. They wielded unique weapons of their own design and eliminated many droids during the battle.

▲ **Taking Aim** Nightsisters used plasma generator-powered energy bows in battle.

▼ **Chant of Resurrection** Before Grievous killed her, Daka, an elder, powerful Nightsister, raised the dead to use as reinforcements against the much larger droid army.

fortress, depriving the Nightsisters of much-needed cover and slowing their defense efforts.

While the Separatists continued their assault with droids and war machines, the Nightsisters turned to their magicks. They had long fostered a connection with Dathomir and its potent dark-side presence. The Nightsisters relied on this rather than technology and fought with methods completely unlike those of the droid army, including raising their dead to assist them. Because of their connection to their home, the Nightsisters managed to make a strong stand against the Separatists despite their lesser numbers. But ultimately, Grievous used the Nightsisters' reliance on magicks against them. With Dooku's assistance he found their weakness and killed the clan's elders.

Though Count Dooku and General Grievous' intent was to exterminate the Nightsisters, they did not achieve their goal. A small number remained. Those who survived waited over the succeeding years and decades for the right moment to avenge their fallen sisters.

Commanders

MOTHER TALZIN (KILLED IN ACTION)
As Clan Mother of the Nightsisters, Talzin used her powerful spells to rain lightning upon the droids. She also used her arcane abilities to torture Count Dooku through an effigy of his body. Dooku retaliated by ordering Grievous to specifically target Talzin.

GENERAL GRIEVOUS
The Nightsisters pushed back the initial Separatist wave, forcing General Grievous to personally intervene. He ordered the destruction of the forest to halt the Nightsisters, and dueled with Ventress before eventually killing Mother Talzin and Daka—thereby ending resistance to the massacre.

▲ **Battle Ready** Ventress felt responsible for the Separatists' attack on the Nightsisters. She used her lightsabers to eliminate multiple enemies, but it was not enough.

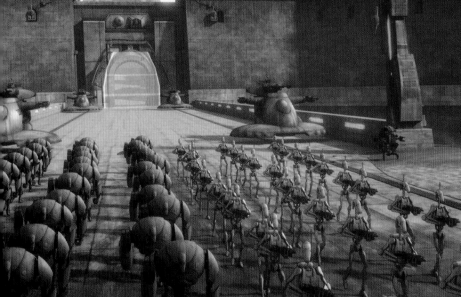

▲ **Endless Reinforcements** B2-series super battle droids flooded into Iziz alongside standard battle droids and HMP gunships after King Sanjay Rash asked Count Dooku for reinforcements. To spare Iziz' civilians from the ensuing battle, Steela Gerrera and the Onderon rebels lured the droids away to the Highlands. This decision saved countless innocent lives.

Commanders

GENERAL STEELA GERRERA (KILLED IN ACTION)
Steela Gerrera's sharp strategic mind and cool head made her an excellent, if reluctant, leader of the Onderon rebels. She died leading them in battle, but her actions restored King Dendup to the throne.

KING SANJAY RASH (EXECUTED)
Installed as Count Dooku's puppet, Sanjay Rash knew nothing about military engagement. Unsure of how to fight the insurgents, Rash depended upon aid from Count Dooku. When Rash failed, the super tactical droid that Dooku had sent to Onderon executed the king.

Onderon

DATE: 1 BFE ■ **LOCATION:** ONDERON, INNER RIM ■ **COMBATANTS:** REPUBLIC/ONDERON REBELS VS. SEPARATISTS ■ **OUTCOME:** ONDERON REBEL VICTORY

GUERRILLA WARFARE

As guardians of peace in the galaxy, the Jedi Order's involvement in the Clone Wars balanced on a wavering line. The Battle of Onderon in particular tested the Jedi's dichotomy between being peacekeepers and war generals. When King Ramsis Dendup, ruler of Onderon, refused to align his planet with either the Republic or the Separatists, the latter organization invaded. Count Dooku deposed Dendup and installed a king of his own: Sanjay Rash.

It was an unusual tactic for the Separatists, and not a successful one, as a group of rebels established a camp in the jungle outside the capital city Iziz to fight the "king" and the droid army that supported him. The Onderon rebels asked the Jedi Council for assistance, but as the current king of the planet stood with the Separatists, the Jedi decided against outright involvement. Instead General Anakin Skywalker made an argument for the Jedi to teach the Onderon rebels how to defend themselves. It was a questionable work-around to the Jedi's decision to not choose a side.

Skywalker led an advisory team to the planet. They showed the rebels, led by the Gerrera siblings, guerrilla tactics such as sabotage, hit-and-run maneuvers, and ambushes. These methods proved fruitful for the group as they shifted from the defensive to the offensive. Indeed, the techniques were so successful that they would later be adopted into the Rebel Alliance's rule book. Rash's Separatist reinforcements were not enough to stop the rebels; they defeated the droid army and reinstated Dendup as king.

▲ **Assisted by Nature** The Separatist and Republic armies comprised machines and organic beings respectively. The conflict on Onderon demonstrated that dichotomy as the rebels rode rupings–flying reptavians–into the fight against the Separatists' droid gunships.

KEY COMBATANT: SAW GERRERA

His spirit hardened in the guerrilla attacks on Onderon, Saw Gerrera carried the spark for rebellion forward. Years after Steela's death, Gerrera organized a group, the Partisans, to fight against the Galactic Empire. The burgeoning Rebel Alliance kept Gerrera at arm's length because he tended to favor extreme tactics.

▲ **Leadership Ambitions** Saw was the self-proclaimed leader of the Onderon rebels, but had much to learn about strategy. He was angered when his sister was later elected leader instead of him.

▲ **Sharpshooter** Steela Gerrera exhibited great skill as a sniper during her training from the Jedi. She wielded her blaster rifle with focus, saving the rebel camp when battle droids suddenly attacked their positions.

Anaxes

DATE: 0 BFE ▪ **LOCATION:** ANAXES, OUTER RIM TERRITORIES ▪
COMBATANTS: REPUBLIC VS. SEPARATISTS ▪
OUTCOME: REPUBLIC VICTORY

DESPERATE COUNTERSTRIKE

In the final weeks of the Clone Wars, Separatist forces led by Admiral Trench disrupted the Outer Rim Sieges by attacking Anaxes, a Republic stronghold located at the Coreward edge of the Outer Rim. Trench's battle droids won a series of key early victories, forcing Jedi Generals Mace Windu, Obi-Wan Kenobi, and Anakin Skywalker to intervene.

Captain Rex suspected that the Separatists had access to a strategic algorithm used by the Republic, implying the ARC trooper Echo had survived his apparent death on Lola Sayu. The 212th Attack Battalion's Commander Cody devised an infiltration mission to test Rex's theory, and called in Clone Force 99, otherwise known as the "Bad Batch." Rex's suspicions proved correct, and Skywalker and the Bad Batch rescued Echo from a Techno Union facility on Skako Minor. Echo proposed feeding Trench strategies that the Republic would know in advance and be able to counteract, and guessed correctly that Wat Tambor, the Techno Union's foreman, would conceal Echo's rescue from Admiral Trench despite the great danger it posed to Separatist forces.

The climactic battle for Anaxes unfolded on two fronts. Windu and Kenobi led troops to retake the shipyards' main assembly complex, while Skywalker, Echo, and the Bad Batch raided Trench's flagship, the *Invulnerable*. Echo engineered a feedback pulse that shut down the Separatist battle droids, but Trench had attached a bomb to the assembly complex's massive fusion reactor. This backup plan failed when Skywalker forced Trench to reveal the deactivation code. He then killed the Separatist admiral.

▲ **Surprise Attack** Anaxes was home to the revered Republic Navy War College, and strongly defended. But Trench's assault caught the Republic by surprise, with his forces repeatedly outflanking Anaxes' defenders.

▲ **Fatal Miscalculation** Trench's uncanny ability to read opponents struck fear into many Republic commanders. But he misread Anakin Skywalker, wrongly concluding that the Jedi would negotiate rather than resort to violence.

Commanders

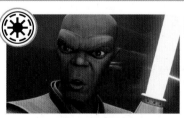

GENERAL MACE WINDU
Windu took the lead in the effort to retake the assembly complex, rallying clone troops and then ordering them to evacuate while he remained behind to disarm a bomb attached to a fusion reactor. Anaxes was one of Windu's final victories in a sterling record as a reluctant but effective Jedi general.

ADMIRAL TRENCH (KILLED IN ACTION)
Trench was a legendary tactician who gained renown in the Andoan Wars and bested Republic forces at Malastare Narrows. But he met his match in Skywalker, who broke his blockade of Christophsis, nearly defeated him at Ringo Vinda, and then killed him at Anaxes.

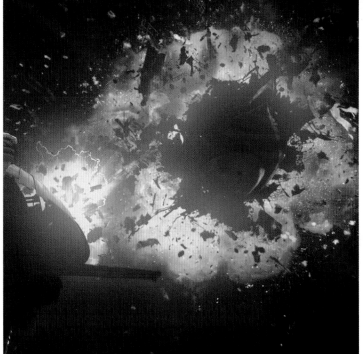

▲ **Commando's Reward** As a fail-safe against capture, Trench rigged the *Invulnerable* to blow, keeping a detonator at his side. Skywalker presented this device to the clone commando Wrecker, who took great pleasure in destroying the flagship.

KEY COMBATANT: THE "BAD BATCH"

Some of the Clone Wars' most dangerous missions fell to clone commandos, with a number of units winning renown during the conflict. One of the most celebrated was Clone Force 99, nicknamed the "Bad Batch." Its members had genetic mutations that proved advantageous in combat, making them highly effective at covert operations. But as more conventional commanders soon discovered, it also made them hard to control.

Wrecker

Sgt. Hunter

Crosshair

Tech

▶ **Never Fail** The unit was reputed to have a 100-percent success rate on operations.

Mandalore

DATE: 0 BFE ▪ **LOCATION:** MANDALORE, OUTER RIM TERRITORIES ▪ **COMBATANTS:** GALACTIC REPUBLIC/MANDALORE RESISTANCE VS. SHADOW COLLECTIVE ▪ **OUTCOME:** GALACTIC REPUBLIC/MANDALORE RESISTANCE VICTORY

UNCIVIL WAR

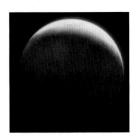

As the Clone Wars drew to its conclusion, Maul, former apprentice of the Sith Lord Darth Sidious, ruled Mandalore from its capital city, Sundari. Blocked from direct rule by Sidious, Maul led from the shadows. He used Prime Minister Almec, who once betrayed the late Duchess Satine Kryze, as his puppet and mouthpiece. Mandalorians loyal to Maul kept a tight grip on Sundari's citizens.

Bo-Katan Kryze, one-time member of the Death Watch and Satine's sister, resolved to remove Maul and his criminal organization from Mandalore.

Kryze asked the Republic for assistance through unconventional means. She approached former Jedi Ahsoka Tano, who then communicated with Generals Anakin Skywalker and Obi-Wan Kenobi. The Republic acquiesced to involvement but with some reluctance. Their forces were already stretched thin with the ongoing Outer Rim Sieges, and when General Grievous kidnapped Supreme Chancellor Palpatine on Coruscant the Republic's numbers were further split.

▲ **Maul's Soldiers** Commander Gar Saxon led Maul's Shadow Collective super commandos against the Republic. They kept the enemy forces occupied while Maul engaged the Jedi. Maul did not stand by his loyal soldiers and ultimately abandoned them.

Without a Jedi to command clone troopers on Mandalore, the Republic contrived a work-around: Skywalker promoted Clone Captain Rex to commander and appointed Tano as an advisor. With Tano, Rex, and a division of troopers from the 501st Clone Battalion, Kryze and her Nite Owl warriors returned to Mandalore.

Maul anticipated their arrival. Tano followed the prescribed strategy for encounters with enemy Force users, focusing on Maul while the clones confronted the remaining enemy units –lethal Mandalorian super commandos rather than battle droids. The super commandos split the clone troopers' numbers with engagements throughout the domed city's surface and Undercity. Meanwhile Kryze's warriors evacuated Sundari's civilians–who were not accepting of the Republic's presence–from the line of fire. Together, Kryze and the Republic claimed victory.

Shortly after Tano and Rex left Mandalore with a captured Maul, Supreme Chancellor Palpatine enacted Order 66. With the new Empire taking over the galaxy, the Republic's victory on Mandalore and the apprehension of Maul were rendered hollow.

Commanders

BO-KATAN KRYZE
Knowing she didn't have the numbers for a siege, Bo-Katan Kryze called upon the Republic for assistance in removing Maul. She flew into battle alongside her Nite Owls, capturing Maul's puppet leader Prime Minister Almec. At the end of the siege, Kryze became Mandalore's regent.

MAUL (CAPTURED)
Maul hoped that Kryze would bring the Republic to Mandalore but he also expected her to bring General Skywalker, who he'd had a vision about, or General Kenobi. Instead, Maul confronted Tano and attempted to make an ally of the former Jedi by telling her about his vision. Tano captured him instead.

KEY LOCATION: MANDALORE

Located in the Outer Rim, the planet Mandalore is the homeworld of the legendary Mandalorian warrior culture. The world's surface is scarred by the centuries of warfare it has endured. The late Duchess Satine Kryze ruled with a pacifist platform, maintaining neutrality in the Clone Wars, but Maul shattered her system when he killed her. As the new leader of the Death Watch, Maul took over the planet.

▲ **Domed Cities** Wars on Mandalore rendered much of the planet a harsh desert, so cities like Sundari were enclosed bio-domes.

▲ **Maul's Offer** Maul told Tano that Skywalker would join Darth Sidious, but she refused to believe him. The duo engaged in an acrobatic and intense lightsaber duel.

Raising Armies

Controlling the entire galaxy requires vast armies of troops for battle. Throughout the ages, regimes have taken many approaches to this problem, from scientific production of soldiers created by cloning biological beings to more traditional manufacturing of mechanical droids. Persuasion in various forms helped others to recruit their soldiers from among the citizenry, while more extreme approaches called for the abduction and brainwashing of children to fill the ranks. While the strengths and weaknesses of each approach could be debated, it is undeniable that the choices made when creating an army would have meaningful effects on the outcomes of the wars they fought.

▲ **Rapid Production** The Republic's clone soldiers' DNA was modified for rapid development, allowing the army to be grown and fielded in just 10 standard years.

CLONING

The Galactic Republic had long opposed maintaining a centralized standing army, but the Separatist crisis in its waning years forced the government to accept a solution that would provide it a fighting force almost instantly. They found it on Kamino, a secretive world whose primary trade was the creation of clones. These biological soldiers benefited from preprogrammed loyalty and obedience, while naturally maintaining the ability to show compassion and improvise in ways that droids could not. But high cost and long production times limited their use in future conflicts.

▲ **Automated Manufacture** The foundries of Geonosis were themselves automated, creating droids by the millions with mechanical precision.

DROID MANUFACTURE

While most armies relied on droids for specialized tasks or support roles, the Confederacy of Independent Systems almost exclusively relied on droids to fill its ranks. Vast sums of corporate wealth and the Banking Clan's credit reserves were funneled into the foundries at Geonosis and elsewhere, producing battle droids by the millions. Given the limited programming of their droids, high-ranking Separatist leadership fell to living beings whose strategies often relied on overwhelming numbers to outweigh the

KEY INFO

IMPERIAL ACADEMIES

To fill its ranks of stormtroopers and pilots, the Empire established a network of academies to train their forces. On planets like Arkanis, Carida, and Lothal, the academies provided a harsh introduction to life in Imperial service, designed to weed out those suited for the infantry from the most promising cadets destined to become pilots. They also served a more sinister purpose, identifying Force-sensitive youths to be redirected toward the Emperor's secret programs.

◀ **Taskmasters** Imperial commandants encouraged competition among cadets, instilling a sense of ruthless ambition among the ranks.

Enlistment documents for rapid processing

Recruiting chief officer rank badge

▲ **Desperate Measures** Imperial recruiters filled their quotas with willing enlistees from the galaxy's downtrodden planets, such as Corellia.

droids' operational shortcomings. Ultimately, it was proven that the standard B1 battle droid was not well-equipped to win a war against clones or Jedi, and their more advanced counterparts were in too limited a supply. Droids continued to serve in other militaries but never in such a significant role as employed by the Separatists.

RECRUITMENT

The Galactic Empire's desire for military expansion required an ever-growing combat force. The clones that initially served this role were phased out in favor of a more cost-efficient and limitless source: the enlistment and conscription of human recruits. Some were attracted by the promise of escaping unremarkable worlds for a life at academies that glamorized Imperial service. Others were attracted by the assurance of order and unity, ideals espoused regularly in Imperial propaganda. While the Emperor's recruits could never match the consistent performance offered by clones or droids, the seemingly limitless supply of troops was a vital tool for projecting Imperial might further than any previous galactic government had ever achieved.

KIDNAPPING AND BRAINWASHING

Three decades after Imperial survivors disappeared into the Unknown Regions, the First Order reappeared in their place, boasting one of the most well-equipped and professionally trained fighting forces the galaxy had ever known. Their ranks were filled by Project Resurrection, a conspiracy to abduct children from their homeworlds and condition them from a young age for life in First Order service. The soldiers of the First Order were more capable than their Imperial predecessors, but in the end the regime was brought down, in part, by former stormtroopers who had broken from their indoctrination.

▲ **True Believers** The First Order's unwavering belief in their cause of order and strength led them to conduct unspeakable war crimes without question.

Coruscant

DATE: 0 BFE ▪ **LOCATION:** CORUSCANT, CORE WORLDS ▪ **COMBATANTS:** REPUBLIC VS. SEPARATISTS ▪
OUTCOME: REPUBLIC VICTORY

ATTACK ON THE CAPITAL

The element of surprise can be a powerful advantage in warfare. By the latter stages of the Clone Wars a Republic victory seemed inevitable, and the Separatists appeared to be trapped in a series of sieges in the Outer Rim. While victory in those battles was proving to be attritional, the military spending and requisition bills passing through the Senate coupled with increasing outputs of clone troopers ensured that momentum was with the Republic.

It was at this point that Count Dooku and General Grievous staged the audacious—and potentially war-winning—raid on Coruscant, the galactic capital. The Republic's most battle-hardened forces had been drawn to the Outer Rim, leaving the interior relatively undefended. Utilizing secret hyperspace routes through the Galactic Core, the Separatist fleet was able to arrive at Coruscant without warning.

With the Coruscant Home Defense Fleet outmaneuvered, General Grievous led an expedition to the Senate District, took Supreme Chancellor Palpatine hostage, and returned to orbit.

Fleets Engaged Above Coruscant the Republic and Separatist fleets merged in a confusing free for all. Capital ships maneuvered to fire on targets of convenience while fighter squadrons attempted to exploit openings and increase damage to unshielded vessels.

Clone Pilots The Kaminoan cloning program had produced various subsets of soldiers suited to the Republic's needs. These included specialist clone pilots who received additional combat training in operating the various fighter craft within the Republic navy.

Commanders

COMMANDER HONOR SALIMA
Having been caught off guard by the Separatist attack, Commander Salima swiftly rallied the Coruscant Home Defense Fleet into action. With the Supreme Chancellor held hostage in orbit, Salima ordered Republic vessels to close to prevent the Separatists from disengaging and escaping.

GENERAL GRIEVOUS
The leader of the Separatist armed forces, Grievous struck the most significant early blow in the battle by personally capturing Palpatine and extracting him from Coruscant. However, having succeeded at this task, Grievous was ordered by Dooku to stay in orbit and engage the Republic fleet at close quarters.

JEDI ON A MISSION

The capture of Supreme Chancellor Palpatine threatened the entire Republic war effort. News that Coruscant was under siege was enough to bring Obi-Wan Kenobi and Anakin Skywalker back from Yerbana with their strike force to assist in the battle.

The two fleets were already fully engaged when the two Jedi arrived, but they were able to make the most of the confusion of battle to home in on General Grievous' flagship, the *Invisible Hand*. The pair fought through Separatist droid fighter squadrons to reach the ship at the cost of many of the clone pilots escorting them. Once aboard, Kenobi and Skywalker were able to navigate up through the vessel to the main viewing platform where Palpatine was held hostage. Upon their arrival they were confronted by Count Dooku, Head of State for the Confederacy of Independent Systems. A duel between the opposing Force users became inevitable.

Jedi Fighter
The ETA-2 *Actis*-class light interceptor was the latest evolution in Jedi starfighters. It lacked shields and a hyperdrive but made up for this in speed and firepower.

Palpatine's Signal Supreme Chancellor Palpatine possessed a homing signal beacon that he activated during his capture to guide rescuers to him.

Coruscant (continued)

If the Separatist fleet had successfully escaped at this point, the capture of Palpatine would almost certainly have forced the Republic to the negotiating table. Victory was within the Separatists' grasp. Instead, Dooku delayed and kept his fleet in orbit. The battle above the planet became increasingly chaotic as Republic *Venator*-class Star Destroyers clashed with Separatist *Munificent*-class frigates and *Lucrehulk*-class battleships. Lines of battle did not simply become blurred, they began to overlap in three dimensions as capital ships from both sides attempted to gain elevation over the opposition using Coruscant's atmosphere

▼ **Passing Broadsides** At the height of the battle, The *Invisible Hand* and the Star Destroyer *Guarlara* engaged in full broadsides at point-blank range. For the *Invisible Hand,* the damage proved fatal.

as a foundation. Packed in close together, the weapons of these ships could be used to devastating effect in full broadsides as vessels passed each other. The Republic forces fought to ensure that the Separatist fleet, particularly Grievous' flagship, the *Invisible Hand,* could not extricate itself from battle. The Separatist battle plan was less apparent, but it appeared they also seemed intent on crippling the enemy fleet above the capital.

Regardless of these overarching strategies, the battle itself swiftly descended into local actions between nearby warships with fighter support on both sides filling the vacuum between them. At this point any coherent control from the commanders on both sides began to break down. Ships fired on targets of convenience or proximity rather than military worth.

KEY WEAPON: MASS-DRIVER CANNON

The weaponry of both Republic and Separatist fleets was designed to facilitate space combat at various distances. During the Battle of Coruscant all of these weapons, even the longest-range turbolasers, were utilized at extremely close quarters, inflicting devastating damage. Turbolaser batteries, mass-drivers, and torpedoes were able to target enemy ships at point-blank range and tear through shields and hull armor. The largest capital ships could survive such assaults for a limited period, but lighter frigates and support vessels could be split in two by a single broadside.

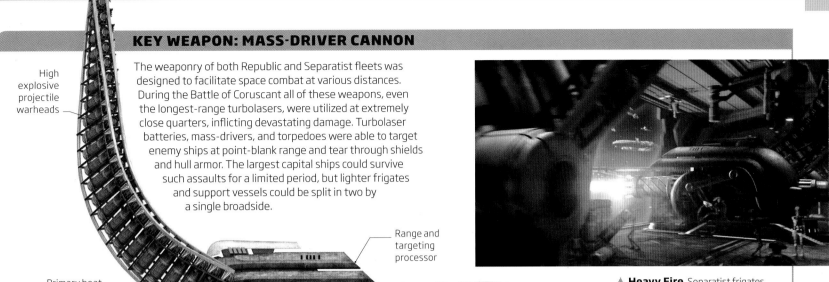

High explosive projectile warheads

Primary heat dissipator

Deck-mounted swiveling platform

Range and targeting processor

Ion cannon

Mass-driver barrel

Automatic shell feeder

▲ **Heavy Fire** Separatist frigates and battleships made use of heavy deck guns to cause enormous damage to enemy targets. Built-in ion cannons disrupted the shields of Republic vessels, allowing the heavy round from the mass-driver cannon to pass through undisturbed and puncture the hull.

◀ **Damage Sustained** Even the heaviest capital ships could not survive long against sustained fire. As the battle raged, the space above Coruscant became choked with shattered hulks and flaming wreckage.

▲ **Clone Casualties** Heavy shells from the *Invisible Hand* smashed through *Guarlara*'s hull and exploded on the gun decks, decimating the gun crews and igniting secondary explosions.

Coruscant (continued)

The rescue of Palpatine on the *Invisible Hand* by Obi-Wan Kenobi and Anakin Skywalker precipitated the battle swinging decisively in the Republic's favor. Not only did they ensure the Supreme Chancellor's safety, but in a lightsaber duel Anakin Skywalker killed Count Dooku. Following a battle on the bridge of the *Invisible Hand* between the Jedi and General Grievous, the Separatist flagship's control functions were destroyed and the vessel became easy prey for nearby Star Destroyers. Ravaged by internal explosions, the *Invisible Hand* fell out of orbit and, although General Grievous and some of the Separatist fleet were able to escape, many ships were left trapped between the Republic navy and Coruscant itself and forced to surrender. What should have been a dramatic and decisive Separatist

▼ **Dangerous Re-entry** After sustaining heavy damage the *Invisible Hand* entered Coruscant's atmosphere and began to break up. The rear half of the ship, including the engines, was torn clear of the main hull and destroyed.

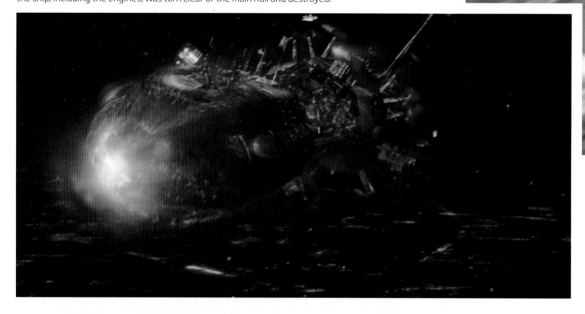

▲ **Emergency Response** Ships that lost repulsor power in orbit, such as the *Invisible Hand*, began to fall into Coruscant's gravity well and enter the atmosphere. If any crashed into the cityscape below, the civilian casualties would be enormous. In response, Coruscant Rescue Operations scrambled fire teams to douse burning vessels and use tractor beams to avert disaster.

▲ **Valuable Hostage** Supreme Chancellor Palpatine was a hugely popular figure. His kidnapping by General Grievous threatened to destabilize the entire Republic war effort. As a result, the Jedi Obi-Wan Kenobi and Anakin Skywalker resolved to rescue him.

victory had turned into a rout. While forces remained in action in the Outer Rim the bulk of the fleet deployed to Coruscant was lost and could not easily be replaced.

In the aftermath, Republic military officials pored over footage of the battle in a bid to discern the Separatist strategy. Why had they stayed in the system so long after capturing Palpatine? What none realized was that escape had never been Dooku's plan. The Clone Wars were being orchestrated by two Sith Lords, one on each side: Count Dooku and his master, Chancellor Palpatine. Palpatine used the battle purely as bait to lure Skywalker back to Coruscant, dispose of Dooku, and prepare the Republic for its final days.

DOOKU'S END

Count Dooku's role as leader of the Separatists had always been a ruse. In conjunction with Supreme Chancellor Palpatine, who was secretly the Sith Lord Darth Sidious, Dooku had orchestrated the war to eliminate the Jedi and claim absolute power. But Dooku had never appreciated that to Palpatine he was just another tool; a charismatic voice to lead the Separatists and distract the Jedi, not someone with whom to share power. Dooku believed his duel with Anakin Skywalker had been arranged so that he could defeat the Jedi. He was wrong. Having literally disarmed Dooku, Skywalker then decapitated him at Palpatine's urging.

▶ **Sith Betrayed** Count Dooku's ego had not permitted him to believe Anakin Skywalker could defeat him. Only as he kneeled at Skywalker's mercy did he realize Palpatine was discarding him.

Kashyyyk

DATE: 0 BFE ▪ **LOCATION:** KASHYYYK, MID RIM ▪ **COMBATANTS:** REPUBLIC VS. SEPARATISTS ▪ **OUTCOME:** REPUBLIC VICTORY

TWILIGHT OF THE WOOKIEES

By the third year of the Clone Wars, the Republic's full industrial might had been harnessed for the war effort, leaving the Separatists unable to keep pace, and Senate action had stripped away decades of bureaucracy, freeing Supreme Chancellor Palpatine and his ministers to direct the war quickly and nimbly.

Republic clone troopers drove the Separatists from the Core and Colonies, chasing them into the Mid Rim and the Outer Rim.

The Republic's 12th Sector Army took aim at the so-called Foundry of the Confederacy, whose factory worlds included Boz Pity, Metalorn, Saleucami, and Felucia. As the Outer Rim Sieges pushed Separatist economies to the brink of collapse, Count Dooku and General Grievous sought to reverse their fortunes by kidnapping Palpatine during a lightning raid on Coruscant. This desperate gambit failed: Dooku died and Grievous fled into the Outer Rim. But the war wasn't over. Kashyyyk occupied a strategic position in the Mid Rim, sitting on the doorstep of the Foundry at a junction of hyperspace routes.

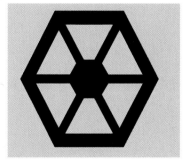

▲ **Attack from the Sea**
Separatist tank droids, dwarf spider droids, and crab droids emerged from the waves like nightmarish beasts from Wookiee tales of the Kashyyyk depths. But Kachirho's defenders showed no fear of these mechanical monsters.

◄ **Heavy Metal**
After months of preparation, Unduli knew the terrain around Kachirho very well. She established a staging area for Republic walkers and Juggernauts in the lowlands beyond the ancient tree-city.

KEY WEAPON: TANK DROID

The NR-N99 droid enforcer bristled with weaponry, packing cheek-mounted heavy blasters and ion cannons. While slower and less agile than other Separatist ground units, its sturdy construction and firepower made up for its deficiencies. Tank droids used their pontoon treads to traverse the shallow Wartaki lagoon before coming ashore at Kachirho.

▼ **Blind Spots**
Tank droids had poor lateral visibility and defenses, which Kachirho's Wookiees were quick to exploit.

Armor shields photoreceptors

Heavy blaster

Commanders

GENERAL LUMINARA UNDULI
The Mirialan Jedi Master Luminara Unduli was shaken by the treachery of her Padawan, Barriss Offee, who betrayed the Jedi Order. She sought solace in repairing the damage done to Kachirho by previous Separatist attacks and preparing new defenses for the city.

GENERAL LINWODO (DESTROYED IN ACTION)
A super tactical droid, Linwodo defended Metalorn and Boz Pity during the Outer Rim Sieges. He studied the battlefield records of Unduli and Vos, and was confident he could outwit them. Ranger Corps scouts tracked him down after the battle and blasted him apart.

Kashyyyk (continued)

Kashyyyk's location was enough to make the Wookiee homeworld an attractive target, but the Separatists also sought the data vault maintained by the Claatuvac Guild in the ancient tree-city of Kachirho. The guild's Wookiee scouts had blazed secret hyperspace routes across the galaxy. Seizing those routes could prolong the war, something the Republic vowed to prevent.

Jedi General Luminara Unduli commanded Kashyyyk's defenses. To bolster her efforts, the Republic reassigned Quinlan Vos from Boz Pity and sent Yoda from Coruscant. The Jedi grand master had helped stop earlier Separatist attacks on Kachirho, earning the honorific "Defender of the Home Tree." Yoda's task force drove a Separatist fleet from Kashyyyk, but invaders had already landed to threaten Kachirho.

▲ **Air Support** Wookiee air vehicles such as the Oevvaor jet catamaran and Raddaugh Gnasp fluttercraft were more maneuverable than Republic gunships, able to evade Separatist fire and swoop in to attack the cumbersome tank droids.

▲ **Battle on the Beach** The lagoon beach offered the only realistic approach to assaulting Kachirho by sea. Merumeru and the Republic clones furiously counterattacked the first wave of Separatist forces, determined to prevent their C-9979 landing craft from exploiting a beachhead.

The forested lowlands and sandy beaches of the Wawaatt Archipelago were ill-suited for both Republic AT-TE walkers and Separatist Multi-Troop Transports. The Republic turned to wheeled HAVw6 A6 Juggernauts, which the Separatists countered with *Persuader*-class tank droids. When tank and spider droids emerged from the Wartaki Sea, Unduli moved to reinforce the defenses from the left flank. Meanwhile, Vos directed an aerial assault led by Wookiee jet catamarans.

Order 66 threw the Republic forces into disarray. As clone troopers sought to neutralize their own Jedi commanders, the Separatists seized a beachhead and prepared to assault Kachirho. But the Republic troops quickly regrouped under Commander Faie, securing final victory.

KEY COMBATANT: THE WOOKIEES

Noting the Wookiees' proud warrior culture, Unduli spent months prior to the battle in consultation with the Wookiee militia, whose leaders included Merumeru, Attichitcuk, and Clausito. When the Separatists attacked, Wookiee warriors defended a key seawall with bowcasters and war clubs, fighting alongside the clone troopers. They also made daring aerial forays from catamarans, swooping in to sabotage tank droids with explosives before they could reach the beach.

▼ **Battle Line** A young Wookiee chieftain, Merumeru commanded ground forces at Kachirho and later fought against Kashyyyk's Imperial occupation.

➤ **Command Post** Unduli offered Yoda command of her forces, but he chose to observe the Separatist assault from a Kachirho command post, assisted by Commander Gree, the Ranger Corps' Captain Jek, and the Wookiees Tarfful and Chewbacca.

AFTERMATH

As night fell on the battlefield, operations shifted to hunting down Separatist stragglers and fugitive Jedi. Unduli was captured and taken into custody, where she ultimately perished, but Yoda escaped offworld with the help of friendly Wookiees and went into exile. Vos' fate remains unknown.

▼ **Clone Patrol** On orders from Faie, clone scout troopers riding All Terrain Recon Transports sought the missing Jedi Yoda and Vos amid Kashyyyk's bogs and forests.

Utapau

DATE: 0 BFE ▪ **LOCATION:** UTAPAU, OUTER RIM TERRITORIES ▪ **COMBATANTS:** REPUBLIC VS. SEPARATISTS ▪
OUTCOME: REPUBLIC VICTORY

DOWNFALL OF GENERAL GRIEVOUS

General Grievous remained a significant obstacle to overall victory for the Republic. Supreme Chancellor Palpatine had warned the Jedi Order that peace would not be considered until Grievous was destroyed. General Obi-Wan Kenobi was tasked with searching the Outer Rim for the Separatist general. While his fleet used the isolated Ak-Hurst system as a staging point, Kenobi arrived on the sinkhole planet Utapau, where the administrators of Pau City informed him that Grievous was holding the

population hostage. While Kenobi searched the city, he ordered his droid, R4-G9, to return his fighter to the fleet carrying a warning for the Republic.

Discovering that Grievous was sending the other Separatist leaders away, and with the Republic fleet not yet in position, Kenobi intervened and engaged Grievous in a lightsaber duel, severing two of the cyborg's hands. The arrival of the Republic fleet decisively swung the battle away from the Separatists by claiming immediate air superiority.

From low orbital positions the Republic deployed clone troopers and LAAT gunships to establish a foothold on Pau City's landing platforms. Sensing that the odds were shifting against him, General Grievous attempted to flee the battle but Kenobi pursued him on a varactyl. After engaging Grievous in hand-to-hand combat, Kenobi used a blaster pistol to shoot and kill the Separatist warlord.

Upon returning to the main battle, Kenobi inspired the clone troopers in an offensive to rout the now leaderless droids. However, following the declaration of Order 66, Commander Cody ordered an AT-TE combat walker to open fire on the Jedi. Kenobi's varactyl was mortally wounded and both fell into the water at the base of the city. Kenobi escaped, but in short order the Republic forces destroyed the remaining battle droids, seized control of the city, and arrested the local administrators.

▼ **Clone Offensive** Deploying from orbiting Republic assault ships, the 7th Sky Corps seized landing platforms on Pau City's 10th level as a foothold from which to attack.

Commanders

GENERAL OBI-WAN KENOBI
General Kenobi was a Jedi Master with a reputation for patient but effective military command. Tasked with locating General Grievous, Kenobi led from the front by personally scouting worlds such as Utapau, and then engaging Grievous to buy time for the Republic fleet to arrive.

GENERAL GRIEVOUS (KILLED IN ACTION)
Following the death of Count Dooku, Grievous assumed full control of the Separatist military. While a fearsome warrior, Grievous was renowned for running from battle if endangered. This proved to be the case at Utapau, where he was killed while attempting to flee.

▲ **Fateful Duel** General Grievous was determined to kill the Jedi Master Obi-Wan Kenobi himself. Utilizing stolen lightsabers and his own combat skills, Grievous engaged Kenobi only to be swiftly disarmed by the superior swordsmanship of the Jedi. Suddenly threatened by the arrival of the Republic troops, Grievous attempted to escape from the battle.

ORDER 66

With the Republic on the verge of victory, Commander Cody received a transmission from Supreme Chancellor Palpatine: "Execute Order 66." This directive was programmed into behavioral chips implanted in the brains of clone troopers and instantly defined all Jedi as enemies of the Republic. Cody followed this new order diligently and instructed his troopers to open fire on General Kenobi. Across the galaxy thousands of other clone troopers would swiftly turn on their Jedi leaders.

▶ **Final Betrayal** Cody had loyally served alongside Kenobi in countless battles, but did not hesitate in trying to kill the general when ordered to.

Mygeeto

DATE: 2–0 BFE ▪ **LOCATION:** MYGEETO, OUTER RIM TERRITORIES ▪ **COMBATANTS:** REPUBLIC VS. SEPARATISTS ▪
OUTCOME: REPUBLIC VICTORY

LONG-SOUGHT PRIZE

The Republic did not claim Mygeeto until the final days of the Clone Wars, but it wasn't for a lack of effort: their troops at last prevailed in the fourth major conflict that convulsed the icy planet. Dubbed part of the "Triad of Evil" by Republic propaganda, Mygeeto was an important InterGalactic Banking Clan hub, trailing only Scipio and Muunilinst in wealth and importance. It was also known for its crystal mines—its name meant "gem" in an ancient Muun trade language—and its kyber crystal deposits were a key target of Republic energy and weapons researchers.

▼ **Elite Unit** The 21st Nova Corps became famous for their ferocity in battle and for their distinctive synthmesh visors, which they wore to filter toxins on the battlefield. Dubbed the Galactic Marines, they were led by CC-1138, nicknamed Bacara.

The Muuns had ruthlessly exploited Mygeeto for centuries, reducing its native Lurmen population to serfdom. Many Lurmen became guerrillas during the Clone Wars, aiding Republic forces.

The Fourth Battle of Mygeeto came just months after the Third, a drawn-out affair in which Mandalorian Protectors came to the assistance of beleaguered Republic troops. By then Mygeeto was a badly tarnished gem: its skies were choked by fuel fires and its crystalline glaciers and cities pitted by years of torpedo impacts. Jedi General Ki-Adi-Mundi commanded the final push to take the world, leading the 21st Nova Corps, but never got to enjoy his victory as he was cut down by his own troops when Supreme Chancellor Palpatine issued Order 66 to the clone army.

THE DEATH OF KI-ADI-MUNDI

Ki-Adi-Mundi was known as one of the more conservative members of the Jedi Council, favoring cool logic and the lessons of tradition over alarmist rhetoric, conspiracy theories, and whispered prophecies. Some in the Order and the Senate found that frustrating, but all respected him on the battlefield. The Cerean's ability to stay calm under fire and his concern for his troops proved critical in many hard-fought campaigns.

▲ **Overwhelmed** When Ki-Adi-Mundi found himself surrounded by heavily armed, well-trained Galactic Marines, not even the Force could shield him from a fatal barrage of laser fire.

▲ **Mobile Troops** The 91st Reconnaissance Corps received special training in using speeder bikes for scouting and infantry support. The unit forged an impressive service record under Commander Neyo.

Saleucami

DATE: 0 BFE ▪ **LOCATION:** SALEUCAMI, OUTER RIM TERRITORIES ▪ **COMBATANTS:** REPUBLIC VS. SEPARATISTS ▪ **OUTCOME:** REPUBLIC VICTORY

DEATH ON THE RIM

Saleucami was branded part of the "Triad of Evil" alongside Mygeeto and Felucia, but the sleepy Outer Rim world didn't seem worthy of such concern, as it housed neither Banking Clan vaults nor Commerce Guild citadels. In the early days of the war, Saleucami was the site of a clash between Separatist warships and Republic forces seeking to rescue the Jedi General Eeth Koth, who had been taken prisoner by General Grievous. After that fight the temperate world seemed destined to become a peaceful backwater again. However, Separatist commanders instead decided to turn it into a trans-shipment point for war materiel generated by the factories of the Foundry of the Confederacy: Saleucami lay close to the Outer Rim's Salin Corridor, a regional hyperlane that became far safer for

Separatist convoys than the increasingly contested Perlemian Trade Route.

Republic intelligence feared Saleucami was more than just a strategically located stockpile: the planet supposedly housed secret labs in which scientists were researching superweapons, genetically engineered plagues, or a clone-soldier

program to rival Kamino's. In the final months of the war, Republic forces under Jedi General Quinlan Vos besieged the planet, finally breaking through and destroying its orbital warehouses. Vos then moved on, leaving Stass Allie and the 91st Mobile Reconnaissance Corps to investigate Saleucami's rumored secrets.

THE DEATH OF STASS ALLIE

A Tholothian Jedi Master, Stass Allie fought ably in the Clone Wars and was granted a seat on the Jedi Council late in the conflict. When Order 66 was issued, she proved easy prey for Commander Neyo and his scouts, who blasted her speeder bike. Similar tragedies unfolded on thousands of worlds, resulting in the deaths of Jedi Masters as well as Knights and Padawans. Surviving Jedi recalled disturbances in the Force that seemed to come from everywhere all at once.

▶ **No Warning** Most clones obeyed Order 66 without anger or fear—their lack of emotion kept the targeted Jedi from sensing danger.

▼ **Restricted Flying** Skywalker, Tano, and the 501st Clone Battalion attempted to stop Separatist invasion of Cato Neimoidia; aerial combat among its bridge cities demanded careful piloting.

Cato Neimoidia

DATE: 0 BFE ▪ **LOCATION:** CATO NEIMOIDIA, OUTER RIM TERRITORIES ▪ **COMBATANTS:** REPUBLIC VS. SEPARATISTS ▪ **OUTCOME:** REPUBLIC VICTORY

BATTLE INTERRUPTED

With so many crises occurring simultaneously around the galaxy, the Jedi Council had to carefully allocate resources. In some cases, as with the Battle of Cato Neimoidia, the Jedi had to put a battle aside in order to handle more urgent matters.

When Separatists forces arrived and began fortifying this Neimoidian purse world, headquarters of the Trade Federation, General Anakin Skywalker and Commander Ahsoka Tano arrived to stop them, alongside the 501st Clone Battalion. They briefly engaged the enemy, but a bombing at the Jedi Temple on Coruscant pulled them away from the conflict, leaving the Separatists free to claim victory.

The Republic returned to the wealthy

Neimoidian colony in the last days of the Clone Wars. They understood its strategic value as center of the Trade Federation and hoped that capturing Cato Neimoidia would be a positive movement toward the end of the war. Jedi Master Plo Koon led the 442nd Siege Battalion and Clone Flight Squad Seven in the battle.

Specializing in assailing enemy barricades, the 442nd Siege Battalion proved critical to the mission's success,

fighting among the planet's distinctive "bridge cities." Commander Verd directed the 442nd's companies as they used AT-RTs and Infantry Support Platforms to besiege the Separatist base in Tarko-se, where the Separatists had housed their forces in a one-time gladiator arena. With aerial support from Clone Flight Squad Seven and Plo Koon, they were eventually able to gain control of the planet from Confederacy General Baik Raaorn and his droid forces.

THE DEATH OF PLO KOON

Order 66 reverberated throughout the galaxy. While patrolling Tarko-se with his squadron of clones after their victory, Jedi Master Plo Koon was caught by surprise when Captain Jag fired upon him. Plo took evasive action, but not even his Jedi abilities helped him. Jag successfully hit Plo's Delta-7 *Aethersprite*-class light interceptor.

▶ **Shot Down** Plo Koon's ship exploded against one of Tarko-se's many bridges, killing the Jedi and destroying his droid.

3rd Felucia

DATE: 0 BFE ▪ **LOCATION:** FELUCIA, OUTER RIM TERRITORIES ▪ **COMBATANTS:** REPUBLIC VS. SEPARATISTS ▪ **OUTCOME:** REPUBLIC VICTORY

OUTER RIM SIEGE

The Clone Wars were nearing their end as Jedi Master Aayla Secura led her clone troopers to Felucia. Their mission was to locate and capture the Presidente of the Commerce Guild and member of the Separatist Council, Shu Mai, and free her hostage, Ormo Hyn, a relative of a Felucian leader who supported the Republic. Mai had kidnapped Hyn in hopes of persuading the Felucians to align with the Separatists. Since Felucia was located along a crucial hyperspace route, both the Republic and the Separatists vied to claim the planet.

▼ **Hard Going** Felucia's tangled jungle surface required a variety of all terrain vehicles–AT-TE, AT-AP, and AT-OT walkers–to traverse its hazardous topography.

Secura brought Commander Bly and the 327th Star Corps to Felucia. Noted for their extraction skills in the most trying of settings, the 327th Star Corps were Secura's safest choice for the operation. While scouting for the Separatist base they encountered HMP droid gunships. Secura piloted her Eta-2 *Actis*-class light interceptor against the enemy.

With the aerial forces dispatched, Secura and the 327th marched through Felucia's dense fungus jungle searching for any sign of Mai and the droid army. Unbeknownst to them, OG-9 homing spider droids and Armored Assault Tanks were slowly closing in on their position. Just as they were about to encounter the enemy, Palpatine issued Order 66 and effectively ended the war. Mai, who had already left Felucia, perished on Mustafar with the other Separatist leaders.

THE DEATH OF AAYLA SECURA

Jedi Master Aayla Secura was in the midst of battle when her clone troopers received Order 66 from Supreme Chancellor Palpatine. They were approaching the Separatists, poised to engage the enemy amid Felucia's fungal lifeforms, when Commander Bly and his clones took aim at Secura's back. Like many other Jedi who fell on this fateful day, she didn't have the opportunity to draw her lightsaber in defense.

▲ **Final Moments** Secura barely had time to react when her clones raised their blasters and started firing. They continued to shoot at Secura after her lifeless body dropped to the ground.

SPARKS OF REBELLION

- **MIMBAN**
  Colonial Warfare

- **ATTACK ON PHOENIX SQUADRON**
  Surgical Strike

- **RYLOTH INSURGENCY**
  Freeing the Twi'leks

- **ATOLLON**
  Rebels Under Siege

- **LOTHAL**
  Fighting for Home

- **WOBANI**
  Prison Break

- **JEDHA**
  Brutal Insurgency

- **EADU**
  Fractured Operation

CHAPTER 2

Sparks of Rebellion: Introduction

GALAXY MAP

Spreading Insurrection

After years of Imperial oppression, planets throughout the galaxy began striving for liberation. The Rebel Alliance monitored these groups and assisted them when they could spare personnel and resources. The new organization slowly expanded their network each time they engaged the Empire.

KEY

1 Mimban
2 Attack on Phoenix Squadron
3 Ryloth Insurgency
4 Atollon
5 Lothal
6 Wobani
7 Jedha
8 Eadu

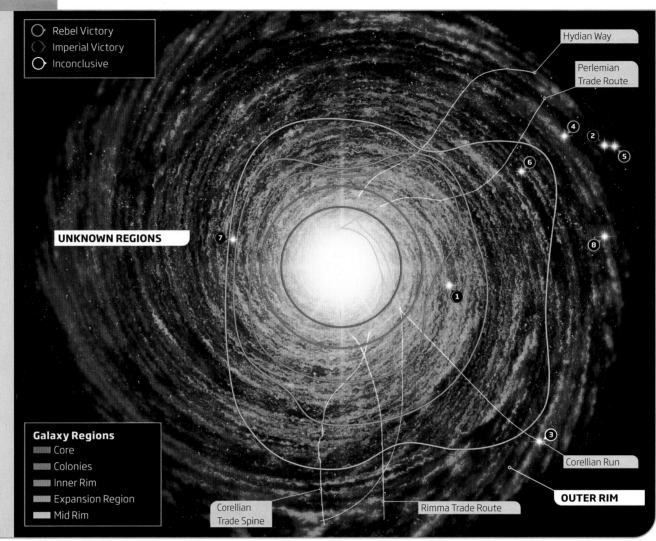

- ◔ Rebel Victory
- ◌ Imperial Victory
- ◯ Inconclusive

Hydian Way

Perlemian Trade Route

UNKNOWN REGIONS

OUTER RIM

Corellian Run

Corellian Trade Spine

Rimma Trade Route

Galaxy Regions
- Core
- Colonies
- Inner Rim
- Expansion Region
- Mid Rim

TIMELINE

AFE: After Formation of Empire

1 Mimban
The Mimbanese Liberation Army took up arms against the Empire after they invaded the planet for its valuable minerals.

3 Ryloth Insurgency
Cham Syndulla's Free Ryloth Movement pushed back against Imperial occupation, claiming some notable and encouraging victories.

9 AFE   10 AFE   11 AFE   12 AFE   13 AFE   14 AFE   15 AFE   16 AFE   17 AFE   18 AFE   19 AFE

2 Attack on Phoenix squadron
Darth Vader's attack against this rebel cell demonstrated how seriously the Empire took the Rebellion.

4 Atollon
Grand Admiral Thrawn attempted to break the Rebel Alliance but instead the rebels escaped.

The Empire exerted control across the galaxy for years, stripping planets of natural resources and dismantling local governments. Imperials arrived promising cooperation and fairness, but instead they simply took what they needed to feed their vast war machine with weaponry, soldiers, and starships. But worlds under various stages of Imperial oppression began to push back. Liberation movements formed through clandestine meetings around the galaxy, while whispers circulated in the Galactic Senate about Emperor Palpatine's true motives for clinging to the emergency powers he received during the Clone Wars.

Birth of the Rebellion

Separate efforts around the galaxy eventually combined into a single mission. Aware of Palpatine's use of Imperial forces to perpetuate violence and injustice, Senators Mon Mothma of Chandrila and Bail Organa of Alderaan realized that politically opposing Emperor Palpatine in the Galactic Senate wasn't enough. They plotted in secret to gather intelligence on the Empire and its vast operations. After pulling the pieces together, they orchestrated the efforts of multiple rebel cells to raid Imperial supplies, stop weapon shipments, and otherwise wreak havoc upon the Imperial machine—a machine that depended on order and precision. The Empire possessed superior might and numbers, but the gathering rebel forces were determined and focused on learning how to best weaken the Empire. They took

their time and gathered resources, allies, and intelligence. The rebels operated from the shadows until Mon Mothma publicly accused the Emperor of tyranny. Her widely broadcast call to arms brought the scattered rebel efforts into an official organization: the Alliance to Restore the Republic.

Increasing Pressure

The Empire put their own propaganda spin on this moment; they pushed the message that the rebels were no more than anarchists, seeking to bring chaos and disorder back to the galaxy after years of peace. Mon Mothma, in exile at this point, countered the claim by publicly issuing a document: the Declaration of Rebellion. The material condemned Palpatine's actions and listed the Empire's crimes against the galaxy. The denunciation also made clear that the rebels supported the institution of a Galactic government and that their intent was to restore the Galactic Republic that had existed before Palpatine dismantled it. Even though they now openly existed, the Rebel Alliance still had to conduct themselves in secrecy. Using an espionage network and leveraging allies on oppressed worlds, the Rebellion made progress in spreading the spark across the galaxy and inspiring beings to fight back. Rebel cells that had once functioned independently began joining together for missions, using secret communications channels to grow their numbers. While the Empire maintained the upper hand with their vast fleet and near-limitless resources, the rebels started landing blows.

5 Lothal
Phoenix Squadron scored a key victory against the Empire by liberating Lothal. The Rebel Alliance did not officially sanction this plan.

7 Jedha
The Empire demonstrated their new superweapon's formidable power. The Death Star obliterated Jedha City.

6 Wobani
The Rebellion freed Jyn Erso from an Imperial labor camp, setting the stage for "Operation Fracture."

8 Eadu
Rebel spies endeavored to extract Galen Erso to gain insight into the Empire's superweapon.

Mimban

DATE: 9 AFE ▪ **LOCATION:** MIMBAN, EXPANSION REGION ▪
COMBATANTS: EMPIRE VS. MIMBANESE ▪ **OUTCOME:** IMPERIAL VICTORY

COLONIAL WARFARE

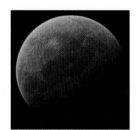

The Mimban Campaign was a notable example of Imperial expansion in the years before the Galactic Civil War. Mimban's heavy mineral deposits had made the world a lucrative addition to the Empire, but ongoing resistance from the native population required an Imperial military response.

Standard Imperial protocol when pacifying unruly worlds was to utilize orbital bombardments followed by mass deployment of ground forces. However, Mimban's dense, ionized atmosphere made aerial support impractical and necessitated the deployment of the 224th Imperial Armored Division. Repeated ground combat turned the surface into a muddy quagmire and the Empire dug in with fortified trench systems.

These conditions presented both a challenge and an opportunity to Imperial command, who implemented a strategy of attrition. The Mimbanese would be forced to engage in repeated battles that were not aimed at any grand strategic objective. Instead, their purpose was simply to grind down the numbers of Mimbanese opposition through relentless ongoing combat. The apparent stalemate on Mimban also allowed further military requisition bills to pass through the Imperial Senate to allow for the ongoing expansion of the armed forces. The reality of the Imperial strategy was not communicated to the soldiers on the ground, who would sustain heavy losses in ill-conceived, futile offensives.

Commanders

ELDER IASENTO
Iasento commanded the Mimbanese during the Imperial pacification campaign. Having been trained by Republic forces in the Clone Wars, he was familiar with the infantry tactics adopted by the Empire. Iasento allowed Imperial forces to push forward before attacking from hidden positions, utilizing the Mimbanese ability to seemingly appear out of the mud.

CAPTAIN ALAYUS BOLANDIN
Alayus Bolandin took control of the 224th Division on Mimban following the death of Major Staz. Bolandin was unerringly loyal to the ideals of the Empire and believed their mission was to affect regime change on Mimban by eradicating the enemy. Before redeploying to the Southern Marshlands he was given a field promotion from lieutenant to captain by General Falk.

▲ **Punishment Duty** Corporal Han Solo was redeployed from the Imperial Naval Academy into the Imperial army and posted to Mimban for insubordination. Considered tantamount to a death sentence, being sent to Mimban was usually a one-way trip.

Fog of War Driven forward by their commanding officers, infantry advancing from their trenches found the battlefield of Mimban a confusing and frightening experience.

KEY COMBATANT: THE MIMBANESE

A tribal species who had previously allied with the Grand Army of the Republic during the Clone Wars, the Mimbanese had shown little interest in wider galactic politics until feuding powers had come to raid the planet's hyperbaride minerals. Fighting first the Separatists and then the Empire, the Mimbanese utilized effective camouflage to hide themselves on the increasingly muddy battlefields and then attack with coordinated aggression. Lacking the industrial capacity to produce their own munitions, the Mimbanese cannibalized old Republic and Imperial weapons to defend their world.

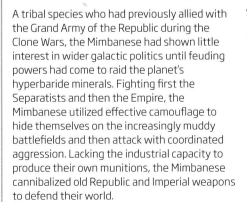

Sedge grass used as camouflage

Armor panel made of woven reeds

Mud-spattered combat fatigues

Republic-era combat webbing

Modified BlasTech F-78 rifle and attached vibroblade

Repurposed Imperial issue army boots

Hostiles Like all native species who resisted imperial invasion, the Mimbanese were simply called "hostiles" by the Empire. The troopers themselves nicknamed their foes "Deadeyes."

Mimban (continued)

Imperial engineers constructed expansive trench systems across Mimban to serve as staging points for the ongoing military campaign. The walls of these defensive positions were reinforced with durasteel to prevent the Mimbanese from tunneling in and launching surprise attacks behind the lines.

The trenches were designed in line with standardized Imperial protocols for the building of fortifications, with command points and medical facilities placed at regular intervals and designated by codes which signified both their location in the trench system and their proximity to the front lines.

Dug below ground level, the trenches existed beneath much of the ionized atmosphere that made combat so difficult and confusing, but they were also liable to fill with water from the damp air. As a result, going "over the top" to attack enemy positions could prove to be a difficult undertaking for soldiers in the 224th, as metal surfaces and ladders became wet and slippery and puddles of mud could prove impossible to escape.

Any appearance of attempting to avoid an order to attack left individual soldiers open to either summary execution or referral to the Imperial Security Bureau agents, who accompanied the division to ensure Imperial loyalty.

◀ **Subterranean Home** Carved out of the muddy landscape, Imperial trenches provided relative safety for the soldiers of the 224th. However, the frontline trenches would rapidly become filled with soldiers before an order to go "over the top," drawing heavy Mimbanese fire.

KEY COMBATANT: MUDTROOPERS

The so-called "mudtroopers" were a mixture of Imperial army soldiers and a specialized detachment of the stormtrooper corps. Trained for operations in extremely wet or muddy conditions, these soldiers led the Imperial efforts against the Mimbanese resistance. The troops made use of specialized equipment such as capes to prevent their armor becoming clogged with mud and waterproof army boots to avoid "trench foot." When not in action these soldiers had to work tirelessly to maintain their trench fortifications and latrines.

▶ **Combat Veterans** The extremely high rates of attrition on Mimban meant that surviving long enough to transfer offworld was a rare occurrence.

▲ **Imperial Trenches** Dug meters below ground level, the trench systems became home for thousands of Imperial soldiers. Navigating the trenches could be confusing for the uninitiated and new arrivals could find themselves lost in the maze of passageways. While notionally safer than above ground, the fortifications could be targeted by Mimbanese mortar fire at any time.

Mimban (continued)

All Terrain Defense Turrets (AT-DTs) provided mobile artillery support and TIE fighters strafed enemy positions. Heavily outgunned and utilizing a mixture of outdated and obsolete weaponry, the Mimbanese relied upon their knowledge of the planet's geography and their own natural abilities. Their eyes, adapted to low light conditions, allowed them to see through the haze of battle, giving them an advantage over Imperial army troopers who lacked helmet visors to assist in spotting targets.

◀ **Imperial Troopers** Regular Imperial army troopers, such as Corporal Han Solo, were equipped with light armor, helmet, and goggles. This basic equipment could deflect some blaster shots, but the goggles did little to help the troopers see through the fog of battle.

Furthermore, the Mimbanese made use of hidden tunnels and camouflaged positions among the ruins of their villages to seemingly appear from nowhere on the battlefield. While leading an attack on a Mimbanese village, Major Staz implored his men to keep moving toward a ridge with the promise that victory was near. However, the ridge disguised a Mimbanese tunnel network and he was swiftly killed by mortar fire.

The Empire made use of airborne reinforcements with AT-DTs being deployed directly onto the field by AT-hauler ships, either from behind the lines or from one of the Star Destroyers holding position above the clouds. While forward momentum was often painstakingly slow for soldiers on the ground, sheer strength of numbers made an ultimate Imperial victory on Mimban inevitable.

▲ **Ravaged World** The ionized fog at ground level made intervention from orbit difficult for the Empire. While TIE fighters strafed beneath the cloud layer, Star Destroyers hovered above and delivered continuous reinforcements to the Imperial outposts below.

KEY COMBATANT: BECKETT'S GANG

Amid the confusion of the Mimban offensive, Tobias Beckett's criminal gang successfully infiltrated the Imperial army. Wearing uniforms and armor liberated from soldiers who had fallen on the battlefield, they fought through fierce Mimbanese resistance to gain access to the Imperial trench system. Their objective was to steal an AT-hauler used to deploy Imperial heavy weaponry directly into combat. Beckett's false captain rank gave him the authority to order Imperial troops to clear his path of enemies.

► **Subterfuge** Beckett used his stolen uniform to reach Imperial lines.

▲ **Coordination** Working together, Beckett's gang fought through strong Mimbanese resistance, though Korso (far left) was killed in action.

▲ **Battlefield Aftermath** As the campaign rolled on, casualties rose on both sides. It was too dangerous to recover Imperial soldiers who fell on the field, and any weapons or heavy equipment that could not be recovered was salvaged by the Mimbanese, or simply lost into the mud.

Attack on Phoenix Squadron

DATE: 15 AFE ▪ **LOCATION:** DEEP SPACE ▪ **COMBATANTS:** PHOENIX CELL VS. EMPIRE ▪ **OUTCOME:** IMPERIAL VICTORY

SURGICAL STRIKE

The Imperial enforcer Darth Vader personally led a crippling attack on one of the early cells of rebels. His target was a combined insurgent force comprising Commander Jun Sato's Phoenix Squadron and a band known as the Spectres. Under its experienced commander, Sato's cell represented one of the largest concentrations of anti-Imperial force in the galaxy at the time, being home to multiple corvettes and a squadron of A-wing starfighters. The Spectres operated from a light freighter known as the *Ghost*, which they had previously used to undertake insurgent activity in and around the Lothal system. Working together allowed the combined cell to conduct regular attacks on Imperial convoys, disrupt Imperial operations in the sector, and successfully evade the Imperial patrols sent to hunt them down. Growing frustrated by the rising Rebellion, Vader laid a trap for the group on Lothal that allowed him to mount a surprise attack in deep space, catching the squadron unprepared.

From his personal TIE fighter, the lone Imperial agent inflicted significant damage on the squadron, destroying the rebel command ship and many of its fighter escorts. However, the three Star Destroyers that arrived to

▲ **Fighter Superiority** Darth Vader took on the entire Phoenix Squadron at the controls of a single TIE Advanced x1 starfighter. This was far from the only occasion where Vader would massacre rebel pilots in space combat.

KEY WEAPON: *PHOENIX HOME*

At the center of the Phoenix Cell's fleet was Commander Sato's *Pelta*-class frigate, *Phoenix Home*. From its well-appointed command center, Sato directed a squadron of A-wing starfighters, which were maintained and outfitted within the ship's internal hangar. Though not equipped for direct combat with larger Imperial warships, the frigate allowed them to conduct smaller raids against less protected targets such as supply convoys. The ship was destroyed in the battle, forcing Sato to relocate his command to a Corellian corvette for a time.

▼ **Countering Rebellion** A tracking device installed on a stolen Imperial cargo shuttle alerted the Empire to the Phoenix Cell's position.

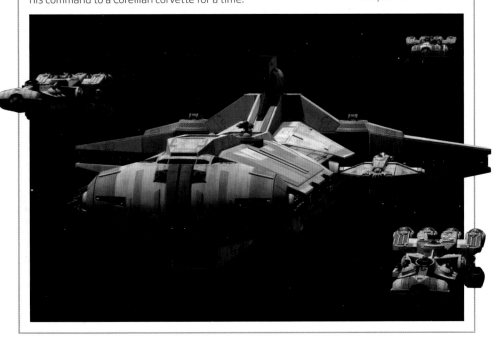

prevent the rebels from escaping failed in their mission, allowing the remnants of the squadron to jump to hyperspace. While the Spectres and five rebel corvettes slipped through the Empire's grasp, the Phoenix rebels took substantial losses against a lone opponent. For a cell of this size, the loss of just one command ship was significant and left them unable to undertake offensive strikes. Though they would ultimately rebuild, the attack was a prime example of just how fragile the early Rebellion was against the might of the Empire.

" How can one fighter best our entire squadron? "

JUN SATO, COMMANDER OF PHOENIX SQUADRON

Commanders

COMMANDER JUN SATO
A native of Mykapo, the principled and level-headed commander of Phoenix Cell led one of the earliest organized cells of rebel resistance. As such, he knew the value of every life and ship under his command. He begrudgingly agreed to abandon his command ship when it became clear the battle was lost.

DARTH VADER
Not only did this shadowy Imperial enforcer seek to destroy all forms of rebellion against the Empire, he personally hunted down fugitive Jedi Knights. Force-sensitive rebels among the Phoenix Cell allowed him to lay a trap that revealed their fleet's location. He arrived in person to annihilate them.

▲ **Fast but Fragile** Valued for their speed and maneuverability, Phoenix Squadron's A-wings had little defense against the precise firepower they faced in this attack. Though bested by Vader, A-wings would continue to serve in combat for decades to come.

Ryloth Insurgency

DATE: 17 AFE ▪ **LOCATION:** RYLOTH, OUTER RIM TERRITORIES ▪
COMBATANTS: PHOENIX CELL/FREE RYLOTH MOVEMENT (FRM) VS. EMPIRE ▪ **OUTCOME:** INCONCLUSIVE

FREEING THE TWI'LEKS

Ryloth's insurgency movement was indicative of the difficulties faced by anti-Imperial resistance groups in the earliest days of the Rebellion. The Clone Wars had caused great damage to the Twi'lek homeworld, and warriors there had helped the Republic defeat the invading Separatists on the understanding that their allies would leave at the conflict's conclusion. They were betrayed when the Republic gave way to the Empire. Isolated from the wider galaxy, Ryloth was regularly bombed by

Imperial forces and the occupation increased steadily as the Empire seized control of key provinces. Even when offered help by his daughter's rebel cell, Cham Syndulla and the Free Ryloth Movement remained wary of outsiders, lest they be betrayed again.

What value could be had in fighting to disrupt the Empire on other planets when their own remained occupied? How could the Rebel Alliance help them when, simply put, there were not enough resources or rebel cells to go round? The FRM did achieve some

▼ **Cruiser-Carrier** The Empire deployed fighters on bombing runs against Ryloth from capital ships in orbit. The rebels resolved to steal one.

▲ **The *Ghost*** This modified light transport served as the main ship for the rebel cell led by Hera Syndulla. Deceptively well-armed, the *Ghost* ran Imperial blockades over Ryloth to help support the FRM.

Commanders

GENERAL CHAM SYNDULLA
Syndulla was deeply suspicious of outside assistance, having been betrayed by the Republic at the end of the Clone Wars. His insurgency aimed to secure liberation for Ryloth alone. As a result, his battle plans often lacked an appreciation of wider strategy and Thrawn was able to outmaneuver him.

GRAND ADMIRAL THRAWN
Thrawn took a different approach toward Ryloth than other Imperial commanders. He still sought to pacify the planet but he also took a keen interest in its culture, art, and history. Through his studies he gained insights into the tactics of the FRM and was able to counter them.

notable victories against the Empire. In conjunction with Hera Syndulla's rebel cell they successfully destroyed an Imperial light cruiser and captured an Imperial *Quasar Fire*-class cruiser-carrier, which became the new home for Phoenix Squadron, *Phoenix Nest*.

In response, however, the Empire began to accelerate its occupation plans and, under the command of Grand Admiral Thrawn, started to forcibly subjugate the population. Some rebel assistance was given to the Free Ryloth Movement at this time but, as before, they were largely left to oppose the might of the Empire alone.

HIJACKING THE CRUISER-CARRIER

The Empire used a cruiser-carrier in orbit above Ryloth to launch TIE bombers to attack positions on the planet's surface. The FRM wanted it destroyed as a symbol; the Phoenix Squadron Cell wanted to capture it for the Rebellion. Cham Syndulla and his followers joined forces with Hera Syndulla and her crew to board the vessel, but then the two groups diverged. The father sought to destroy it, the daughter to capture it. Only by working together were they able to defeat the carrier's crew, capture the vessel, and destroy the escorting light cruiser to give Ryloth a symbol of resistance.

▲ **Imperial Task Force** The cruiser-carrier and its TIE bombers brought fear to Ryloth. In rebel possession they would bring hope.

Hyperspace and Warfare

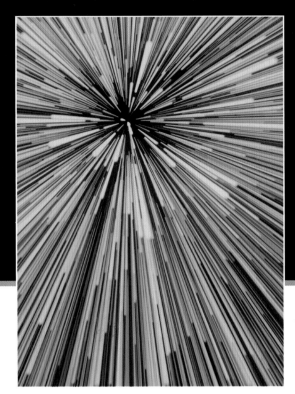

Faster than Light Without hyperdrives, it would take starships thousands or even tens of thousands of years to reach other systems. Denying or controlling access to hyperspace has therefore been crucial in every galactic-scale war ever fought.

The hyperdrive created galactic civilization. Invented millennia ago, it allowed explorers to travel between impossibly distant star systems in days or even hours, knitting isolated cultures into a single dynamic, galaxy-spanning society—and offering raiders and would-be conquerors the chance to target countless new worlds. From the start, militaries sought to control hyperspace travel. Battlefield tacticians focused on preventing enemies from escaping into hyperspace, while strategists studied how to prevent travel along established routes between systems, discover new, faster-than-light lanes to gain the strategic upper hand, and find ways to track starships across the galaxy.

HYPERSPACE DANGERS

Every object in realspace casts a "mass shadow" in the dimension known as hyperspace. Collision with a large mass shadow, such as that cast by a celestial body, will spell instant destruction for a vessel. A ship traveling blindly through hyperspace will inevitably encounter one of these mass shadows, forcing it to drop out of hyperspace to avoid a collision, with no control over where it ends up in realspace. To avoid this fate, ships follow stable routes established by hyperspace

scouts and maintained by constant surveying that keeps them safe to use. For millennia, onboard navicomputers lacked the power to track the movement of so many mass shadows and calculate routes. Instead, these calculations were performed and sent to ships by jump beacons—supercomputers sited at key locations along hyperspace routes. Centuries of exploration created a "lighthouse network" of such beacons allowing passage across settled space. During this era, disabling a beacon was

KEY INFO

INTERDICTORS

Gravity-well projectors generate artificial mass shadows, blocking ships from entering hyperspace or yanking them back into realspace. For centuries this technology demanded massive, immobile power sources, and projectors were primarily used to prevent travel near vital installations. Research into more efficient projectors began during the Clone Wars, leading to Imperial field tests of projectors mounted on a spaceframe. The *Interdictor*-class cruiser soon became a key element of the Imperial navy, and was used effectively during engagements such as Atollon.

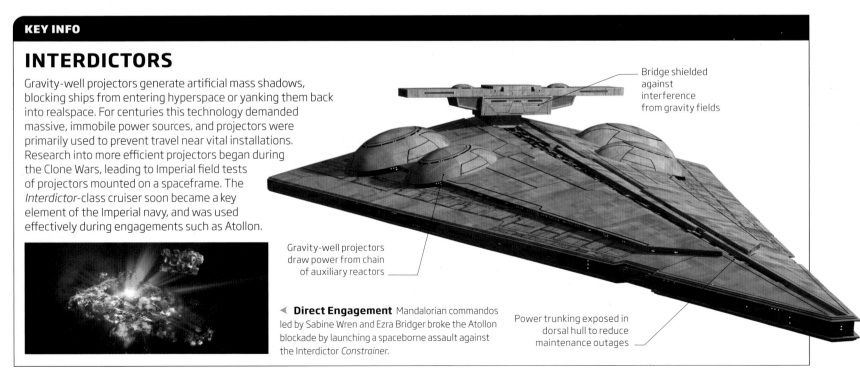

Bridge shielded against interference from gravity fields

Gravity-well projectors draw power from chain of auxiliary reactors

Direct Engagement Mandalorian commandos led by Sabine Wren and Ezra Bridger broke the Atollon blockade by launching a spaceborne assault against the Interdictor *Constrainer*.

Power trunking exposed in dorsal hull to reduce maintenance outages

▲ **Blockades** Galactic militaries routinely blockaded space around restive planets, waiting to intercept starships before they could make the calculations required to escape into hyperspace.

enough to pin ships in realspace; a favored tactic of militaries and pirates alike.

NAVICOMPUTERS

The jump-beacon era ended when technological advances allowed every starship to have its own navicomputer, complicating the quest to control hyperspace. Militaries turned to techniques used by generations of pirates—blockading planets and disrupting hyperspace lanes by scattering debris or "mass mines" across routes. The problem with such tactics was that they complicated travel for friend and foe alike. A more effective approach didn't emerge until the Galactic Civil War, when the Empire deployed Interdictor warships outfitted with gravity-well projectors, which could snatch ships out of hyperspace and prevent them escaping. Once freed of jump beacons, species,

guilds, and even lone smugglers could blaze their own routes through hyperspace. Such routes decayed if not surveyed regularly, but the few stable ones became invaluable secrets, offering critical advantages to merchant fleets and military forces alike. Several Clone Wars campaigns were fought over access to the Nexus Route, secret Hutt lanes, and rumored Wookiee hyperlanes, and the Alliance used the Empire's own Sanctuary Pipeline to travel from Sullust to Endor.

HYPERSPACE TRACKING

Tracking ships once they entered hyperspace was another long-standing challenge. Bursts of Cronau radiation emitted by ships entering hyperspace allowed pursuers to pinpoint a quarry's trajectory and estimate its course, but a fleeing ship needed only to drop to sublight speed and change trajectory to make pursuit impossible. The First Order built on Imperial research to solve this problem, finally achieving their goal via brute force: They gathered astrogational data that had been collected over millennia by militaries, spaceports, and guilds; then used arrays of supercomputers to analyze trajectories and past sightings against these data sets, determining the most likely courses with startling precision.

▲ **Holdo Maneuver** Vice Admiral Holdo's devastating collision with the *Supremacy* occurred precisely as her ship was entering hyperspace. This meant the *Raddus* was already traveling at a significant percentage of the speed of light, but its mass had not entirely transitioned into hyperspace, unleashing vast amounts of energy on impact.

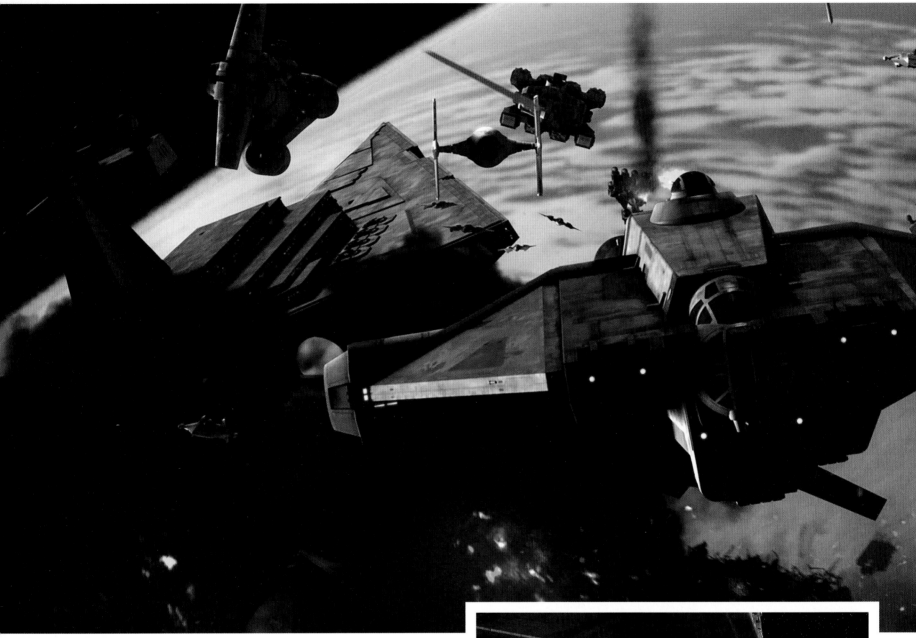

Commanders

GENERAL JAN DODONNA
General Dodonna was known by
the Empire as a courageous
opponent. Upon realizing that
escape through hyperspace was
impossible, Dodonna ordered his
surviving ships to ground. During
the Empire's surface attack he
organized the initial defense, which
destroyed several Imperial walkers.

GRAND ADMIRAL THRAWN
Thrawn was widely recognized as
a military genius. By studying the
artwork created by his adversaries,
Thrawn designed his strategies to
exploit psychological blindspots.
At Atollon, Thrawn intended not
only to destroy the rebel forces
but also cripple their morale by
inflicting a crushing defeat.

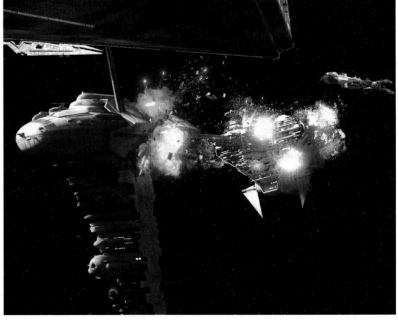

▲ **Rebel Losses** While attempting to charge the Imperial blockade the Rebel
Alliance suffered serious losses. The fleet at Atollon contained a number of Nebulon-B
escort frigates which, while formidable anti-starfighter vessels, could not withstand
sustained long-range fire from Imperial Star Destroyers. As a result numerous rebel
ships were destroyed before they could organize a sustained response.

Atollon

DATE: 17 AFE ■ **LOCATION:** ATOLLON, OUTER RIM ■
COMBATANTS: EMPIRE VS. REBEL ALLIANCE ■ **OUTCOME:** IMPERIAL VICTORY

REBELS UNDER SIEGE

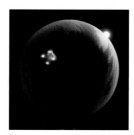

Grand Admiral Thrawn's plan to destroy the Rebel Alliance almost came to fruition over Atollon. Believing, mistakenly, the planet to be the base for the entire rebel fleet, Thrawn initiated a blockade with a squadron of Star Destroyers, supported by two Interdictor cruisers that would prevent his quarry from escaping into hyperspace.

Initial attempts by the rebel fleet to break the blockade resulted in heavy losses, with only light damage inflicted by Y-wings to the Star Destroyer *Dark Omen,* commanded by Captain Corf Ferno. To allow the young Jedi Ezra Bridger to escape and seek reinforcements, Commander Sato sacrificed himself and his ship, *Phoenix Nest,* in a collision with Admiral Kassius Konstantine's Interdictor. The surviving rebels retreated to Atollon's surface. Thrawn began an orbital bombardment of the planet's surface intended to break the rebels' morale, but an energy shield prevented serious damage. Thrawn then personally led a surface assault to capture the rebel leadership, but interference by a mysterious creature known as the "Bendu" disrupted the attack. The arrival of Mandalorian reinforcements for the rebels resulted in the destruction of the second Interdictor cruiser, clearing an escape route for the survivors through hyperspace.

The remaining rebel ships pushed through a gap between Thrawn's *Chimaera* and the *Dark Omen* and fled, ensuring that–despite heavy losses–the battle was merely a defeat rather than a total disaster.

▲ **Escaping Atollon** Thrawn's blockade of Atollon and the subsequent space battle resulted in heavy losses for the Rebel Alliance. Only late reinforcements and good fortune allowed the survivors to escape.

DEATH OF COMMANDER SATO

At the opening of the battle Commander Sato ordered rebel forces to charge the Imperial blockade, but swiftly realized the Interdictor cruisers made escape impossible. To ensure that Ezra Bridger could break through, and to prevent further losses, Sato ordered the crew of the *Phoenix Nest* to abandon ship. Imperial Admiral Konstantine saw an opportunity to claim personal glory by destroying Sato's flagship and disregarded orders from Thrawn. When Sato ordered his ship into a hard portside turn Konstantine realized his error, but it was too late. The resulting collision destroyed both vessels and gave Bridger his opening.

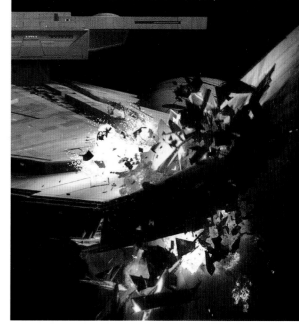

▶ **Sato's Sacrifice** By colliding the *Phoenix Nest* with one of the Interdictor cruisers, Commander Sato severely disrupted Thrawn's blockade, saving many rebel lives.

▲ **Orbital Bombardment** The rebels activated an experimental shield generator to protect their base on Atollon's surface moments before the Imperial fleet began an orbital bombardment. Despite the ferocity of the assault, the shield held. Thrawn then launched a surface attack.

Lothal

DATE: 19 AFE ▪ **LOCATION:** LOTHAL, OUTER RIM TERRITORIES ▪
COMBATANTS: LOTHAL RESISTANCE/SPECTRE CELL VS. EMPIRE ▪
OUTCOME: LOTHAL RESISTANCE VICTORY

FIGHTING FOR HOME

Lothal, an Outer Rim world, was quiet before the Empire came. The rebel cell known as the Spectres carried out multiple strikes against the Empire on the planet over the span of years, culminating in the Liberation of Lothal. This final battle represented an instance of military strategy coming together with personal interest. Ezra Bridger, call sign Spectre-6, called Lothal home; he longed to save it from total ruin. The Empire had established an Imperial Planetary Occupation Facility in Capital City, known to Lothal's inhabitants as the "Dome," and a factory crafting TIE defender starfighters; they ravaged the planet's natural resources in the process. Freeing Lothal would accomplish two objectives.

The Spectres gathered allies, but even with assistance they were a small crew trying to eliminate a full Imperial outpost. The larger Rebellion did not sanction the mission. Tactics were key, as was the knowledge and experience the Spectres had acquired over their years attacking the Imperial forces on the planet. They were familiar with Lothal's Imperial leader, Governor Arihnda Pryce, due to previous encounters. Those factors combined, along with the element of surprise, gave the lean group an advantage.

They formulated a careful plan with the ultimate goal of destroying the Dome. It began with luring Pryce into a trap and capturing her.

Commanders

▲ **Imperial Blockade** Despite the six *Imperial I*-class Star Destroyers stationed above Lothal to prevent incoming attacks, Syndulla and her allies slipped past the blockade.

GENERAL HERA SYNDULLA
To liberate Lothal, General Syndulla recruited old friends and allies to strengthen the Spectres' position. Operating from the *Ghost*'s pilot seat, Syndulla delivered reinforcements and strafed Imperial gunships. She also ensured the destruction of the Dome to free Lothal.

**GRAND ADMIRAL THRAWN
(MISSING IN ACTION)**
An intelligent tactician, Thrawn faced the rebel cell known as the Spectres on numerous occasions. When he learned the group had taken over Imperial headquarters in Capital City, he bombarded the planet before Ezra Bridger intervened to stop him.

▲ **Drawing Fire** The rebels expunged the Imperials from Lothal with a ragtag and nimble crew. They combined their individual talents and knowledge to stay ahead of the Empire's much greater numbers.

◄ **Cliff Attack** Bridger and Ryder Azadi lured Governor Pryce to a Lothal cliff dwelling where Loth-wolves joined the melee, assisting the rebels.

Lothal (continued)

Because the Spectres knew Pryce wanted to please Thrawn they were able to offer the precise thing to draw her out: they pretended Ryder Azadi, a longtime insurgent on Lothal, would surrender and share his intel on the Spectres. She took the bait.

Upon capturing Pryce, they used her clearance codes to access the Dome. The rebels then targeted the command center and subdued the command staff. With former Imperial Security Bureau agent Alexsandr Kallus on their side, the rebels had detailed knowledge of Imperial procedures and used Protocol 13 to evacuate all Imperial forces from Lothal to the Dome, where

the rebels had planted explosives. Grand Admiral Thrawn waylaid those plans by ordering his fleet to bombard the planet. Bridger, who anticipated Thrawn's arrival, had a backup plan in place to handle the Imperial commander. With Thrawn removed from the situation, the Spectres enacted their plan to launch and blow up the Dome. Observing civilians witnessed the explosion and recognized that it meant the end of Imperial rule on their planet. While the Rebellion didn't officially support the Liberation of Lothal, they would cite its success numerous times during the Galactic Civil War.

▲ **Purrgil Arrival** Bridger enacted his backup plan to stop Thrawn: the *Ghost* transmitted on Frequency Zero, summoning a pod of purrgil. The creatures eliminated Thrawn's entire fleet.

▲ **Dome Destruction** The Imperial Planetary Occupation Facility loomed over Capital City, housing Imperial offices, barracks, and hangar bays. The rebels used a faux Protocol 13 to get all Imperial forces to evacuate to the Dome, then detonated explosives and destroyed it as it took off.

THE END OF ADMIRAL THRAWN

The Bendu, a Force-sensitive entity, once warned Grand Admiral Thrawn that he saw his defeat: "like many arms surrounding you in a cold embrace." That vision came to fruition in the sky above Lothal. After Bridger surrendered to the Chiss aboard the *Chimaera*, he summoned a pod of purrgil and used the Force to push Thrawn into their tentacles. The purrgil, capable of traveling through hyperspace, pulled the *Chimaera* and its occupants into deep space. Thrawn's location remained unknown for years.

▲ **Final Act** Knowing Thrawn planned to destroy Lothal, Bridger escaped imprisonment and stormed the *Chimaera*'s bridge. He risked himself rather than letting Thrawn continue to bombard his homeworld.

Wobani

DATE: 19 AFE ▪ **LOCATION:** WOBANI, MID RIM ▪ **COMBATANTS:**
EMPIRE VS. REBEL ALLIANCE ▪ **OUTCOME:** REBEL ALLIANCE VICTORY

PRISON BREAK

The Rebel Alliance continually had to weigh cost against benefit when deciding which missions to pursue and which intelligence leads to follow. While they were still building their forces against the massive Empire, the rebels established a widespread and reliable intelligence network early on. Operatives worked undercover throughout the galaxy and relayed reports through encoded transmissions and closely guarded rendezvouses. One such assignation led to murmurs of a new Imperial superweapon. This led the Rebellion to Jyn Erso. Once the Rebel Alliance high command deemed Erso highly pivotal in pursuing the lead about the superweapon, they located her in an Imperial labor camp on Wobani. Senator Mon Mothma ordered her extraction. As they operated from the shadows with minimal resources, rebel strike teams excelled at these types of missions.

Extraction Team Bravo traveled to Wobani in *Bravo One*, a U-wing starfighter. There, they identified the extraction point with the highest likelihood of success. The rebel team included K-2SO, a former Imperial security droid who was instrumental in helping them gain access to the prison world without discovery. The extraction team freed Jyn Erso from her imprisonment and rebel ships arrived to escort them to safety. Though the extraction encountered resistance and the Alliance lost a CR90 corvette, Erso's rescue was a success, setting the stage for the climactic battles of Scarif and Yavin.

Commanders

SERGEANT RUESCOTT MELSHI
Sergeant Ruescott Melshi joined the Rebel Alliance in its early days. He led the extraction team on Wobani and successfully planned the rescue, pinpointing the exact location and moment when his team could free Jyn Erso. He then demonstrated calm leadership when the extraction went awry.

CAPTAIN ADRE L'MENDI
Notified of a rebel ship above Wobani, Captain Adre L'Mendi arrived on the *Tenacious*. She destroyed a rebel corvette and halted the U-wing's escape with a tractor beam. However, rebel reinforcements arrived and broke the connection. Her failure would have devastating consequences for the Empire.

RESCUING JYN ERSO

With intel that Imperial scientist Galen Erso possessed knowledge of a superweapon, the Alliance opted to locate Erso's daughter. She would have access to the Partisan Saw Gerrera, who held the relevant information, and potentially Galen himself. They discovered she was a prisoner at Imperial Detention Center & Labor Camp LEG-817 on Wobani. The rebels mounted a rescue operation, successfully freeing Jyn from a modified turbo tank prison transport.

▶ **In Captivity** Jyn Erso, alias Liana Hallik, carried a twenty-year sentence for her crimes.

▲ **X-wing Reinforcements**
Answering K-2SO's distress call,
a squadron of X-wings engaged
the *Tenacious* above Wobani. They
bought time for K-2SO to repair *Bravo
One*'s navicomputer and escape.

➤ **Efficient Rescue**
Red Leader, Samala Loené,
led her pilots into battle,
eliminating a number of TIE
fighters before destroying the
Tenacious' targeting array.

Jedha

DATE: 19 AFE ■ **LOCATION:** JEDHA, MID RIM ■ **COMBATANTS:** PARTISANS VS. EMPIRE ■ **OUTCOME:** IMPERIAL VICTORY

BRUTAL INSURGENCY

Beings from across the galaxy traveled to Jedha, a cold desert moon in the Mid Rim with over 11 million citizens. Home to ancient structures–some of the earliest known in the galaxy–Jedha attracted many explorers and pilgrims. The moon also caught the attention of Saw Gerrera and his Partisans. Already suspicious about the Empire's focus on kyber crystals, Gerrera made his way to Jedha City when he learned the Empire was extracting large quantities of crystals from the moon. He discovered a city in turmoil with local insurgent cells striking at the Imperials from the shadows. The environment was turbulent, teetering on the edge of chaos. Gerrera saw an opportunity.

The leader of the Partisans gathered intelligence on the local rebel cells and started recruiting. Operating in rebellion but not as part of the Rebel Alliance, Gerrera was comfortable using unorthodox methods, as were his followers. In the case of Baze Malbus and Chirrut Îmwe, Gerrera offered provisions for the insurgents' skills; Malbus and Îmwe gave those provisions to orphans. The Partisans attracted other local extremists with promises of retribution and ending the Imperial occupation, and together they operated from a hidden base in the Catacombs of Cadera. Their forces grew to include ships for conducting air raids. They targeted the Imperials where they were most vulnerable: when they were either mining or transporting kyber crystals. The Partisans focused on hit-and-run missions, slowly picking away at the Empire's defenses.

KEY COMBATANT: GERRERA'S PARTISANS

After working with the Republic to remove the Separatists from his homeworld of Onderon, Saw Gerrera formed the Partisans. They grew from resisting Imperial occupation on Onderon to later working with the burgeoning Rebellion, until the Rebellion deemed the Partisans' methods too extreme. Ruthless in their campaign against the Empire, the Partisans were willing to do whatever it took to terrorize the enemy–including risking civilian casualties. The militia group moved to Jedha where Gerrera continued to recruit.

◀ **Lookout** Sul Fansord signaled the Partisans when Imperials arrived at the inflection point.

▼ **Street Battles** Imperial combat drivers used TX-225 combat assault tanks to escort precious kyber shipments out of Jedha. Even when flanked by escorting stormtroopers, the convoys made a tempting target for insurgents.

▲ **In Harm's Way** Making a stand against the Empire in Jedha City's narrow passages put civilians at risk. The insurgency destroyed families who were caught in the crossfire.

▲ **Fiery Surprise** Explosives expert Weeteef Cyu-Bee, one of Gerrera's Partisans, crafted sticky bombs and canister explosives for the insurgents to wield against Imperial patrols and vehicles.

As the Partisans' violent strikes increased, the Imperial reprisals became more severe. The Empire bolstered their presence in the Holy City in response to the militia group. They brought in the *Dauntless*, an *Imperial I*-class Star Destroyer, from orbit to hover directly above Jedha City's densely populated plateau. Imperial patrols increased significantly as well, with more stormtroopers and All Terrain Scout Transports on the city's cramped streets. The constant engagements between the Partisans and the Empire put the locals on near constant alert.

Jyn Erso and Cassian Andor, representatives of the Rebel Alliance, arrived into this tense situation while conducting Operation Fracture. They were searching for information on Galen Erso–Jyn's father and an Imperial scientist–from an Imperial pilot who had defected and was now in the custody of Saw Gerrera, Jyn's one-time guardian. The Partisans attacked a kyber convoy not long after the rebels' arrival, entangling Erso and Andor in the fracas. It was then that Erso witnessed Gerrera's extremism firsthand as the insurgents exhibited no care for innocent bystanders.

Commanders

SAW GERRERA (KILLED IN ACTION)
Gerrera led his Partisans with fervor and decisiveness; the militia's members loyally followed his directives. Suspecting the Empire were using the kyber crystals for a weapon, he had his Partisans strategically hit the stolen shipments and was killed when the Imperial forces retaliated.

DIRECTOR ORSON KRENNIC
Director of Advanced Weapons Research for the Imperial Security Bureau, Orson Krennic was eager to show the Death Star's capabilities. Viewing Jedha as merely a resource to be exploited, he ordered his stormtrooper battalions to ruthlessly crush any attempt to disrupt the kyber program.

Jedha: Map

Surrounded by the desert, Jedha City jutted above the desolate landscape in a bustling jumble of structures, temples, open-air markets, and catacombs. Precious few open areas dotted the city's surface, making any kind of ground combat challenging. Insurgents marked their targets from rooftops and from around corners along the Empire's common transport routes. As soon as the Empire pinpointed sources of attacks, the Partisans would utilize new locations to hide. With such a large area to cover, the Imperials couldn't establish enough checkpoints in the sprawling avenues to identify and capture potential insurgents, who were more familiar with the city's layout. The Imperial forces were at a disadvantage on the ground, but they could get a clearer picture of Jedha City from the Star Destroyer stationed just above the surface. The Partisans countered this by breaking down the walls between houses, allowing them to avoid the streets and move through the city unseen.

WAR-TORN CITY

Situated on the Mid Rim moon of Jedha, Jedha City, also known as NiJedha or the Holy City, was a chaotic place. Its narrow streets spread like a labyrinth atop a plateau, and hosted pilgrims coming to visit the Temple of the Kyber as well as locals, Saw Gerrera's Partisans, and the Empire. Imperials conducted mining operations to extract kyber crystals from the planet and scarred the natural environment. Meanwhile Gerrera's militia targeted the Empire regularly; civilians never knew when or where an attack would occur, making the Holy City an extremely dangerous place.

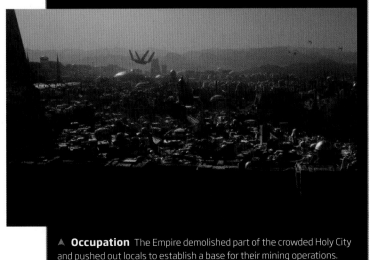

▲ **Occupation** The Empire demolished part of the crowded Holy City and pushed out locals to establish a base for their mining operations.

1 Air Cover Flights of TIE fighters launched from the *Dauntless* above Jedha for regular patrols of the city and the surrounding area.

2 Dome of the Anointed The Partisans established a secondary base here to stage missions in the city. They launched their final onslaught from this location.

3 Checkpoint 7 Imperials maintained checkpoints in the streets to monitor the population, stopping suspicious individuals for interrogation.

4 Pilgrim's Gate Visitors to Jedha City funneled through this ancient entry point. It was the scene of several firefights with the Imperial garrison.

5 Outpost J-33 The Empire established multiple hidden outposts through the city in order to spy on the Partisans as well as newcomers.

Tight Quarters Both the Empire and Saw Gerrera's Partisans leveraged Jedha City's narrow corridors. The Empire deployed TX-225 GAVw "Occupier" combat assault tanks and AT-ST walkers—both vehicles capable of navigating smaller spaces. Lacking ground vehicles, the insurgents found the Holy City's close quarters to be ideal for striking from hidden vantage points.

6 Tythoni Square
Jyn Erso and Cassian Endor were caught up in a skirmish between the Empire and Partisans in this area of the city.

7 Landing Zone The Empire moved the kyber crystal containers here to be airlifted from the surface.

8 Vehicle Base The Empire used Occupier combat assault tanks to move kyber crystal containers. They used this site as a maintenance hub.

9 Tunnel Bomb
Insurgents tunneled under the Imperial vehicle base in Varnos Square and detonated a massive explosive device.

10 Resupply Base No. 4
The Empire held multiple locations to house the garrison assigned to the planet and store supplies. These sites were vulnerable to attack.

11 Imperial Headquarters The strongest Imperial presence was concentrated in the Temple Quarter, nearest to the largest kyber deposits.

12 The Temple The Temple of the Kyber loomed above the city wall. The temple's guardians kept it safe before the Empire's arrival.

Jedha (continued)

The Partisans had focused on stealing kyber crystals from the stormtroopers and attacking the occupation forces, but the situation changed when they captured an Imperial defector, pilot Bodhi Rook. The Empire knew that Rook had traveled to Jedha, though were unaware of the message he carried from Galen Erso. Having largely exhausted Jedha's kyber deposits, and wanting to stop Rook from sharing any secrets, the Empire chose the moon to test their new weapon, the Death Star.

Caught in the midst of a firefight, Jyn Erso and Cassian Andor were captured by an increasingly paranoid Gerrera and taken to his base in the Catacombs of Cadera. Shortly afterward, the Empire issued a Protocol 13 order and the garrison suddenly evacuated, provoking an all-too-brief celebration by the local population.

▲ **Repeating Fire** Baze Malbus, a former Guardian of the Whills, carried an illegal repeating blaster with enough firepower to penetrate the armor of Occupier tanks and AT-ST walkers.

▲ **Lesson in Underestimation** Stormtroopers believed Chirrut Îmwe was harmless because he was blind. He proved otherwise, using his walking staff to incapacitate a number of troopers with precision. He helped Jyn Erso and Cassian Andor escape Imperial detainment.

THE DESTRUCTION OF JEDHA

Jedha City became the first site to be ravaged by the Death Star's superlaser. The test, operating on a single reactor, obliterated the Holy City. Imperial forces evacuated before the weapon fired but countless civilians were not as fortunate. The cataclysmic effects were instantaneous with no corner of the city escaping annihilation. The Empire viewed the test as a great achievement and continued work to further hone the Death Star. Not wanting word of their secret weapon to spread throughout the galaxy, the Empire fabricated a story and blamed the explosion on a mining accident.

➤ **Catastrophic Consequences** Though the Empire only targeted the Holy City, the shock wave caused significant damage across the moon and made Jedha uninhabitable for native lifeforms.

The events leading up to this moment demonstrated the importance of a unified Rebel Alliance. A formal rebel cell in the Holy City may have been more successful in discovering the Empire's use for the kyber crystals and done so without attracting further retaliation from the Empire.

Cassian, Erso, and Rook escaped Jedha as the Death Star's blast tore open the moon's crust. The destruction of Jedha City served the Empire in more ways than one. They deemed their new superweapon ready for further use to serve their agenda, and though they did not terminate the defector Bodhi Rook as they intended, they did destroy the Temple of the Kyber and many ancient sites connected to the Jedi—locations believed to be sacred by the Church of the Force. By leaving the temple in ruins, the Empire demolished a symbol of the Force and of hope.

CASUALTIES

EMPIRE: The Imperial occupation force lost several companies of stormtroopers and a handful of ground combat vehicles in attacks by the Partisans.
PARTISANS: Several dozen Partisans died in insurgent attacks against the Empire, while a number of Partisan X-wings were shot down.
CIVILIANS: The Death Star's superlaser strike wiped out Jedha's entire population.

➤ **Innocent Victims** As in so many insurgencies, Jedha's civilians found themselves caught in the middle, and the population suffered at the hands of both sides.

Propaganda

Propaganda has been a key factor in every war. All factions wielded propaganda internally and externally as a weapon to promote and publicize their own political causes or to defame the opposing party. The Galactic Republic, the Separatists, the Galactic Empire, the Rebel Alliance, the First Order, and the Resistance invested resources into crafting propaganda in a variety of mediums to further their goals, whether those goals be recruitment, winning public sentiment, or unveiling the "truth." Who controlled the narrative broadcast to the galaxy was nearly as important as battles won or lost, as that control meant affecting the view of citizens across hundreds of worlds.

▲ **Breaking News** In the aftermath of the Battle of Endor, holonet footage of the second Death Star's destruction was beamed around the galaxy, igniting a wave of celebrations and revolutionary uprisings.

WORDS MATTER

The most common form of propaganda throughout the multiple galactic wars was words. Speeches, pamphlets, and declarations spread important messages for both sides—all biased and some misleading. Words could be easily broadcast through the holonet if the proper channels were available, and sometimes those words reached throughout the galaxy. When Emperor Palpatine declared his New Order, he stated a thousand years of peace would begin that day. Trillions of citizens heard his proclamation. Weary from years of battles during the Clone Wars and looking for reasons to be optimistic about unity, they believed Palpatine—just as the Emperor knew they would.

THE POWER OF ART

Another method all factions leaned upon was the dissemination of posters. Numerous artists contributed their skills and vision from the Clone Wars through the First Order-Resistance War. Some voluntarily used their art to support their beliefs while others were coerced with threats. Imagery promoting and disparaging all sides appeared everywhere from densely populated cities to rural outposts throughout the conflicts. The propagandists employed different techniques depending on the desired result: they appealed to fear; they used repetition; they played upon the hope for peace; they pulled at strings of grief. Colorful posters made bold statements and the accompanying art supported them. Artists particularly experimented with overt messaging combined with

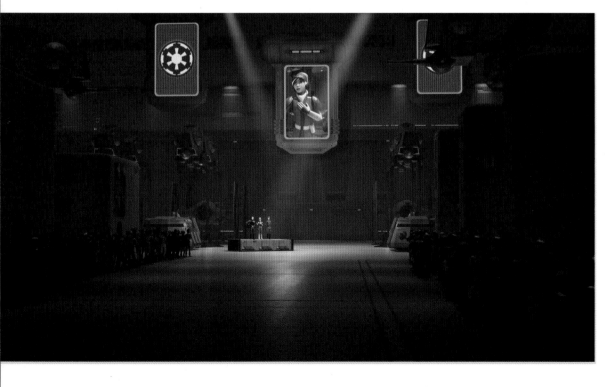

◄ **Empire Day** To celebrate the day the Clone Wars ended, the Empire instituted a galaxy-wide holiday featuring parades. Attending the festivities was mandatory.

◀ **Economic Benefits** Saespo Choffrey painted this mural, displayed around Lothal, to garner support for Sienar Fleet Systems' TIE fighter factory and the jobs it provided.

▶ **Building the Future** One of artist Coba Dunivee's messaging tactics was to induce a feeling of missing out. This poster tempts potential Imperial recruits by telling them, "Be part of tomorrow today."

subtle imagery communicating the true information. Imperial posters might emphasize the opportunity to aid Darth Vader, while Resistance posters glamorized being an X-wing pilot. Grotesque caricatures, the glory of victory, and outright lies featured prominently. Artists elevated key figures from their respective organizations in the posters too, including Emperor Palpatine and Princess Leia Organa. It all contributed to swaying citizens into aligning with one side or the other.

PATRIOTISM

More manipulative propaganda played upon the patriotism of citizens. The establishment of national holidays such as Republic Day and Empire Day with mandatory participation was one example. The Empire also utilized celebratory anthems to embed itself into the hearts of the beings it ruled. The organization issued flags and banners for its devotees to display–whether they wanted to or not–and harshly punished any outward signs of disloyalty.

MEDIA

Holos played a vital role in communicating propaganda as well. The Rebel Alliance released holo recordings of their victories for a variety of purposes, especially recruitment; the Alliance propaganda chiefs later made holos to support the legitimacy of the New Republic. The Empire crafted holos for the holonet, which they largely controlled throughout the Galactic Civil War. The First Order even utilized holos to bolster the subliminal messaging they played for recruits.

KEY INFO

COMPNOR

The Commission for the Preservation of the New Order (COMPNOR) promoted Imperial ideology as an official Galactic Empire government agency. The organization had its roots in the Galactic Republic, when it promoted wartime propaganda supporting the Republic in the war against the Separatists. In the age of the Empire, COMPNOR used propaganda campaigns to support the Emperor's missives, releasing art to encourage citizens (particularly humanoids) across the galaxy to join the Imperial military. COMPNOR persisted after Palpatine's death at the Battle of Endor; the group shifted its focus and became the Office of Imperial Promotion, Galactic Truth, and Fact Correction, or OIP.

▶ **"Explore the Galaxy"** Coba Dunivee, an artist for COMPNOR, strove to entice those who wanted to see the galaxy; her work here posits joining the Imperial navy as a means to travel.

> **Desperate Defense** Stormtroopers from the 975th garrison were deployed to safeguard the Eadu lab and its high-value personnel, but could do little against the superior firepower of rebel starfighters.

Eadu

DATE: 19 AFE ▪ **LOCATION:** EADU, OUTER RIM TERRITORIES ▪ **COMBATANTS:** EMPIRE VS. REBEL ALLIANCE ▪ **OUTCOME:** REBEL ALLIANCE VICTORY

FRACTURED OPERATION

Alliance Intelligence approved the mission codenamed Operation Fracture amid rumors that the Empire were building a planet-killing superweapon that threatened to end all resistance to Palpatine's rule. Rebel spies learned that Galen Erso, a key scientist for the Empire's Advanced Weapons Research program, had persuaded Imperial cargo pilot Bodhi Rook to defect and deliver a message about the program to Saw Gerrera's rebel splinter group on Jedha.

The Alliance freed the petty criminal Jyn Erso, Galen's daughter and a former protégé of Gerrera's, from Imperial custody in hopes that she could help Captain Cassian Andor find her father. Officially, Andor's mission was to deliver Erso to the Alliance so he could testify about the Empire's plans before the Senate. But Alliance Intelligence chief Davits Draven gave Andor secret orders: he was to kill Galen Erso, not rescue him.

Draven was acting without approval from Mon Mothma, the Alliance's political leader. His rogue action was revealed years later, when slicers sympathetic to the New Republic's Centrist

▲ **Secret Installation** Eadu was the property of the powerful Tarkin family, and Grand Moff Tarkin himself gave the planet to the Empire. That helped Tarkin maximize his influence on the secret program to create a superlaser battle station, which depended on advances made by his Tarkin Initiative think tank.

KEY CASUALTY: GALEN ERSO

A brilliant but naïve scientist, Erso tried to escape the Empire once he realized his research into kyber crystals' energy potential would be used for a horrific superweapon. He fled to Lah'mu, but was tracked down by Krennic and forced to resume his work. He did so as slowly as he could, and created a trap by way of revenge, hiding a flaw in the Death Star's systems that could allow it to be destroyed. He then alerted the Rebel Alliance.

▶ **Trapped** Erso admitted he was the Imperial traitor, but Krennic still executed the other scientists.

Commanders

CAPTAIN CASSIAN ANDOR
Few rebel operatives were as experienced as Andor, who had first taken up arms as a child. But by Operation Fracture, Cassian was struggling with the burden of dark deeds he'd done in the name of freedom and the question of whether the "greater good" could ever justify such acts.

DIRECTOR ORSON KRENNIC
Despite the Death Star's successful test at Jedha, Krennic was becoming desperate: someone in his research lab was funneling intelligence to the Alliance. His rival, Wilhuff Tarkin, was eager to take advantage of the opportunity, using it to undermine Krennic with the Emperor and take credit for the battle station.

faction broke into data-stacks housing Alliance archives, offering Draven's actions as proof of "rebel" intolerance and violence.

The truth was more nuanced: the Alliance was badly divided, quarreling over whether to oppose the Empire through Senate politics, carefully targeted covert missions, or all-out war. As Draven saw it, Mothma felt obligated to work through the Senate, but she knew that approach was doomed and would be secretly relieved if that option were taken away from her–so he did.

Captain Andor's team escaped Jedha without a copy of Galen Erso's message–which only Jyn had heard. Their U-wing then crashed on Eadu, the site of Galen's weapons lab. With Andor's fate unknown, Draven ordered Blue Squadron to launch a raid on Eadu under the command of General Antoc Merrick.

Eadu (continued)

Meanwhile, Andor was dealing with complications of his own. Having survived the U-wing crash, he had moved to observe the Imperial base and, if the opportunity presented itself, complete his mission. An Imperial shuttle then arrived at Eadu, carrying Orson Krennic, director of the Advanced Weapons Research program. He gathered the lab's energy researchers, executing all but Erso. Andor disobeyed orders, passing up the chance to target Erso with a long-range rifle shot, but learned that Alliance starfighters were inbound. That endangered both Rook, who had been sent ahead by Andor to find a transport the team could steal, and Jyn Erso, who was trying to reach her father.

Andor contacted Yavin 4, urging that the attack be called off, but it was too late: Blue Squadron had already been detected by

▲ **Target Destroyed** General Merrick's pilots shook off their lack of preparation and the challenging conditions at Eadu to catch the Empire unawares. Nimble X-wings ran interference for bomb-laden Y-wings, ensuring the lab's destruction.

▼ **Strafing Runs** Trapped on the surface with minimal cover, the stormtrooper garrison were decimated by accurate laser fire from the attacking rebel X-wings.

the enemy, and aborting the mission now would let the Imperials entrench, leaving Andor's team without support and vulnerable to capture. The rebel starfighters attacked the lab, skirmishing with the TIE fighters that scrambled to intercept, and dropped limpet charges and proton torpedoes. The lab was badly damaged and Galen Erso was killed.

The raid on Eadu was over within minutes, with Blue Squadron disengaging and heading home. Amid the chaos, Andor's team stole a *Zeta*-class cargo shuttle and evacuated. Jyn Erso brought her father's message to a frightened and skeptical Alliance, insisting he'd hidden a vulnerability in the Death Star and urging the rebels to steal the schematics that would give them a chance to destroy the battle station.

▲ **Heavy Fire** Imperial forces fought back by launching TIE fighters to shoot down the rebel raiders and engaging them with heavy turbolasers. But the speedy X-wings evaded most of the fire, while rebel insurgents on-site added to the chaos.

KEY WEAPON: T-65 X-WING STARFIGHTER

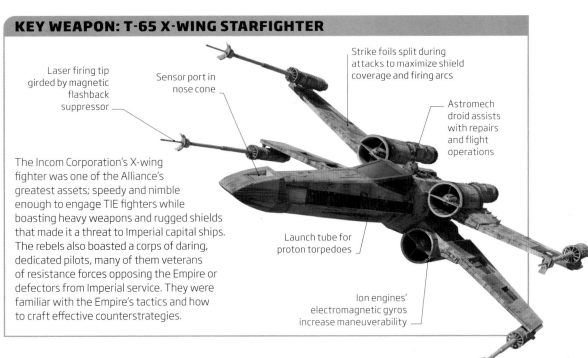

Laser firing tip girded by magnetic flashback suppressor

Sensor port in nose cone

Strike foils split during attacks to maximize shield coverage and firing arcs

Astromech droid assists with repairs and flight operations

The Incom Corporation's X-wing fighter was one of the Alliance's greatest assets; speedy and nimble enough to engage TIE fighters while boasting heavy weapons and rugged shields that made it a threat to Imperial capital ships. The rebels also boasted a corps of daring, dedicated pilots, many of them veterans of resistance forces opposing the Empire or defectors from Imperial service. They were familiar with the Empire's tactics and how to craft effective counterstrategies.

Launch tube for proton torpedoes

Ion engines' electromagnetic gyros increase maneuverability

GALACTIC CIVIL WAR

- **SCARIF**
  Beginning of the Civil War

- **BOARDING OF THE *TANTIVE IV***
  Scarif Aftermath

- **YAVIN**
  Most Desperate Hour

- **CYMOON 1**
  Raid on the Weapons Factory

- **VROGAS VAS**
  Vader Unleashed

- **MUTINY AT MON CALA**
  Dawn of the Rebel Fleet

- **MAKO-TA**
  Assault on the Space Docks

- **HOTH**
  Fighting Retreat

- **SULLUST**
  Changing Plans

- **ENDOR**
  Palpatine's Downfall

- **NABOO (THEED)**
  The Contingency

- **ZAVIAN ABYSS**
  Stalking the *Starhawk*

- **NADIRI DOCKYARDS**
  Imperial Vengeance

- **GALITAN**
  New Republic Trap

- **JAKKU**
  The End of the War

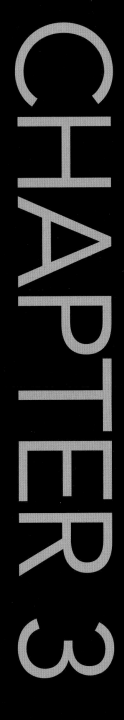

CHAPTER 3

Galactic Civil War: Introduction

GALAXY MAP

Galactic Operations

The Rebel Alliance could not survive a direct confrontation with the Empire and largely confined their activities to the Outer Rim. The Imperial fleet expended much energy trying to stamp out the Rebellion and force the Alliance into a decisive battle.

KEY

1 Scarif
2 Boarding of the *Tantive IV*
3 Yavin
4 Cymoon 1
5 Vrogas Vas
6 Mutiny at Mon Cala
7 Mako-Ta
8 Hoth
9 Sullust
10 Endor
11 Naboo (Theed)
12 Zavian Abyss
13 Nadiri Dockyards
14 Galitan
15 Jakku

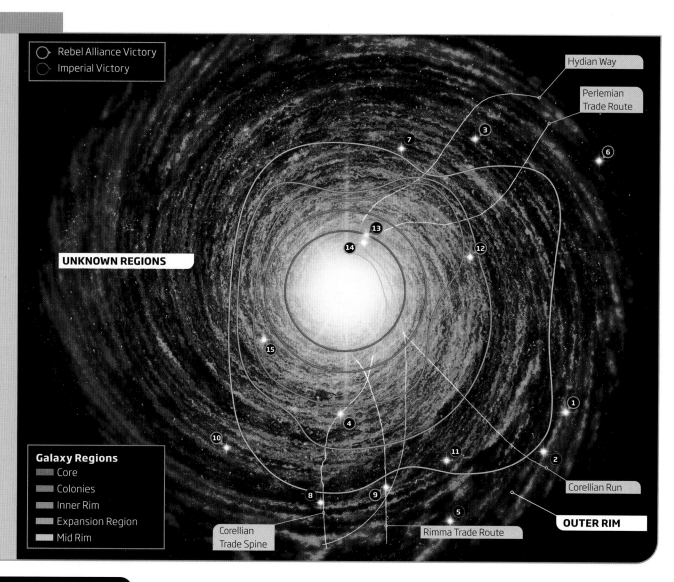

Rebel Alliance Victory
Imperial Victory

Hydian Way
Perlemian Trade Route
UNKNOWN REGIONS
OUTER RIM
Corellian Run
Rimma Trade Route
Corellian Trade Spine

Galaxy Regions
- Core
- Colonies
- Inner Rim
- Expansion Region
- Mid Rim

TIMELINE

1 Scarif
The battle at Scarif marked the outbreak of the Galactic Civil War and provided the Alliance with their first key strategic victory.

3 Yavin
The destruction of the Death Star proved that the Empire's technological superiority was not enough to quash the Rebellion.

6 Mutiny at Mon Cala
An uprising on Mon Cala provided the Rebel Alliance with the heart of a new fleet and further destabilized the Empire.

19 AFE

2 Boarding of the *Tantive IV*
Desperate to reclaim the Death Star plans, the Empire captured Princess Leia's ship above Tatooine.

4 Cymoon 1
The rebel strike on a key weapons factory cost the Empire valuable resources.

5 Vrogas Vas
The Rebellion attempted to kill Darth Vader but he proved far too powerful.

The Galactic Civil War was, on appearances, the most lopsided conflict in military history. The overwhelming might of the Galactic Empire, which had ruled the galaxy since the Clone Wars, was arrayed against an insurgent movement a fraction of its size. Most military analysis would conclude that such an asymmetric balance of power could only result in an Imperial victory. But such analysis would be wrong. The Galactic Empire held many advantages, but the rebel strategy of maintaining secrecy where possible and stirring up insurrections while playing for time proved highly effective against their rigid opponent.

The Outbreak of War

The Battle of Scarif saw the Rebel Alliance declare open war against the Empire and, though it cost them much of their fleet, it paved the way for their future success. The Imperial fleet may have dwarfed their opponents', but the ideology of the Empire eschewed flexibility of thought and sophistication of strategy. For much of the war the Empire aimed to locate the central rebel headquarters and destroy the Alliance in a single blow, nearly achieving this at Hoth. But despite this, the Empire failed to grasp that the strengths of the Alliance lay in their ability to hide while also motivating others to join. While the Empire built ever greater fleets and starships, the Rebellion was built on hope, cultivating support in the Outer Rim to ensure their long-term survivability. As a result, Imperial aims of forcing the Alliance into decisive battles were often thwarted by the aversion of the rebel military leadership to commit to set-piece battles that served no key strategic importance.

Rebellion Triumphant

The longer that the Galactic Civil War lasted, the more complicated issues became for the Empire. Ordinarily uprisings on isolated worlds would be brutally suppressed, but the demands of fighting an elusive enemy, and constructing superweapons like the Death Stars, sucked in resources. The Emperor decided the easiest way to force the Rebellion into a decisive confrontation was to provide them with bait that could not be ignored. The location of the second Death Star, and the fact that Palpatine himself was to inspect it, forced the Alliance fleet out of hiding only to fall into a trap that could have cost them everything. However, the Alliance leaders had learned much from years of war while the same could not be said for their opposition. The ability of rebel forces to display flexibility in tactics and bravery in combat—upon which their survival had depended for years—enabled them to outthink the Empire at Endor and subsequently outfight them too. The destruction of the Death Star and the deaths of most of the Imperial hierarchy, including Palpatine himself, shattered the Empire. The key historical lesson is that a well-organized and dedicated band of insurgents toppled a technologically superior opponent through a mixture of wise strategy, careful tactics, and good fortune.

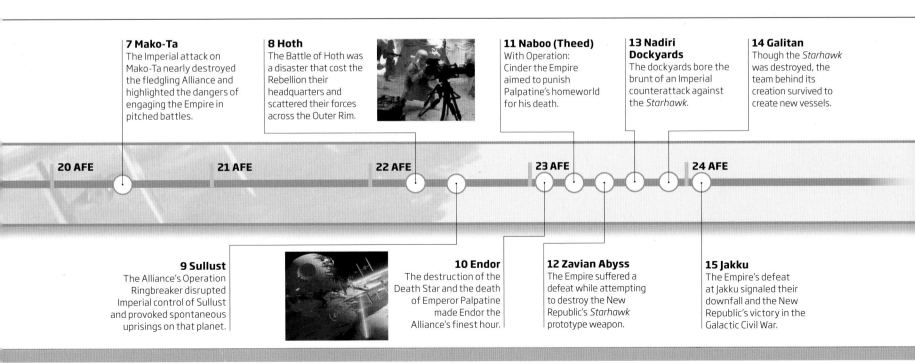

7 Mako-Ta
The Imperial attack on Mako-Ta nearly destroyed the fledgling Alliance and highlighted the dangers of engaging the Empire in pitched battles.

8 Hoth
The Battle of Hoth was a disaster that cost the Rebellion their headquarters and scattered their forces across the Outer Rim.

11 Naboo (Theed)
With Operation: Cinder the Empire aimed to punish Palpatine's homeworld for his death.

13 Nadiri Dockyards
The dockyards bore the brunt of an Imperial counterattack against the Starhawk.

14 Galitan
Though the Starhawk was destroyed, the team behind its creation survived to create new vessels.

20 AFE | **21 AFE** | **22 AFE** | **23 AFE** | **24 AFE**

9 Sullust
The Alliance's Operation Ringbreaker disrupted Imperial control of Sullust and provoked spontaneous uprisings on that planet.

10 Endor
The destruction of the Death Star and the death of Emperor Palpatine made Endor the Alliance's finest hour.

12 Zavian Abyss
The Empire suffered a defeat while attempting to destroy the New Republic's Starhawk prototype weapon.

15 Jakku
The Empire's defeat at Jakku signaled their downfall and the New Republic's victory in the Galactic Civil War.

Scarif

DATE: 19 AFE ▪ **LOCATION:** SCARIF, OUTER RIM TERRITORIES ▪
COMBATANTS: EMPIRE VS. REBEL ALLIANCE ▪
OUTCOME: REBEL ALLIANCE VICTORY

BEGINNING OF THE CIVIL WAR

The Death Star's destruction shook the foundations of Imperial rule, but that victory had depended on a rebel raid just a few days earlier on Scarif. The planet housed a data vault protecting key Imperial military secrets, including a full readout of the Death Star and the weak point Galen Erso had created in its systems. The Battle of Scarif was the first major Alliance victory of the Galactic Civil War. It was also chaotic and improvised, fought on the ground and in space by rebel units acting without the authorization of Alliance high command. The twin victories at Scarif and Yavin not only struck a key blow for freedom but also forced the fractious rebels to finally unite against the threat of the Empire.

As prelude to the battle, Cassian Andor and Jyn Erso returned from Eadu with news that the Empire's rumored "planet killer" was real—and that Jyn's father had hidden a weakness inside it. Erso urged the Alliance to steal the plans from Scarif, but the divided rebels rejected the idea. So a defiant Erso struck out on her own, accompanied by Andor and veteran rebel Pathfinders sympathetic to her plea. Calling themselves Rogue One, the team headed for Scarif aboard a stolen cargo shuttle.

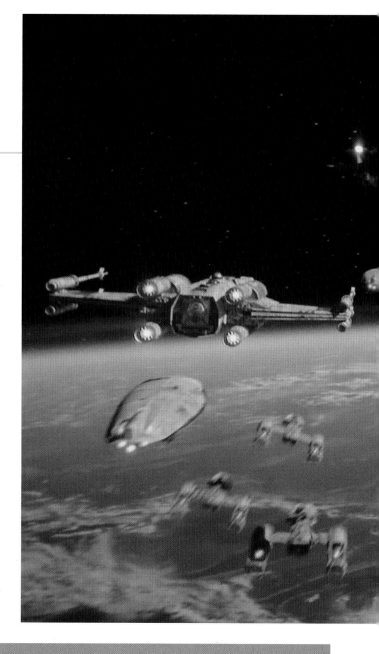

▶ **Ragtag Fleet** Raddus' flagship, the MC75 star cruiser *Profundity*, led the rebel fleet against the shield gate.

KEY LOCATION: THE CITADEL

Scarif was located far from the Core and the eyes of the Senate, making it a perfect location for sensitive Imperial military projects. Its tropical islands were dotted with bunkers and labs linked by repulsor railways. At the center of the complex was the Citadel, a towering fortress built around a secure vault, the repository of zettanodes of cutting-edge Imperial military research data. Inside the heavily guarded vault, datatapes including a technical readout of the Death Star were stored "cold," disconnected from data networks as an additional precaution against electronic intrusion and theft.

◀ **A Quiet Posting** Warm, languid Scarif was a prized post for Imperial officers, who found it hard to believe war could intrude on their tranquility.

Commanders

**ADMIRAL RADDUS
(KILLED IN ACTION)**
Raddus escaped the Imperial occupation of Mon Cala to become a key early member of the Alliance, commanding its nascent fleet. He disobeyed orders and supported Jyn Erso's raid on Scarif, engaging the Imperial forces in orbit. His sacrifice made him a rebel legend.

**DIRECTOR ORSON KRENNIC
(KILLED IN ACTION)**
Following the Death Star test at Jedha, Orson Krennic fought to keep control of the battle station, but Tarkin outmaneuvered him. Krennic died when Tarkin fired the Death Star's superlaser at Scarif in an effort to stop the rebels from extracting the Death Star plans.

▲ **Taking Command** After arriving at Scarif, Krennic was disgusted to find discipline entirely too lax given the secrets the Citadel protected. But before he could clean house, explosions rocked the complex. The rebels were already there–and he knew their goal was the data vault and the Death Star plans.

Scarif (continued)

Erso's improvised plan depended on catching the Empire unawares: the rebel Pathfinders would fan out and attack targets of opportunity, causing a distraction that would allow Erso, Andor, and the reprogrammed Imperial security droid K-2SO to infiltrate the Citadel security complex and find the Death Star plans. The team would then engineer an escape and return to Yavin 4 with proof of the danger the galaxy faced.

The first part of the plan succeeded, as troops led by Sergeant Ruescott Melshi drew out the Imperial garrison. But Orson Krennic had arrived on Scarif to investigate Galen Erso's treachery, and taken command of the Citadel's defenses. As AT-ACTs and death troopers engaged the Pathfinders, unexpected rebel support further complicated matters. Admiral Raddus, the Alliance fleet commander, defied orders and brought a task force to Scarif to try and assist Erso. But that led to the Empire closing the portal in Scarif's planetary defense shield, trapping the Rogue One team and leaving them unable to transmit the plans.

Reinforcements for the rebel ground team were offloaded via U-wing transport, but the losses soon mounted. K-2SO was destroyed defending Andor and Erso while they located the plans, while Chirrut Îmwe, Baze Malbus, and Bodhi Rook died– along with most of the rebel ground troops–re-establishing a communications link to the Citadel that allowed Rogue One to talk with the rebel fleet. Rook's last words were a stark warning: if the defensive shield remained in place, the plans would never leave Scarif and Rogue One's sacrifices would go for naught.

▲ **Battle on the Beach** After Krennic ordered the Scarif garrison deployed, shoretroopers led infantry squads of stormtroopers through the island jungles in search of insurgents. Shoretroopers' lighter armor allowed for greater mobility during operations.

▲ **Airborne Cavalry** Having broken through the orbital shield gate before it closed, General Antoc Merrick led Blue Squadron's X-wings and U-wings against Scarif's AT-ACTs, assisting rebels fighting on the beaches.

KEY COMBATANT: DEATH TROOPERS

Elite stormtroopers clad in gleaming black armor, death troopers defended high-value Imperial military leaders and helped secure vital operations. Candidates were tapped during stormtrooper training and then subjected to classified medical procedures that augmented their senses, strength, and stamina. Rumors about far stranger alterations to death troopers' bodies were rife within the Imperial ranks, causing even veteran stormtroopers to give them a wide berth.

▲ **Personal Guard** To quell the incursion on Scarif, Krennic sent in his personal guard of death troopers.

Scarif: Map

The Scarif raid depended on misdirection, with veteran rebel Pathfinders led by Sergeant Ruescott Melshi making "ten men look like a hundred," drawing Imperial eyes away from the Citadel so that Jyn Erso, Cassian Andor, and K-2SO could access the data vault, find the Death Star plans, and transmit them to the Alliance. After being caught unawares, the Imperials mounted a furious counterassault, stiffened by the battle-hardened death troopers of Orson Krennic's personal guard. The Alliance's SpecForces went into battle knowing they were unlikely to survive, and willing to pay that price for the greater good of the rebel cause.

INFILTRATING THE VAULT

Disguised in gear taken from incapacitated Imperial personnel, Erso, Andor, and K-2SO located the plans in the Citadel's data vault. But their intrusion was detected, alerting Krennic to their true goal. And the closure of the shield gate forced the Rogue One team to improvise yet again and find a new way to get the plans into Alliance hands—an outcome both Krennic and Grand Moff Tarkin were determined to prevent at any cost.

▲ **In Disguise** Jyn Erso wore the uniform of a luckless Imperial ground technician during the Citadel raid—complete with traffic wands used to direct starships on landing pads.

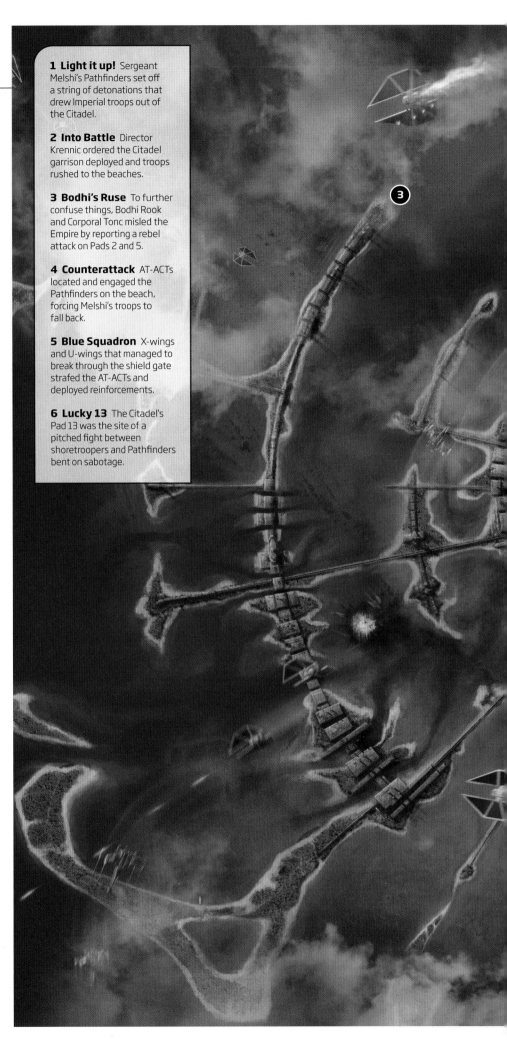

1 Light it up! Sergeant Melshi's Pathfinders set off a string of detonations that drew Imperial troops out of the Citadel.

2 Into Battle Director Krennic ordered the Citadel garrison deployed and troops rushed to the beaches.

3 Bodhi's Ruse To further confuse things, Bodhi Rook and Corporal Tonc misled the Empire by reporting a rebel attack on Pads 2 and 5.

4 Counterattack AT-ACTs located and engaged the Pathfinders on the beach, forcing Melshi's troops to fall back.

5 Blue Squadron X-wings and U-wings that managed to break through the shield gate strafed the AT-ACTs and deployed reinforcements.

6 Lucky 13 The Citadel's Pad 13 was the site of a pitched fight between shoretroopers and Pathfinders bent on sabotage.

7 Blue Leader Down
General Antoc Merrick was shot down and killed by a TIE striker.

8 Master Switch Chirrut Îmwe died after opening a comms channel allowing Bodhi to send a message to the rebel fleet.

9 Noble Sacrifice Bodhi told the rebels of the need to destroy the shield gate, but was killed by a grenade.

10 Surgical Strike Jyn Erso successfully transmitted the plans, but shortly afterward Tarkin ordered the Death Star superlaser to fire at the Citadel dish, dooming all in the complex.

11 Heroes' End Erso and Cassian Andor embraced on a beach as the shock wave approached, having given their lives for the Alliance.

Scarif (continued)

In orbit above the planet, Admiral Raddus adapted lessons from skirmishes with the Empire at Nexator and Carsanza, deploying his forces to tie up the Imperial defenders until he could find a weakness. He split his task force into thirds, supporting Red, Gold, and Green Squadrons, and sent Blue Squadron to support the Rogue One team below.

When the Empire responded by shutting the planetary shield, Raddus sent Red Squadron to attack the shield gate orbital station while his other ships harried the two Star Destroyers stationed at Scarif, the *Persecutor* and *Intimidator*, keeping them from concentrating their superior firepower. That gambit succeeded, but the shield gate proved heavily armored and well defended by TIE squadrons–too hard a target for even Y-wing bombers to neutralize.

Raddus had achieved a draw despite being outgunned. That would have satisfied him just an hour earlier, when his goal was to buy time, extract Rogue One, and retreat with the plans. But now it was no longer enough: the team were trapped and unable to transmit. Raddus needed a victory, not a stalemate.

He achieved it using the Star Destroyers. First, he flanked the *Persecutor*, enabling a frontal attack by Y-wings that disabled it. Then, while fighters boxed in the *Intimidator*, Raddus ordered a Hammerhead corvette to act as a tug, shoving the *Persecutor* into the other Star Destroyer. Finally, the two ruined battleships destroyed the shield gate, letting Erso transmit the plans.

▲ **Searching for a Weakness** After most of Blue Squadron made it through the shield gate, Red and Gold Squadrons conducted repeated attack runs on the station's defense turrets and control linkages. But it soon became clear that the starfighters lacked the firepower to destroy the station.

▼ **Desperate Hours** Blue and Green Squadrons were all but destroyed at Scarif. Just days later, Massassi Base's techs had to cobble together enough ships for Red and Gold Squadrons to attack the Death Star.

KEY LOCATION: THE SHIELD GATE

A planetary deflector shield enveloped Scarif, with cargo shuttles and other traffic passing through a portal at the center of a ring-shaped Golan M3185 space station, known as the shield gate. Such defenses were rare, as full planetary shields were prohibitively expensive and demanded enormous amounts of power. A stolen cargo shuttle and a rebel squadron made it through the portal before it was closed, but the shield then resisted attacks from starfighters scrambled from Yavin 4, and the Empire fought back with squadrons of TIE fighters and Scarif's complement of Star Destroyers. Only a daring, improvised attack by Admiral Raddus destroyed the station.

➤ **Ample Defenses** Twelve squadrons of TIE fighters were aboard the shield gate to respond to any attack, deploying from hangars built into the Golan station.

Scarif: Decisive Moment

The Battle of Scarif turned on an improvised tactic from Admiral Raddus. He saw the key to victory was bringing down the defensive shield encircling Scarif that was preventing Rogue One from transmitting the Death Star plans from the Citadel. But the shield gate had proved too tough a target for the Alliance's X-wings and Y-wings to crack, and Raddus' task force was taking a frightful beating from the Star Destroyers *Persecutor* and *Intimidator* and squadrons of TIE fighters. Raddus decided to attack the Star Destroyers, hoping to draw off the shield gate's defensive screen of TIEs and give the rebel pilots a chance to inflict more serious damage. This change in tactics would prove far more damaging than Raddus expected.

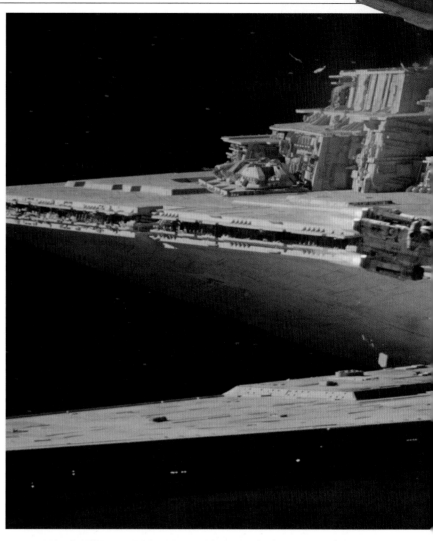

▲ **First Blow** Flying as Blue Four, Barion Raner just missed passing through the shield gate with the rest of Blue Squadron. But his X-wing struck a far more important blow for the Alliance, destroying the starboard deflector-shield generator of the *Persecutor*.

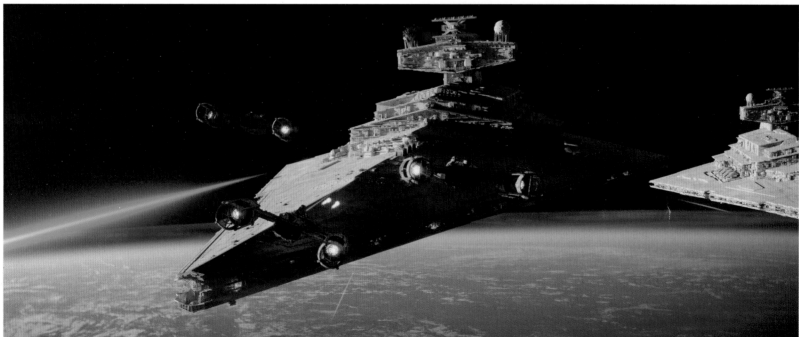

▲ **A Weak Spot** With his own flagship's shields failing, Raddus ordered Gold Squadron to engage the Star Destroyers. Y-wings led by Wona Goban (Gold Nine) strafed the *Persecutor* with ion torpedoes, a barrage that penetrated the Star Destroyer's weakened shields and caused a systems shutdown that left it disabled.

▲ **Admiral's Gambit** Seeing his chance, Raddus ordered a damaged Hammerhead corvette, the *Lightmaker*, to ram the *Persecutor*. Captain Kado Oquoné engaged the corvette's sublight engines, driving the *Persecutor* into the nearby *Intimidator*.

An attack run by Y-wing bombers disabled the *Persecutor*, leaving it dead in space. Raddus then turned the tide with an unlikely asset: the Hammerhead corvette *Lightmaker*, which had been damaged, largely evacuated, and sent to cover the line of retreat.

The *Lightmaker* rammed the *Persecutor* amidships with its heavily armored prow, then engaged its sublight engines at full throttle. Aboard the *Intimidator*, Admiral Gorin watched helplessly as the *Persecutor* gained momentum. The *Persecutor* ripped through the Imperial flagship and both plowed into the shield gate. A corvette that had been out of the fight had succeeded where the best Alliance starfighter pilots had failed: Scarif's shield was down, and the *Profundity* could now receive the Death Star plans from the Rogue One team below.

▶ **Target Destroyed** The wrecks of the two Star Destroyers slammed into the shield gate, destroying the station and bringing down Scarif's planetary shield. The Alliance now had a chance.

Scarif (continued)

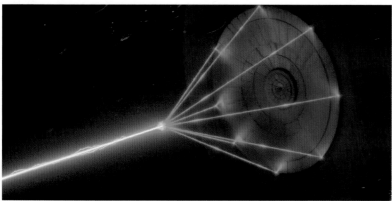

▲ **Chilling Calculus** Grand Moff Tarkin ordered the Death Star to fire at the Citadel tower in an effort to prevent the transmission of the stolen plans, brushing off the casualties that would result as acceptable collateral damage.

The Alliance stood on the verge of victory, but the Empire had two surprises up its sleeve. Another Star Destroyer, Darth Vader's personal flagship the *Devastator*, emerged from hyperspace, cutting off the *Profundity*'s retreat. With it came an even greater threat: the Death Star itself. The battle station targeted the Imperial Citadel with its superlaser, wiping out all survivors on the surface–rebel and Imperial alike.

The rebel retreat became a scramble, but the *Devastator*'s elite gunners made short work of the Alliance fleet, battering down the *Profundity*'s shields and leaving it dead in space. As an Imperial boarding party closed in, Raddus prepared once again to buy time: his crew would make a last stand while the plans were evacuated aboard the *Tantive IV*, a Corellian corvette belonging

▲ **Dark Enforcer** In a last-ditch effort to reclaim the Death Star plans, Darth Vader boarded the disabled *Profundity*, stalking rebel soldiers through its halls. But the blockade runner *Tantive IV* escaped from the crippled flagship, bearing the rebels' prize away from Scarif.

CASUALTIES

REBEL ALLIANCE: While Scarif was a rebel victory, it was a costly one, partially justifying the Alliance's caution about engaging the Empire in a full-scale battle. Admiral Raddus died aboard the *Profundity*, which fell into Imperial hands; the fleet was ravaged; Massassi Base's roster of starfighter pilots was decimated; and every member of the Rogue One mission died, either killed by Imperial troops or incinerated by the Death Star.
EMPIRE: The losses at Scarif were a stunning blow to the Empire: two Star Destroyers, the shield gate station, and the entire complement of the Citadel complex. In response to this brazen rebel attack and his (accurate) suspicions that the rebels were aided and abetted by conspirators in the Imperial Senate, Palpatine disbanded the galactic government. No one dreamed that the rebel raid at Scarif would lead to a far more damaging defeat—one that would threaten the Empire's very hold on power.

▼ **Heroes of the Alliance** Rogue One's principals, such as Baze Malbus and Chirrut Îmwe, died at Scarif but inspired generations of freedom fighters.

▲ **A World Scarred** The single-reactor firing, similar to the Jedha test, incinerated the top of the Citadel and ignited a firestorm kilometers offshore, creating a devastating shock wave that expanded in all directions. A cloud of plasma and superheated debris wiped the Citadel complex off Scarif's surface.

to Alderaan's House Organa and commanded by Princess Leia. The ship had been damaged on a mission and was being repaired aboard the *Profundity* when the rebel fleet left for Scarif.

The Death Star plans became the object of a frantic relay race, with the *Profundity*'s crew handing the schematics to troopers aboard the *Tantive IV* just moments before Darth Vader would have recaptured them. Organa's ship, still only partially repaired, lurched away from the doomed *Profundity* and escaped into hyperspace, custodian of hope for the galaxy.

Boarding of the *Tantive IV*

DATE: 19 AFE ▪ **LOCATION:** TATOOINE ▪ **COMBATANTS:** EMPIRE VS. REBEL ALLIANCE ▪ **OUTCOME:** TACTICAL IMPERIAL VICTORY

SCARIF AFTERMATH

Having escaped from Scarif with the Death Star plans, the *Tantive IV* made a direct course to Tatooine with the aim of locating the Jedi Master Obi-Wan Kenobi. However, a faulty hyperdrive subsystem saw the vessel pursued by the Imperial Star Destroyer *Devastator* and intercepted in orbit. The rebel ship was unable to outrun the *Devastator* and turbolaser fire from the Star Destroyer breached its shields, damaging the main reactor. Captain Raymus Antilles ordered the reactor to be shut down to save the ship from destruction but left it dead in space. Using tractor beams, the *Devastator* drew the stricken vessel into the main hanger.

In preparation for a boarding attempt, rebel soldiers took up defensive positions at the main docking ports on the corvette's flanks. There was no cover for the defenders and little chance of escape for the ship or its crew, but the rebel personnel were loyal to Princess Leia Organa of Alderaan and prepared to lay down their lives to protect her.

In a textbook boarding action, stormtroopers used cutting lasers to blow open the portside boarding

▲ **Boarding Operations** Imperial stormtroopers from the 501st Legion, also known as "Vader's Fist," breached the *Tantive IV* and stormed the ship. Smoke and debris caused by the boarding impeded the ability of rebel soldiers to hit their targets and hold the corridor.

◀ **Bitter End** In an attempt to contain any leaks about the Death Star, all of the rebel survivors were executed and the *Tantive IV* was flagged for disposal. After Alderaan was destroyed the ship was no longer a priority and was forgotten.

hatch and then advanced into the ship. Their helmets provided visual and targeting information that nullified the clouds of smoke resulting from the hull breach, giving them a combat advantage over the rebels. Utilizing small unit tactics, stormtroopers moved in cohesive zigzag patterns down the corridors to maintain clear lines of fire, killing many rebels and forcing the rest back toward the ship's bridge.

With the ship overrun, Darth Vader boarded the vessel and personally executed Captain Antilles. Princess Leia was captured shortly afterward, but not before the plans for the Death Star were jettisoned in an escape pod that slipped past the *Devastator*'s gunners and descended to the planet below.

Commanders

PRINCESS LEIA ORGANA (CAPTURED)
The adopted daughter of Bail Organa, Princess Leia was an Imperial Senator and, secretly, a member of the Rebel Alliance. A fearless battle commander, Leia inspired great loyalty in the crew of the *Tantive IV*, many of whom laid down their lives for her.

DARTH VADER
The Sith Lord Darth Vader was known for his aggressive strategies and ruthlessness toward those who failed him. Having been unable to capture the *Tantive IV* at Scarif, Vader pursued it with his flagship and supervised the subsequent boarding by members of the 501st Stormtrooper Legion.

▲ **Antilles' Death** Captain Antilles attempted to use the exemption of diplomatic immunity to avoid Imperial reprisal, a tactic that had worked in the past, but the situation was too grave for that to work now.

KEY LOCATION: THE *TANTIVE IV*

The *Tantive IV* was a CR90 Corellian corvette, a vessel type sometimes affectionately referred to as a "blockade runner." Utilized in service to the Alderaanian House of Organa, the ship was used by Princess Leia to carry out missions in support of the Rebel Alliance, taking advantage of Leia's cover as an Imperial Senator. This subterfuge survived for a time until the vessel was seen escaping the Battle of Scarif by Darth Vader, who pursued it to Tatooine. Decades later, the ship would serve Leia again in the war against the First Order.

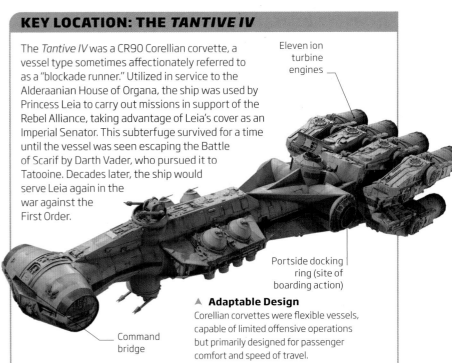

Eleven ion turbine engines

Portside docking ring (site of boarding action)

▲ **Adaptable Design**
Corellian corvettes were flexible vessels, capable of limited offensive operations but primarily designed for passenger comfort and speed of travel.

Command bridge

Yavin

DATE: 19 AFE ▪ **LOCATION:** YAVIN, OUTER RIM TERRITORIES ▪
COMBATANTS: EMPIRE VS. REBEL ALLIANCE ▪
OUTCOME: REBEL ALLIANCE VICTORY

MOST DESPERATE HOUR

The Battle of Yavin saw the Rebel Alliance, armed with only a small number of starfighters, facing the most powerful superweapon that had ever been fielded by the Galactic Empire. The Death Star, a moon-sized space station with more firepower than half of the Imperial star fleet combined, was en route to its target on the fourth moon of Yavin, where the Alliance kept their most vital base and housed much of their leadership. If the Death Star could orbit around the planet Yavin, the station's kyber-crystal-powered superlaser would destroy the entire moon and with it any hope of victory for the Rebellion.

Despite their technological disadvantage, the Alliance had received complete technical readouts of the station from the Rogue One team at Scarif, together with intelligence that a weakness had been planted inside. The rebels formulated a plan to strike a weak point on the surface of the station. The approach was dangerous, requiring a trio of fighters to skim along the surface of a meridian trench to give their targeting computers enough time to lock on to the station's weak point and fire torpedoes. More difficult still, the attackers had only 15 minutes to deal a crippling blow before the Death Star would be in firing range of Yavin 4.

▶ **Defiant Underdogs** Red and Gold Squadrons launched from the fourth moon of Yavin knowing that if they failed, the moon and most of the Rebel Alliance would be destroyed in a single blast.

Commanders

GENERAL JAN DODONNA
With the loss of Admiral Raddus at Scarif, it fell to Jan Dodonna to lead the analysis of the Death Star plans and find the weakness hidden in its design. He attempted to instill confidence in the strategy in his pilots, but he knew the heavy odds against them. Even if they were victorious, few would return.

GRAND MOFF WILHUFF TARKIN (KILLED IN ACTION)
Though Imperial analysts discovered the Rebellion's attack strategy and the danger it posed, Tarkin's hubris got the best of him. He refused to launch additional TIE squadrons or evacuate the station, believing—as many did—that the Death Star was the ultimate power in the universe.

▲ **Stafighter Strike** The Death Star's defenses were designed to repel a direct, large-scale assault by an enemy fleet. The Alliance sent only starfighters for a precision strike.

As expected, the battle station's anti-ship weapons dealt minimal casualties to the attacking starfighters, having been designed for larger capital-ship-scale targets, while the Death Star's stationary defense towers were vulnerable to strafing runs by the nimble fighter craft. The tide of the battle turned with the arrival of Imperial TIE fighters, and the ensuing dogfights were fierce. Though rebel losses were mounting, these skirmishes served their purpose as a distraction from the real target, a bombing run conducted by Gold Squadron's Y-wing bombers.

▲ **Easy Targets** The long approach down the narrow polar trench left rebel pilots little room to maneuver, making them easy targets for TIE fighters in pursuit.

KEY COMBATANT: REBEL STARPILOTS

The fate of the Rebellion–and the galaxy–rested at the hands of just 30 fighter pilots. This band of Imperial defectors, political idealists, and backwoods bush pilots had little idea what they were to face when they reached the Death Star. All but a few gave their lives for the mission, but their bravery saved the Rebellion and ultimately led to the downfall of the Empire.

► **Pilots' Bond**
A pair of wingmates accompanied the lead fighter on each bombing run, risking their lives to bravely shield their leader from attack.

Yavin: Decisive Moment

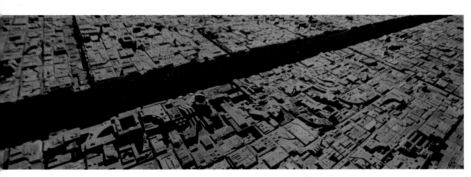

▲ **Trench Run** Skywalker's target lay at the end of a narrow meridian trench. He ordered his wingmates to make the approach at full speed in an attempt to outrun the trailing TIE fighters. This risky decision could have meant his targeting computer would not have been able to acquire the target in time.

With minutes left before the battle station was in firing range, Imperial analysts discovered the meaning of the rebel attack strategy and requested that additional squadrons be launched to counter the bombers. Tarkin, who retained sole authority to deploy them, declined. The leaders of Gold and Red Squadrons both attempted bombing runs, but both met the same fate as they were run down by a flight of TIEs that had been commandeered by Darth Vader. With the squadrons' ranks dwindling and leadership gone, it fell to Red Squadron's newest recruit to make one final attempt. His attack run would have likely ended in failure had it not been for a last-minute reinforcement. In the heat of battle, Han Solo joined the fight

◄ **In Vader's Sights** At the controls of his TIE fighter, Darth Vader quickly dispatched the first two bombing attempts. When a third group formed up for the attack, he disabled one defending wingman and destroyed the other, feeling confident that only a single rebel starfighter lay between him and complete Imperial victory.

▼ **An Unlikely Hope** Pilot Luke Skywalker, call sign Red 5, was an improbable hero of Yavin who had never been at the controls of an X-wing prior to the battle. The young pilot betrayed conventional wisdom by disabling his targeting computer in the final moments of his bombing run, choosing to rely upon something other than technology in this most critical moment.

▲ **Surprise Reinforcements** The pursuing TIE fighters had no room for evasive action when caught in a surprise attack from a lone rebel-aligned freighter, the *Millennium Falcon*. Vader's wingmates were killed, and his TIE fighter spun out of control.

in a highly modified freighter and provided vital covering fire for Skywalker in the final moments of his attack run. By the time Skywalker reached his target, the Death Star had already commenced its firing sequence. The station was but seconds away from firing when his proton torpedoes found their target, entering the two-meter-wide exhaust port and causing a chain reaction that led to the volatile main reactor. The hasty analysis of the plans provided earlier by Rogue One proved correct, and the Rebellion let out a collective sigh of relief as the station exploded before their eyes. Thanks to the collective actions of a few Alliance heroes, the Rebellion had toppled the most powerful weapon in the galaxy.

▲ **Hard Target** With ray shielding that protected the thermal exhaust port, proton torpedoes were the only armament in Alliance armories that could make the final strike.

Yavin (continued)

▲ **Shot Heard Round the Galaxy** The Empire's prolific propaganda machine worked hard to hide the truth about Yavin. While they tried to conceal the facts about the station's destruction, the massive debris field in the Yavin system left little doubt that something of great significance had transpired there.

Skywalker's strike caused a chain reaction that destroyed the Empire's most imposing superweapon and sent political ripples throughout the galaxy. The victory at Yavin sent a clear message to the Empire and rebel sympathizers alike: the initial triumph at Scarif was not a fluke and Palpatine's Empire was exposed. The Galactic Civil War was now in full swing and holonet footage of the battle station's destruction provided the rebels with a powerful recruiting tool.

Despite the Alliance's success, ultimate victory remained far from certain. Immediately following the attack, they were once again on the defensive as the Empire doubled its resolve to find and eliminate the Rebellion. The Alliance leadership left little time for celebrating before calling for a complete

evacuation of their hidden base on Yavin 4, rightly concerned that Imperial retaliation would be swift and severe.

Though the Death Star was destroyed, the intact Imperial star fleet continued to grow. The gargantuan cost and loss of the Death Star platform caused Imperial commanders—at least for a time—to reconsider their approach, and they diverted resources to other programs, such as the Super Star Destroyers. These gigantic battleships were championed by the likes of Grand General Tagge, one of the few survivors to have departed the

CASUALTIES

REBEL ALLIANCE: Of the thirty rebel starfighter pilots who took part in the battle, only three survived: Luke Skywalker, Wedge Antilles, and Evaan Verlaine. The pilots' sacrifice saved all of the personnel on the ground and secured the survival of the Rebellion.

EMPIRE: The destruction of the Death Star cost the Empire over a million lives and more than a trillion galactic credits. In addition to the station's substantial crew complement, made up of some of the Empire's finest recruits, the loss of Grand Moff Tarkin was particularly noteworthy. Tarkin was a generational military mind and trusted associate of the Emperor, and his ideologies had shaped Imperial doctrine from its very beginnings.

▶ **Heavy Sacrifice** After heavy losses at Scarif and Yavin, the Rebellion's starfighter squadrons were nearly depleted.

▲ **Fleeting Victory** The Rebel Alliance celebrated their new heroes and commemorated those they lost. But with their location now known, the celebration did not last long. The Alliance were forced to evacuate, scattering teams across the galaxy in search of a new base.

Death Star before the attack, leaving him in a position to fill the leadership void left by the station's destruction. In a rebuke of its former commander, Tagge dubbed the Death Star program "Tarkin's Folly." Another notable survivor, Darth Vader, evaded death but not the immense embarrassment of losing the Emperor's prized superweapon to a band of defectors and farmhands. He would personally lead the effort to hunt down the Rebel Alliance and its new hero, Luke Skywalker.

MEDAL OF BRAVERY

This ornate medal was among the highest honors given to heroes of the Alliance to Restore the Republic. Unlike their enemies in the Empire, the Rebellion rarely displayed such military fanfare and pageantry, but the heroics demonstrated at Yavin by pilots Luke Skywalker, Han Solo, and Chewbacca called for open recognition.

▶ **Deeper Meaning** The medal's design features a stylized flower symbolizing hope.

Cymoon 1

DATE: 19 AFE ▪ **LOCATION:** CYMOON 1, EXPANSION REGION ▪
COMBATANTS: EMPIRE VS. REBEL ALLIANCE ▪
OUTCOME: REBEL ALLIANCE VICTORY

RAID ON THE WEAPONS FACTORY

Eliminating the Death Star was a remarkable win for the scrappy Rebel Alliance. They seized the momentum of this major victory and pressed their advantage throughout the galaxy with daring offensives. In one such mission, Princess Leia Organa assembled a small strike team to sneak into an Imperial factory mass-producing weapons on Cymoon 1. Their objective: to destroy Weapons Factory Alpha.

To access the secure facility, the rebels intercepted an emissary of Jabba the Hutt who was going to offer an Imperial negotiator resources in exchange for weapons. The smuggler Han Solo took the place of the emissary. The deception gained the rebels entry, and they wasted no time getting to the facility's power core. But in a terrible case of bad luck, Darth Vader's shuttle arrived on Cymoon 1. Vader was the Empire's negotiator.

The Sith Lord engaged Luke Skywalker while Organa, Solo, Chewbacca, C-3PO, and R2-D2 continued to focus on the mission. The astromech droid R2-D2 proved particularly useful to the team, distracting stormtroopers and repairing weaponry on an AT-AT the rebels commandeered. Skywalker eventually triggered a meltdown of the factory core and destroyed the structure, but he disobeyed direct orders from Organa in the process. This willingness to bend the rules depending upon the situation was a trait of

Commanders

PRINCESS LEIA ORGANA
Leia Organa enacted a straightforward plan to eviscerate Cymoon 1's weapons factory. When Darth Vader's arrival interfered with her strategy, she quickly pivoted—an important skill for a leader. She maximized the talents of her small team to stand against Imperial forces and leaped into action herself. The rebels left with their mission accomplished.

DARTH VADER
Darth Vader arrived on Cymoon 1 to negotiate between the Empire and what he believed to be Jabba the Hutt's emissary. When he discovered the presence of the pilot who destroyed the Death Star, he went after him with laser focus. His pursuit of the rebel, who unbeknownst to him was his son, meant the Empire lost the factory.

▶ **AT-AT Power** Han Solo attempted to crush Darth Vader using an AT-AT he commandeered from the factory, but Vader fought back with the Force and toppled the walker.

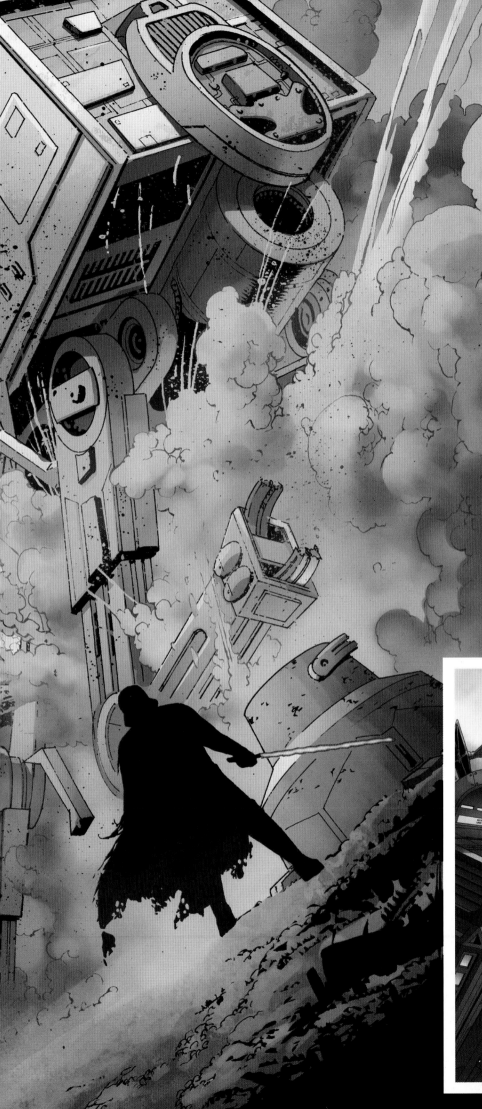

a rebel soldier, whereas Imperial ranks were built upon a foundation of order and chain of command. Disobeying an order from a commanding officer in the Empire led to punishment–severe, probably lethal punishment if that officer was Darth Vader.

With the successful eradication of the weapons factory, the Rebel Alliance removed a significant portion of the Empire's resources. This likely spared the lives of countless civilians and rebel soldiers. The quick and decisive victory also served as further proof to the Empire that they should not underestimate their foes.

▲ **Facing Fear** Though lacking confidence in his Jedi skills, Skywalker faced Darth Vader head on.

KEY LOCATION: WEAPONS FACTORY ALPHA

The Empire's massive forces required a substantial amount of weaponry. Across the galaxy planets were assessed to see if they could offer the myriad resources necessary to manufacture arms. Sometimes those resources were ferried offworld to giant arms factories. Weapons Factory Alpha on Cymoon 1, part of the Corellian Industrial Cluster, was one such location–the largest weapons factory in the galaxy. Though the Empire proclaimed that the factory was fully automated, in reality they used slaves to operate the machinery.

▼ **Controlled Entry** As the factory was a vital strategic location, Overseer Aggadeen carefully screened all incoming craft to Cymoon-1.

Vrogas Vas

DATE: 19 AFE ■ **LOCATION:** VROGAS VAS, OUTER RIM TERRITORIES ■ **COMBATANTS:** EMPIRE VS. REBEL ALLIANCE ■
OUTCOME: IMPERIAL VICTORY

VADER UNLEASHED

Determined to find the rebel pilot who destroyed the Death Star, Darth Vader traveled to Vrogas Vas after the archaeologist Doctor Aphra shared with him that Luke Skywalker would be on the planet. Vader set out alone in his TIE Advanced x1 fighter, and on arrival at the planet instantly found himself among rebel starfighters practicing maneuvers. The Sith Lord leveraged the momentum of his surprise

appearance and fought the entirety of Red, Blue, and Yellow Squadrons by himself; he destroyed most of the ships and used the Force to veer the rebels' torpedoes off course. The space battle transitioned to a battle on the surface when Red Five–Skywalker–flew directly into Vader's TIE, causing both ships to spin down to the planet. Skywalker and Vader survived their respective crashes unscathed.

Sensing an opportunity to capture one of their most dangerous enemies, soldiers and pilots rushed into action from the secret Rebel Alliance refueling

▼ **Vader Takes All** Red, Blue, and Yellow Squadrons were practicing maneuvers when Darth Vader arrived at Vrogas Vas. The Sith Lord immediately engaged them in battle.

base on Vrogas Vas. Rebel infantry and Gray Squadron's Y-wings soon arrived at Vader's crash site. However, Vader wiped out Gray Squadron with Force-thrown debris from his crashed TIE Advanced and then proceeded to kill an entire platoon of infantry troopers that attempted to capture him.

Meanwhile, General Dodonna ordered a battalion to the planet to support the rebels' numbers. Princess Leia Organa, Han Solo, and Chewbacca joined them. Vader's allies traveled to Vrogas Vas too: Doctor Aphra and her droids, Triple-Zero and BT-1. A rival of Vader's also joined the fray: the cyborg Mon Calamari Commander Karbin. The fellow Imperial stood against Vader in hopes of remanding Luke Skywalker into custody to gain favor with Emperor Palpatine.

Organa targeted Vader while the various other parties fought one another. She was willing to sacrifice herself to kill Vader, but Karbin and his stormtroopers interrupted her scheme. Vader ultimately killed Karbin and foiled the commander's plan to capture Skywalker. Though Luke and his friends escaped, Vader had inflicted a significant defeat on the Rebel Alliance.

KEY LOCATION: ALLIANCE REFUELING STATION

Vrogas Vas was once home to a Jedi temple that fell to ruin. A barren world with no known native lifeforms, it was an ideal location for the rebels to establish a hidden base. The station, secretly built sometime after the Battle of Yavin, held numerous personnel and ships, including X-wings and Y-wings. All forces at the base were deployed to locate and eliminate Darth Vader, suffering serious casualties in the process. With its location now known to the Empire, the facility was abandoned.

▲ **One-Way Trip** Infantry soldiers and pilots were scrambled from the refueling base to track down and capture Darth Vader. Few of them returned.

▲ **Fear and Dead Men** The rebels surrounded Darth Vader. Seeing that they had him vastly outnumbered and believing that they had the upper hand, they demanded his surrender. Vader interpreted it as the rebels giving up, and taunted them. He then used the Force to detonate the rebels' own grenades, wiping out most of the unit.

Commanders

PRINCESS LEIA ORGANA
Leia Organa seized the opportunity to corner Darth Vader and led rebel soldiers to his location. Willing to sacrifice herself to take down the Sith Lord, she ordered the bombers of Amber Wing to hit her and Vader with everything they had, but Karbin's forces intervened.

DARTH VADER
Darth Vader flexed his powerful Force abilities during the battle. He took down two whole fighter squadrons, Delta Squad, and many rebel troopers. Effectively a one-man army, he emerged victorious, having inflicted severe damage on the rebel forces.

▶ **Pitched Battle** Admiral Ackbar's task force arrived at Mon Cala without a formal battle plan and found itself in a chaotic brawl. Rebel starfighters and warships sought to buy time as Ackbar looked for a way to break the Empire's blockade and free the trade fleet.

Mutiny at Mon Cala

DATE: 19 AFE ▪ **LOCATION:** MON CALA, OUTER RIM TERRITORIES ▪ **COMBATANTS:** EMPIRE VS. REBEL ALLIANCE ▪ **OUTCOME:** REBEL ALLIANCE VICTORY

DAWN OF THE REBEL FLEET

The Death Star's destruction left the Empire's military strategy in disarray and inspired a surge in funding and recruits to the Alliance. Though emboldened, the Alliance knew the Empire would soon strike back, and rebel forces had to be prepared. Alliance high command's most pressing goal was to strengthen the rebel fleet, which had been barely worthy of the name even before its losses at Scarif: it was a ragtag gaggle of ships begged from sympathetic planetary governments, surreptitiously "borrowed" from salvage yards, and stolen from Imperial facilities.

Since the Alliance lacked the credits and access to shipyards necessary to build their own fleet, Leia Organa and Admiral Ackbar set their sights on recruiting the Mon Calamari to join their cause. The Mon Cala Trade Fleet was one of the galaxy's largest merchant fleets, and its cruisers could be refitted into effective warships. Unfortunately, the Empire knew the Mon Calamari's capabilities and sympathies all too well, and had kept a stranglehold on the planet since occupying it soon after the Clone Wars.

THE MUTINY

After the Empire seized Mon Cala, Dors Urtya remained on his homeworld rather than join the nascent Rebel Alliance with his friends Raddus and Ackbar. Urtya feared what the Empire would do to his planet, and concluded that he could best serve the Mon Calamari by shielding them from the Empire's vengeance. Named regent for the imprisoned King Lee-Char, he cooperated with Mon Cala's Imperial occupiers, putting its trade fleet at their disposal. But Urtya was never reviled as a collaborator; rather, the Mon Calamari saw him as a protector who did the best that he could in a bad situation.

▶ **Showdown** Though disappointed by Urtya's refusal to aid the Alliance, Leia respected the difficult choices he faced as regent. Her faith in Urtya paid off when he decided to transmit Lee-Char's last message.

▲ **The Price of Mutiny** After the trade fleet's escape, Imperial Star Destroyers targeted Mon Cala. An orbital bombardment erased the ancient regency complex, killing Urtya.

Grand Admiral Dors Urtya, Mon Cala's regent and warden for the imprisoned King Lee-Char, refused the rebels' entreaties, fearing devastating Imperial reprisals. Stymied, Organa opted for an audacious jailbreak to free Lee-Char from Imperial custody. Though near death, Lee-Char recorded a message urging the Mon Calamari to break with their Imperial captors regardless of the cost.

Still fearful for his planet, Urtya confiscated this message, but broadcast it when the Empire tried to seize the trade fleet. Mon Calamari crews rose up against the Empire, and Ackbar led a rebel task force that helped their ships break the Imperial blockade. The Alliance had their fleet.

Commanders

ADMIRAL GIAL ACKBAR
Gial Ackbar took command of the Alliance fleet after Raddus died at Scarif. Though he found personal motives unbecoming in a commander, he admitted taking pride in victory at Mon Cala: his homeworld's ships and crews were now the backbone of the rebel fleet.

ADMIRAL TYRUS MEORI
Tyrus Meori was promoted to admiral for victories at Hargawi and the Narrant Shoals, and was admired for both his ruthlessness and his knack for quotes that played well on Holonet News. He survived the debacle at Mon Cala, but both his flagship and his career were seriously damaged.

KEY WEAPON: THE *AURORA FLARE*

The key to breaking the Imperial blockade lay in the cargoes carried by the trade fleet. Ackbar studied manifests sent to him by the mutinous Mon Calamari captains and discovered the *Aurora Flare* was loaded with coaxium bound for the great refineries at Redhurne. The *Flare*'s captain, Pysk Lila, sacrificed herself and her vessel by setting it on a collision course with Admiral Meori's flagship, the *Aquilifer*. The coaxium ignited, destroying the *Aurora Flare* and doing catastrophic damage to the *Aquilifer*. The trade fleet then escaped through the hole Lila had punched in the blockade.

▶ **Too Late** Meori neglected to order a scan of cargoes on the Mon Calamari merchant ships, and only discovered the peril posed by the *Aurora Flare* when evasive action was no longer possible.

Mako-Ta

DATE: 20 AFE ■ **LOCATION:** MAKO-TA, OUTER RIM TERRITORIES ■ **COMBATANTS:** EMPIRE VS. REBEL ALLIANCE ■
OUTCOME: TACTICAL IMPERIAL VICTORY

ASSAULT ON THE SPACE DOCKS

The Imperial assault at Mako-Ta nearly broke the Alliance. The rebels had to scatter their forces to survive, and star systems that had voiced opposition to the Empire after the destruction of the first Death Star no longer dared to do so.

Botajef Shipyards had built the Mako-Ta Space Docks as an auxiliary facility, but abandoned them after solar flares erupted on binary stars Mako and Ta. By the time the stellar weather ebbed, shifting trade routes had left Mako-Ta a backwater–unprofitable for Botajef, but ideal for the Alliance.

The Alliance restarted the docks, and Princess Leia Organa recruited Queen Trios of Shu-Torun to refit a dozen Mon Calamari star cruisers into warships, dramatically bolstering the rebel fleet. But Trios was a double agent serving Darth Vader. When the Alliance gathered its leaders and ambassadors to unveil the new fleet, Vader sprung his trap. Programs hidden in their Shu-Torun-built systems shut down the rebel cruisers' hyperdrives, turbolasers, and communications networks and locked down their starfighter hangars. Vader's Death Squadron then emerged from hyperspace, led by the Super Star Destroyer *Executor*, and began systematically destroying the rebel fleet.

The Alliance barely escaped total destruction. Han Solo and Luke Skywalker managed to free the starfighters, allowing the Alliance to engage the Star Destroyers, while Organa and Davits Draven led a daring raid on the *Executor* that secured override codes to bring the rebel ships back online. Mon Mothma and the ambassadors escaped, but the Empire won an enormous tactical and propaganda victory: 6 of the 12 new rebel cruisers were destroyed, along with more than 90 percent of the starfighters.

▶ **Facing Vader**
General Draven had studied Darth Vader's attack on the *Profundity* at Scarif and created combat strategies to slow down the Sith Lord. These tactics allowed Leia Organa to escape the rebel raid on the *Executor*.

Commanders

GENERAL JAN DODONNA (KILLED IN ACTION)
A veteran naval officer, Jan Dodonna commanded Yavin's rebel cell and planned the attack on the first Death Star. He escaped the ambush at Mako-Ta aboard the *Republic*, but returned to rescue Mon Mothma and the rest of the rebel fleet, sacrificing his flagship and his life in the process.

DARTH VADER
After their defeat at Yavin, the Imperials were stuck chasing rebel task forces across the galaxy, an inefficient strategy that made them look impotent. Vader opted for a new strategy: allowing the Alliance time to concentrate its forces, making them easier to destroy. At Mako-Ta, his plan came within a whisper of ending the Galactic Civil War.

A HERO'S DEATH

Blunt and ruthless, Davits Draven played an invaluable role in the early Alliance, harrying the Empire through sabotage, espionage, and assassination. He made no apologies for the disquiet such missions caused among the Alliance's leaders and supporters, going behind Mon Mothma's back when he felt he must. Draven's great regret was misjudging Jyn Erso, whom he dismissed as incapable of loyalty. At Mako-Ta, he joined Leia Organa in raiding the *Executor*, buying time for her to flee with the codes that saved the Alliance, before meeting his end at the hands of Darth Vader.

▶ **Last words** Draven's farewell to Organa was a request that she avenge Shu-Torun's betrayal of the Alliance: "What I want is payback against Trios... You'll be better at it than me."

◄ **Rogue Attack** Once freed to join the battle, Luke Skywalker formed an ad hoc squadron that also included Wedge Antilles, Zev Senesca, and Hobbie Klivian. In honor of Jyn Erso, Skywalker dubbed the fighter group Rogue Squadron. The Rogues would become one of the most celebrated starfighter units in the Alliance and New Republic.

▲ **Heavy Casualties** The first cruiser destroyed at Mako-Ta was the *Yavin's Hope*, under the command of Vanden Willard. Commanders Dodonna, Cor, Lajaie, Hudsol, and Draven also died in the battle, thinning the Alliance of veteran leaders at a critical time.

Intelligence and Espionage

Battles are often won or lost by the quality of intelligence that guides the battlefield strategy. Throughout the ages, warring factions have engaged in an ever-increasing race for information to give them the upper hand, whether sourced from battlefield observation, intercepting communications, employing covert operatives, or engaging in counter-intelligence to mislead the enemy. The more paranoid regimes even focused their efforts internally, ruthlessly seeking out any insubordination or insurrection within the ranks. Those tasked with the business of intelligence and espionage often risked their lives for the information they sought, for being discovered was too often a death sentence.

▲ **Listening Posts** The wide-ranging fronts of the Clone Wars led both the Republic and Separatists to employ stationary listening posts to intercept enemy transmissions that would provide information on troop movements.

ORGANIZED INTELLIGENCE

Though Emperor Palpatine claimed complete control of the galaxy, his regime employed many layers of intelligence gathering to monitor for acts of sedition. These included Imperial Intelligence and its many subdivisions as well as the Imperial Security Bureau (ISB). The latter was notable for its far-reaching remit of intelligence gathering, surveillance, internal affairs, investigations, counter-insurgency, and security. This multifaceted military and bureaucratic

▲ **Agent Fulcrum** The Rebel Alliance relied heavily on insights provided by Imperial defectors. Alexsandr Kallus was an ISB agent who went on to become a key rebel operative.

hierarchy created a complex web of agents working to uphold the complete and unwavering rule of the Emperor,

KEY INFO

SPY SHIPS

The Galactic Empire used specially outfitted vessels to provide mobile reconnaissance while hunting for rebel activity. The IGV-55 surveillance vessel was a modified *Gozanti*-class cruiser boasting an array of advanced espionage equipment used to scan a multitude of data for any sign of disobedience. Each vessel was staffed with a team of dedicated Imperial Information Office analysts with the ability to remotely tap into security holovids, information networks, and comms frequencies.

▲ **Enhanced Intelligence** A cybernetic device helped Imperial Intelligence controllers process large amounts of data.

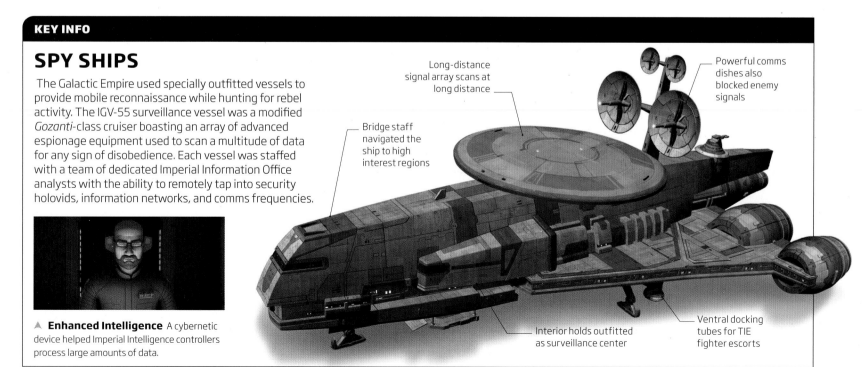

Long-distance signal array scans at long distance

Powerful comms dishes also blocked enemy signals

Bridge staff navigated the ship to high interest regions

Interior holds outfitted as surveillance center

Ventral docking tubes for TIE fighter escorts

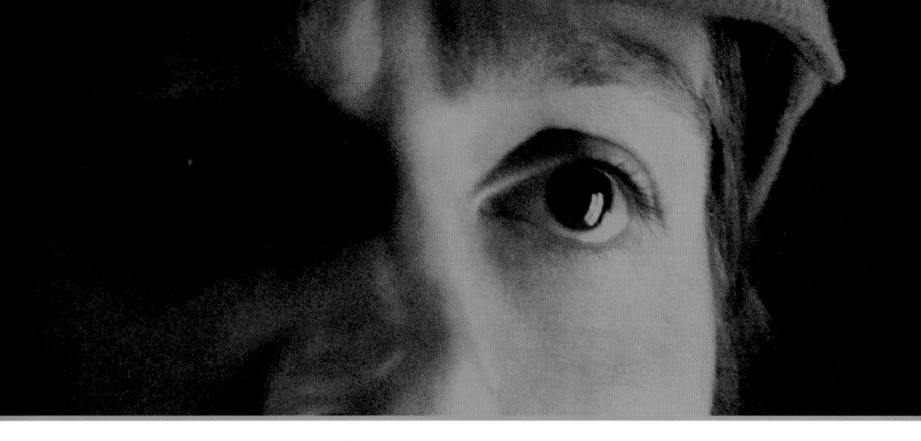

▲ **In Disguise** Cassian Andor of the Rebel Alliance regularly operated behind enemy lines. His clandestine missions sometimes required questionable methods.

an authority that was shaken to its core by the rise of the Rebel Alliance. The rebel attack on the Death Star at Yavin led to a galaxy-wide search for the Alliance's main operating base. Designated Project Swarm, the Empire dispatched hundreds of thousands of probe droids to scan the star systems for any sign of the rebels.

SPY GAMES

Unlike the Empire, the Rebel Alliance had no large-scale intelligence gathering organizations, instead relying on smaller teams of field operatives. Early in the Galactic Civil War, it fell to generals like Airen Cracken and Davits Draven to organize these highly secretive field agents, extraction teams, and spy networks. During these opening years

of the war, the Alliance lacked the military strength to mount a large-scale strike, instead relying on their agents to sabotage Imperial operations, create counter-intelligence, and even assassinate Imperial officials. The attacks on and subsequent destruction of both Death Star battle stations were the result of Alliance espionage activity, and both were costly for the teams involved. Rogue One's mission to retrieve the first Death Star plans led to 100 percent casualties. Later, the Battle of Endor was notable for the sacrifices made by rebel-aligned Bothans,

unaware that the intelligence they received was a trap by the Emperor himself.

INTELLIGENCE FOR HIRE

During the Cold War between the First Order and Resistance, Snoke's forces bolstered their own military intelligence with contracted spies that had infiltrated key points across the galaxy. General Leia Organa's Resistance relied on a network of unassuming droid intelligence agents.

▼ **Hiding in Plain Sight** The mercenary Bazine Netal posed as a patron at Maz Kanata's castle, concealing her well-paid role as a spy for the First Order.

Hoth

DATE: 22 AFE ▪ **LOCATION:** HOTH, OUTER RIM TERRITORIES ▪
COMBATANTS: EMPIRE VS. REBEL ALLIANCE ▪
OUTCOME: TACTICAL IMPERIAL VICTORY

FIGHTING RETREAT

The Battle of Hoth was the Alliance's worst defeat during the Galactic Civil War, a rout that badly strained already-stretched rebel resources. But while holonet propagandists trumpeted Hoth as an Imperial victory, it was actually a failure. A combination of tactical errors and misplaced priorities—along with the rebels' discipline and fortitude in battle—allowed the escape of key rebel leaders, along with personnel and equipment. The Empire seized the chance to strike back at the Alliance, but missed landing a death blow.

Hoth, first surveyed by a Gigoran rebel scout, offered the Alliance a number of advantages. The icy world was very close to the Corellian Trade Spine but on a lesser hyperlane plagued by navigational anomalies, making it rarely if ever visited. An extensive asteroid field snarled in-system travel, and regular asteroid impacts on Hoth created thermal signatures that would hide signs of habitation. If such signs were detected, observers would most likely conclude that yet another band of smugglers was trying to use Hoth as a bolthole. Such efforts inevitably came to nothing, given Hoth's punishing climate and savage storm seasons.

But the Alliance had the resources to succeed where smuggling rings had failed. Rebel engineers spent two years expanding ice caverns into

KEY COMBATANT: DEATH SQUADRON

Darth Vader supervised the hunt for the rebels' new base from his flagship, the *Executor*—a massive Star Dreadnought of terrifying power. The Sith Lord's Super Star Destroyer was typically accompanied by five other Star Destroyers—*Tyrant*, *Avenger*, *Devastator*, *Conquest*, and *Ultimatum*—to form Death Squadron. Vader could requisition additional ships as needed, with *Stalker* attached to Death Squadron shortly before the Battle of Hoth. The Alliance faced a greatly expanded Death Squadron at the Battle of Endor.

▲ **Imperial March** The ships of Death Squadron represented a massive concentration of naval firepower. However, every ship in the squadron suffered damage in Hoth's asteroid field, with a strike to its bridge destroying the *Ultimatum*.

▲ **Buying Time** Echo Base's rebel troopers cheered as snowspeeders from Corona and Rogue Squadrons streaked overhead. But the troops knew they were a rear guard, sacrificing their lives to save as many comrades as possible.

a formidable base built around a giant ion cannon, powered by a reactor stolen from a *Praetor*-class battlecruiser and buried a kilometer below the surface ice. The battle-worn, cautious General Carlist Rieekan ensured Echo Base—named for its caverns' eerie acoustics—would be a fortress, with heavy blast doors protecting its north and south entrances, rings of trenches for infantry, and anti-vehicle and anti-personnel emplacements built into the mountainside and set on the surrounding ice fields. Establishing Echo Base was an enormous undertaking intended to give the Alliance a principal base for the rest of the Galactic Civil War; because of some truly bad luck, the rebels called it home for less than a month.

Commanders

GENERAL CARLIST RIEEKAN
Carlist Rieekan was away from his homeworld of Alderaan when the Death Star incinerated it, and vowed no such tragedy would happen on his watch. After a probe droid scouted Echo Base's defenses, he overruled other rebel leaders who thought evacuating was an overreaction.

GENERAL MAXIMILIAN VEERS
Like Rieekan, Maximilian Veers had narrowly escaped doom, having been called away from the Death Star just before the Battle of Yavin. This brush with fate caused him to redouble his efforts in the war. He was badly injured when Hobbie Klivian's snowspeeder plowed into the head of his AT-AT, Blizzard 1.

▲ **Fire Control** Protecting the rebel transports demanded pinpoint timing, with the planetary shield opened just long enough for Echo Base's v-150 Planet Defender ion cannon to fire along a precisely calculated vector. Miss by even a little and the ion pulse would disable the craft it was meant to protect. This critical job belonged to communications officer Toryn Farr, whose sister, Samoc, flew with Rogue Squadron.

Hoth (continued)

▼ **Armored Monsters** AT-ATs had limited fields of fire and their legs demanded constant maintenance. However they were singularly effective terror weapons, in the face of which even hardened troops broke and ran.

The Imperial hunt for Echo Base intensified after the ambush of a rebel convoy at Derra. While that clash didn't reveal the base's location, it dovetailed with chatter tracked by Imperial Intelligence about increased rebel operations in the region. Star Destroyers blanketed sector after sector with probe droids; one launched from the *Stalker* descended to Hoth and captured an image of Echo Base's main power generator before self-destructing. Admiral Kendal Ozzel, commander of the Super Star Destroyer *Executor*, dismissed the sighting as an uncharted settlement or smugglers' outpost, but Darth Vader overruled him and ordered Death Squadron to Hoth.

Standard tactics called for Ozzel to assemble his squadron on the edge of the Hoth system and approach using its asteroid belt as cover, but Ozzel feared the rebels would call in the Alliance fleet, catching his task force amid the chaos of the asteroids. So he opted for surprise, decanting from hyperspace close to the planet. The rebels activated a planetary shield to protect their base—a potent defense the Empire did not know they had. Furious, Vader strangled Ozzel and promoted Firmus Piett in his stead.

With an orbital bombardment now impossible, General Maximilian Veers moved immediately to execute a ground assault: he would land Blizzard Force's dozen AT-ATs beyond the shield's perimeter, march overland to the shield generator, and destroy it. Meanwhile, Admiral Piett deployed his Star Destroyers as a blockade, ready to intercept fleeing rebel ships.

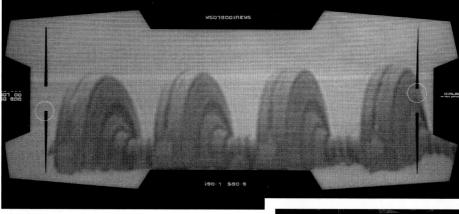

▲ ▶ **Tempting Target** Echo Base's power generator created large amounts of waste heat, which threatened to collapse its ice caverns. Engineers persuaded a reluctant Rieekan to accept leaving the generator exposed on the ice fields.

Fortunately for the Alliance, Rieekan had ordered evacuation preparations immediately after the encounter with the *Stalker*'s probe droid. The rebels were still on Hoth, but all of their critical equipment had already been loaded. Thirty rebel transports would have to run the Imperial blockade and escape to hyperspace, but Rieekan had planned for that: Echo Base would briefly lower the shield to fire blasts from its ion cannon at the Star Destroyers overhead, allowing X-wings to escort the transports to safety. Meanwhile, snowspeeders and ground forces would delay the Imperial ground assault as long as possible. The rebels would suffer grievous losses, but if they kept their heads, total disaster could be averted.

KEY WEAPON: ECHO BASE DEFENSES

To defend against ground vehicles and infantry, Echo Base relied on revolving DF.9 turrets and 1.4 FD P-Towers, the latter known for their distinctive energy dishes. Despite being larger, DF.9s were anti-infantry units and the smaller P-Towers were the installations used to target vehicles. Both were rugged and able to operate in Hoth's punishing cold, but neither packed enough of a punch to penetrate an AT-AT's frontal armor. They were more effective against enemy stormtroopers, but Veers kept most of his infantry inside the bellies of Blizzard Force's walkers until the rebel defensive lines had been broken.

▶ **Tough Veterans** The Alliance's fabled Special Forces bore the brunt of the fighting in the Hoth trenches.

Hoth: Decisive Moment

▲ **Change of Plans** Rogue Squadron's initial attack run at Blizzard Force's walkers yielded bad news: The walkers' armor was too powerful for the snowspeeders' laser cannons to pierce. Another strategy would be needed to stop them.

▼ **A Theory Tested** Wedge Antilles and Wes Janson tried a tactic the Rogue pilots had discussed: firing a harpoon at an AT-AT's leg and using their T-47's tow cable to bind the walker's limbs together. It was a daring maneuver born of desperation.

The rebels' hastily upgraded and modified T-47 airspeeders were highly maneuverable, but still civilian craft: just "punched-up cargo haulers," in the words of Wedge Antilles. The snowspeeders' laser cannons could only penetrate an AT-AT's weak neck, belly, or leg joints, which were difficult to target in battle. That forced the Rogues to try a novel tactic they'd debated in their ready rooms: using harpoons and tow cables to entangle the walkers' limbs. No one knew if that would actually work, and it required a perfect shot to fix the harpoon, followed by precise flying: too wide and you would snap the cable; too narrow and you would clip the target. The result, gunner Wes Janson recalled, was "thirty seconds of terror."

Rogue Three's maneuver went down in Alliance lore, but Antilles routinely dismissed his own legend, reminding wide-eyed young pilots that it was the only time the tactic worked that day.

▶ **No Good Choice** Brigadier General Nevar, commander of Blizzard 2, faced a dilemma: remain still and become an easy target for precision fire from rebel gunners, or advance and hope to break the tow cable. He chose to try and move forward.

▶ **A Giant Falls** To the Rogues' relief, the cable held. Blizzard 2 crumpled into the snow, the impact of its fall shaking the battlefield. The downed AT-AT was easy prey for Antilles, who came around for another pass and targeted its vulnerable neck.

▼ **A New Hope** The rebels still faced long odds, but the success of the Rogues' unorthodox tactic rallied the troops and the pilots trying to protect them. The Empire wasn't invulnerable: even their mightiest war machines could be toppled through bravery and ingenuity.

Hoth (continued)

Veers worried that X-wings would swarm his AT-ATs before they could deploy from their dropships, so he used nimble *Gozanti*-class cruisers to deliver the walkers, escorted by TIEs. But Blizzard Force landed unmolested at the Moorsh Moraine—the X-wings had other orders, which saw them providing support to the convoy evacuating the planet. It was also quickly apparent that Hoth's frigid winds robbed the TIEs of their maneuverability, and Veers ordered them back into space.

Three walkers stumbled into a crevasse attempting a southerly traverse of the Kerane Valley, but Veers knew speed was critical and advanced across the Nev Ice Flow with his remaining nine, leaving the laggards to be extracted after the battle. The AT-ATs obliterated Echo Base's sentry outposts and advanced on its defensive trenches. In response, the Alliance scrambled its compliment

CASUALTIES

REBEL ALLIANCE: More than half of Echo Base's 7,500 rebels were killed in action, died aboard their transports, or were captured while trying to escape.
EMPIRE: Around 500 Imperial troops died on Hoth, but the Empire would endure much heavier losses while trying to negotiate Hoth's asteroid field.

▼ **Grim Odds**
Zev Senesca and his gunner, Kit Valent, were among the first pilots killed in Rogue Group.

▼ **Enter the 501st** After landing on the battlefield, Vader and snowtroopers from the feared 501st Legion stormed Echo Base and targeted the *Millennium Falcon* with an E-web heavy repeating blaster. But the freighter managed to escape.

of T-47 airspeeders that had been modified to operate in the cold—a desperate effort that rebel techs had only just completed. But these "snowspeeders" lacked the firepower of starfighters and were unable to penetrate the AT-AT's armor. In desperation, Luke Skywalker ordered Rogue Squadron to use harpoons and tow cables to entangle the walkers' legs.

Alliance pilots destroyed three AT-ATs and disabled a fourth, but the Imperial march proved unstoppable. Veers destroyed the power generator, bringing down Echo Base's shields and allowing Imperial troops led by Vader to storm the base. By that point, however, nearly all the transports were away—and Vader's raid netted no high-value targets. Rather than try and track the fleeing rebel transports, Vader ordered Death Squadron and its TIE fighters after the *Millennium Falcon* in hopes of capturing Skywalker. The rebels had suffered painful losses, and struggled to regroup. But in one of the ironies of history, the rebel

▲ **Manhunt** While capturing the pilot who destroyed the Death Star was an obvious priority for the Empire, Vader's obsession with finding Luke Skywalker baffled many in the Imperial ranks.

leadership also began to wonder if the Alliance's best bet at victory was to amass their forces for a single strike at the heart of Imperial power. That strike would fall in a backwater system that would become famous across the galaxy: Endor.

▼ **Toll of War** The first rebel GR-75 medium transport to escape was the *Quantum Storm*, which slipped by the *Tyrant* to hyperspace and safety. But too many others weren't so lucky: only 13 of Echo Base's 30 transports made it through the blockade. Few of those captured were ever seen again.

Sullust

DATE: 22 AFE ▪ **LOCATION:** SULLUST, OUTER RIM TERRITORIES ▪ **COMBATANTS:** EMPIRE VS. REBEL ALLIANCE ▪
OUTCOME: REBEL ALLIANCE VICTORY

CHANGING PLANS

To increase the likelihood of a successful attack on the Imperial shipyards at Kuat Drive Yards, the Rebel Alliance devised Operation Ringbreaker. Everi Chalis, an Imperial defector and one-time governor of Haidoral Prime, presented the campaign to the 61st Mobile Infantry, a.k.a. Twilight Company. It involved attacking Imperial outposts along the Rimma Trade Route in order to pull forces away from Kuat Drive Yards and leave the ship manufacturer more vulnerable. The Siege of Inyusu Tor on Sullust

comprised one prong of the campaign; the rebels would target the Imperials' Inyusu Tor refinery complex.

After jumping to a point dangerously close to Sullust to gain the element of surprise, the rebels used dropships to reach the surface. They captured the Inyusu Tor facility in short order. However, the Empire had correctly deduced where the rebels would strike next. A TIE fighter squadron ambushed the rebels' ships, *Thunderstrike* and *Apailana's Promise*, and left Twilight Company stranded on Sullust.

▲ **Fighting Spirit** Members of the 61st Mobile Infantry were strongly committed to the ideals of freedom and justice for the galaxy. Stranded on Sullust without a ready escape, the rebels were prepared for a last stand against the Imperial stormtroopers.

Commanders

CAPTAIN HAZRAM NAMIR
Captain Hazram Namir was one of Twilight Company's most valuable members and led Operation Ringbreaker. After encountering setbacks taking a key processing facility on the planet, Namir determined the better course of action was to help the Sullustans free their home.

PRELATE VERGE (KILLED IN ACTION)
The youngest member of Emperor Palpatine's Ruling Council, Prelate Verge was pursuing leads on Imperial defector Governor Everi Chalis. He followed the information to Sullust, where he located Chalis at Inyusu Tor, but was later killed by one of his own officers.

▲ **Diversion Tactics** Two T-65B X-wing starfighters from *Apailana's Promise* returned to Sullust to distract the Star Destroyer *Herald* from bombarding the Twilight Company squads on the ground.

Upon convening with the Sullustan resistance in the capital city of Pinyumb, Twilight Company's leader, Hazram Namir, realized the Rebellion could attain a greater victory by fighting for the planet. Twilight Company put Operation Ringbreaker aside to aid the Sullustans and together they successfully took back Pinyumb from the Empire. Their actions inspired further uprisings around the planet. Eager to help other citizens on other occupied planets, Nien Nunb and several other Sullustans joined the Rebel Alliance. Following its capture, Sullust would become the main staging point for the Alliance fleet prior to the Battle of Endor.

ATTACKING KUAT DRIVE YARDS

After manufacturing starships and vehicles for the Galactic Republic, Kuat Drive Yards continued to fulfill orders for the new Galactic Empire. The factories that ringed Kuat were a primary source of Star Destroyers and AT-AT walkers, as well as several other formidable designs for the Imperial navy. The constant influx of orders meant huge profits for the manufacturer. Given its role in the Galactic Civil War, Kuat Drive Yards' facilities became an imperative, if difficult, target for the Rebel Alliance. Operation Ringbreaker was an intricate campaign to incapacitate the massive ship-building operation, and though the plan was abandoned, the New Republic would eventually authorize a direct attack on Kuat Drive Yards.

▲ **The Fall of Kuat** The New Republic bombed the KDY shipyards in 24 AFE. After weeks of battle, the Empire finally surrendered.

Endor

DATE: 23 AFE ▪ **LOCATION:** ENDOR, OUTER RIM TERRITORIES ▪
COMBATANTS: EMPIRE VS. REBEL ALLIANCE ▪
OUTCOME: DECISIVE REBEL ALLIANCE VICTORY

PALPATINE'S DOWNFALL

The Battle of Endor was the most significant military engagement in modern galactic history. Despite having been lured into a trap, the forces of the Rebel Alliance won a victory which effectively decapitated the Imperial hierarchy and dealt a mortal wound to the Empire's military.

The Emperor had baited the perfect trap for the Rebel Alliance. The construction of a new and more powerful Death Star above Endor forced the rebels into an infiltration mission to destroy the protective shield generator on the moon itself before launching an attack on the battle station. But when the rebel fleet arrived, they discovered that the shield was still up. The Imperial fleet appeared from behind Endor to block their escape while the Death Star's superlaser targeted rebel capital ships.

While an Imperial victory seemed assured, the seeds of disaster had already been planted. The first wave of Imperial TIE fighters caused havoc among the rebel fleet but, on Palpatine's orders, Admiral Piett held the Star Destroyers back. The unsupported TIEs suffered badly as the rebels counterattacked.

When the rebel capital ships unexpectedly moved to engage the Star Destroyers at point-blank range, the reduced Imperial fighter screen meant that the rebel ships had less fear of being swamped by TIEs. Imperial doctrine had never envisioned such an engagement, and the subsequent hesitation squandered both the element of surprise and momentum.

▲ **Rebels Cornered** Caught between the Imperial fleet and the still-shielded Death Star, the rebels had no choice but to turn and fight. The first wave of Imperial fighters tore through their formation.

Commanders

ADMIRAL GIAL ACKBAR
Ackbar was the highest-ranking military officer in the Rebel Alliance. Aboard the Mon Calamari cruiser *Home One*, Ackbar commanded the rebel fleet at Endor. Upon realizing that Endor was a trap, Ackbar reorganized his forces and led them into short-range combat with the Imperial fleet.

EMPEROR PALPATINE (KILLED IN ACTION)
Palpatine's rule over the Empire was absolute; even when his orders placed tight restrictions on his officers, they still obeyed them without question. While Palpatine focused his energies on Luke Skywalker, his paralyzed fleet began to struggle.

▲ **Blade Squadron** Rebel B-wing fighters isolated the Star Destroyer *Devastator* during the battle. The hard-hitting starfighters broke through the vessel's shields and successfully destroyed Darth Vader's former flagship. It would be one of many Star Destroyers to fall at Endor.

THE EMPEROR'S TRAP

An under-construction Death Star was a threat so grave that the Rebel Alliance had no option but to launch an attack. Emperor Palpatine had known this to be true when he leaked word of the station to the Bothan spy network. His own presence aboard the Death Star only increased the likelihood that the rebels would fall into his trap. Palpatine intended to use the destruction of the rebel fleet as a tool to turn Luke Skywalker to the dark side. He needed the drama of battle to achieve this goal. But to produce it he placed hugely restrictive orders on his military.

▶ **Fully Operational** At the Emperor's command, the Death Star's superlaser opened fire on the rebel fleet. After destroying the cruiser *Liberty*, its second target was the *Nautilian*.

Endor (continued)

On Endor's surface, rebel forces were engaged in a frantic battle against the Imperial garrison manning the shield generator, who had been reinforced with some of the Empire's finest soldiers. Having located a back door into the shield bunker, rebel commandos led by General Han Solo and Princess Leia Organa had initially stormed the building before being captured.

However, though they were elite soldiers, the Imperial forces at the bunker had paid scant attention to the supposedly "primitive" Ewok species who were indigenous to the moon. The Empire had not noticed the Ewoks' fiercely proud warrior culture, or that they had been preparing defensive positions around the bunker for several weeks.

When the Ewoks attacked, the Imperial military found themselves fighting from a surrounded position against an enemy who had prepared the battlefield against them. While the Empire possessed a marked technological advantage it was effectively nullified by an adversary who knew the terrain and could seemingly disappear at will.

Imperial combat discipline began to disintegrate. Using a captured AT-ST walker, General Solo tricked the bunker commander into opening the facility's blast doors. Solo then planted and detonated explosives that destroyed the facility.

▲ **Ground Combat** With General Solo's rebel commando team captured, the forces of the Empire appeared to have won the day on Endor's surface. However, an attack by the Ewoks distracted the Imperial troops and allowed the rebels to gain the advantage.

▲ **Shields Down** After winning the ground battle, General Solo planted a series of explosives within the shield bunker. Upon detonation they tore the shield generator apart, leaving the Death Star open to attack.

KEY COMBATANT: THE EWOKS

As it had on countless other worlds with native populations, the Empire had largely dismissed the presence of the Ewok tribes on Endor as either an inconvenience or an irrelevance. Tribal regions had been cleared to make way for the shield generator bunker. But the Ewoks were both competent and cunning warriors. They would not engage the Empire directly, but instead prepared a series of traps around the bunker just in case an opportune moment arose. Having been won over to the rebels' cause by stories of their past heroism, the Ewoks decisively intervened in the ground combat outside the shield bunker. While they defeated the stormtroopers, the battle also cost many Ewoks their lives.

▲ **Cunning Warriors** The Ewoks had constructed a series of traps and obstacles, such as tripwires and swinging logs, that could be deployed against the Imperial military.

Endor: Map

The fleet movements at Endor remained a source of interest for military historians decades after the battle. The Empire initially took up a perfect position by pinning the rebel fleet against Endor's gravity well and then blocking their avenues of escape. However, as the battle unfolded, the rebels made use of the superior shielding on their own fighters and the Empire's seeming unwillingness to advance their battle lines. The two fleets intermingled, thereby nullifying the firepower of the Death Star. By pushing between Star Destroyers, rebel cruisers were able to concentrate their fire on isolated ships. This culminated in the destruction of the *Executor*, which temporarily paralyzed Imperial operations moments before the Death Star itself was destroyed.

CLIMACTIC CONFLICT

The Imperial captains at Endor had waited years for this moment: they finally had the entire rebel fleet trapped and at their mercy. For so long they had chased the Alliance around the galaxy, fruitlessly trying to force them into a full-scale battle, but now it had happened. Faced with such an overwhelming force, the rebels would surely try to surrender—a request that would certainly be refused. They were shocked when the rebel fleet did not capitulate, and instead charged directly at their waiting Star Destroyers.

▲ **Command Ship** At the center of the Imperial fleet loomed Admiral Piett's flagship, the *Executor*, which had come close to annihilating the entire Rebellion at Mako-Ta and then again at Hoth. Rebel pilots regarded the ship with fear and awe in equal measure.

1 Initial Arrival The rebel fleet exited hyperspace and made directly for the Death Star. Hoping that the shield was down the rebels attempted a scan, but upon discovering their sensors were being jammed they realized that it was a trap. Rebel fighters began immediate evasive maneuvers.

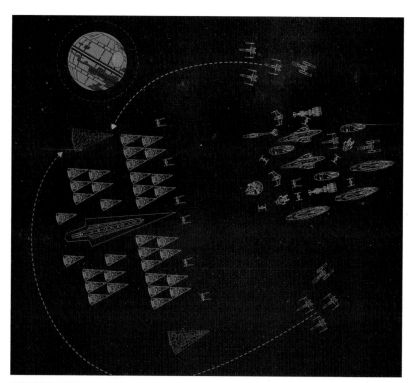

4 Point Blank General Calrissian and Admiral Ackbar ordered the rebels to close in on the Star Destroyers, ensuring the Death Star could not fire without hitting Imperial vessels. Rebel fighters of Blue and Green Squadrons outflanked the Imperial fleet to begin attacking the Interdictors and disrupt Imperial comms.

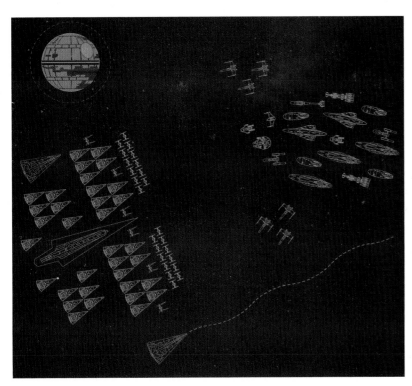

2 Imperial Blockade The Imperial fleet had been hiding behind Endor and moved into position to block an immediate escape while Interdictors activated their gravity-well generators to trap the rebel fleet. The first wave of TIEs engaged the Alliance ships and disrupted their formation.

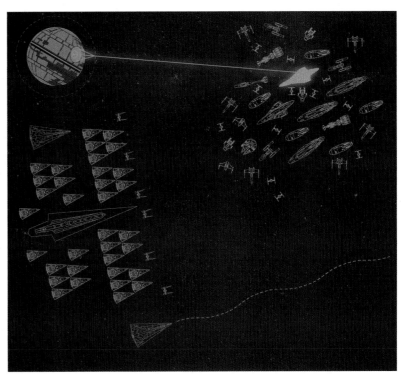

3 Superlaser Blast The rebels initially kept their distance from the Imperial fleet, wary of being swarmed by TIEs and attacked by Star Destroyers. At this point the Death Star opened fire and destroyed the cruiser *Liberty* in a single blast. The rebels had no choice but to advance.

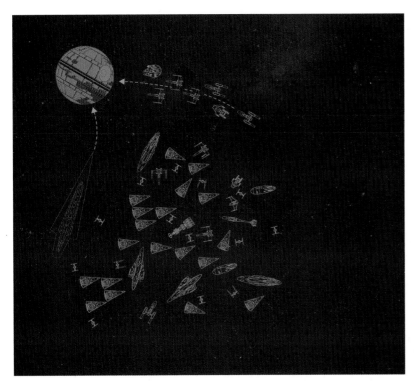

5 *Executor*'s Fall With the battle lines completely blurred, the rebels were able to isolate individual Star Destroyers and destroy them. When the Death Star's shield collapsed, rebel fighters entered its structure while the Alliance fleet concentrated its fire on the *Executor* and sent it crashing into the battle station.

6 Last Movements With confirmation that the Death Star was about to explode, the rebel fleet disengaged and evacuated the immediate area. Coming to the same realization, the Imperial fleet reorganized around Admiral Rae Sloane's *Vigilance*. The Imperial survivors then fled into hyperspace.

Endor: Decisive Moment

▲ **Imperial Command** Admiral Piett (right) was a highly competent battle commander—he would not have survived serving under Darth Vader otherwise. But the Emperor's commands robbed him of the chance to use his initiative and skills.

◀▼ **Crynyd's Sacrifice** Arvel Crynyd served as Green Leader at Endor. Post-battle analysis of his flight data showed that Crynyd purposely wrestled his fighter onto a collision course with the *Executor*'s bridge as a final sacrifice for the Rebellion.

The *Executor* was not only the Empire's command ship at Endor, it was also arguably the most important vessel in the entire Imperial navy. Serving on Lord Vader's flagship was, if you could survive his temper, a fast track to promotion.

At Endor the ship was the centerpiece of the largest fleet the Empire had ever committed to battle. Commanded by Admiral Piett, who was following the highly restrictive orders of the Emperor, the *Executor* held position after trapping the rebels.

When the rebel ships closed to short range the advantages held by the Empire began to dissipate. The *Executor* could feasibly have destroyed whole fleets by itself, but not when penned in on all sides by other Star Destroyers and rebel cruisers.

After Admiral Ackbar ordered rebel ships to converge on the *Executor*, a strafing run by A-wings destroyed its bridge shield generators, leaving the enormous vessel vulnerable.

Admiral Piett directed weapons control to intensify the firepower of the forward point-defense batteries to prevent anything breaking through, but it was too late. The *Executor*'s fire damaged an A-wing piloted by Captain Arvel Crynyd. Badly wounded and realizing his fighter was doomed, Crynyd steered his disintegrating craft so that it collided with the *Executor*'s bridge, killing Piett and the entire fleet command staff.

The subsequent loss of power resulted in the *Executor* falling into the gravity well generated by the enormous Death Star. The crew of the secondary bridge were unable to regain control and the Super Star Destroyer collided with the battle station and exploded. With it went the Empire's hopes for victory and the best and brightest of the Imperial navy.

▲ **Bridge Destroyed** Crynyd's A-wing plowed directly into the *Executor*'s command bridge, killing all inside and opening the tower to the vacuum of space. Power to the ship's engines and helm immediately failed.

▼ **Giant's Fall** Though incomplete, the Death Star still possessed considerable mass and exerted a gravity well over the surrounding area. With power to the engines and helm severed, the stricken *Executor* fell into the Death Star's gravity well. The subsequent collision and explosion claimed the lives of its entire crew—more than 300,000 personnel.

Endor (continued)

Stripped of its energy shield, the Death Star's unfinished superstructure was left open and vulnerable. Rebel fighters, led by General Calrissian in the *Millennium Falcon*, abandoned the main fleet battle and began to enter the Death Star itself. A number of brave or foolhardy Imperial pilots followed the rebel ships into the battle station's interior, but Yellow Squadron's Captain Ribeiro and her second-in-command, Lieutenant Malena, formed a protective screen over the entrance to the superstructure to prevent further TIEs from pursuing those inside.

In the Death Star's throne room, Emperor Palpatine's grand plan was also unraveling. He had believed that the Jedi Knight Luke Skywalker could be turned to the dark side as his new apprentice. He was wrong. His torturing of Skywalker cracked through the dark side to the good within Darth Vader, the former Jedi Anakin Skywalker. Anakin sacrificed his own life to kill the Emperor by throwing him into a reactor shaft. Palpatine's foresight had failed, costing him his corporeal form and his Empire. With his demise, the outcome of the battle became a foregone conclusion.

Within the Death Star, General Calrissian and Captain Wedge Antilles flew ever deeper into the battle station's superstructure, aware that every second they spent flying further inside was one they would also have to spend escaping. They ordered the other rebel fighters to split off and draw some of their pursuers away. Upon reaching their target the pair destroyed the main reactor before racing back the way they had come.

▲ **Chain Reaction** Wedge Antilles destroyed the Death Star's power regulator, meaning that when General Calrissian opened fire on the reactor itself it suffered a catastrophic collapse. A huge explosion was inevitable.

▶ **Skywalker Redeemed**
The Emperor believed that Darth Vader's spirit had long been broken. But watching on as his master tortured his son, Anakin's true self was awakened. He seized Palpatine and threw the screaming Emperor into the abyss.

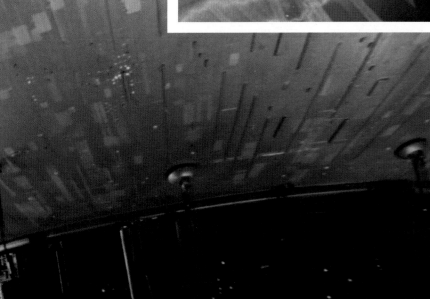

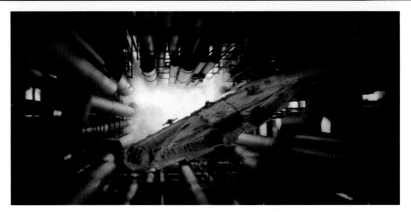

▲ **Frantic Escape** As the reactor collapsed, the *Millennium Falcon* raced ahead of the fiery shock wave that was now consuming the Death Star, escaping by mere moments.

KEY COMBATANT: WEDGE ANTILLES

One of the finest starfighter pilots the galaxy has ever known, Wedge Antilles was also considered among the greatest heroes of the Rebellion. Having been present at most of the major battles of the Galactic Civil War, including Yavin and Hoth, Antilles was the only person alive to have fought against two Death Stars and survived them both. He was a supremely talented pilot and squadron leader.

▶ **Rebel Hero** Antilles commanded Red Squadron during the battle, playing a decisive role in destroying the Death Star.

Endor (continued)

▼ **Rebel Dawn** The destruction of the Death Star's main reactor unleashed a powerful chain reaction that tore through the battle station. The subsequent explosion lit up the sky above Endor and hurled debris across the system.

To buy time for the rebel fighters inside the Death Star, Admiral Ackbar ordered all ships to concentrate their fire on Admiral Piett's flagship, the Super Star Destroyer *Executor*. Shorn of its shields, the Imperial command ship was overwhelmed and, following the loss of its bridge, crashed into the Death Star.

With the *Executor*'s destruction and Piett's death, the Imperial fleet was left in chaos until Admiral Sloane took command. When informed that the rebel fleet was swiftly evacuating the area and that the Death Star's power readings were fluctuating, Sloane realized that the battle was lost. While her Star Destroyer, the *Vigilance*, screened the Imperial fleet, Sloane ordered a recall of all TIEs and issued orders to prepare for an immediate retreat into hyperspace.

KEY LOCATION: DEATH STAR DEBRIS

While the explosion consumed much of the Death Star's superstructure, the battle station was too vast to be destroyed completely. An extensive debris field was formed and wreckage was scattered across the nine moons of Endor. The remains of Emperor Palpatine's throne room tower crashed onto the ocean moon Kef Bir, where it would be discovered by the Resistance decades later.

▲ **Imperial Graveyard** Many pieces of the Death Star were too large to simply burn up in Kef Bir's atmosphere and crashed, largely intact, onto its surface.

▲ **Galactic Uprising** Across the galaxy word of the Emperor's death sparked wild celebrations. On Tatooine, a world that had been annexed by the Empire, people took to the streets of Mos Eisley in a spontaneous act of joy.

MOPPING-UP OPERATIONS

The retreat of their fleet left Imperial forces abandoned on Endor. While some surrendered, others dug into positions across the moon and continued to wage a guerrilla campaign against the Alliance. Rebel Pathfinders undertook numerous missions to locate and destroy these Imperial holdouts. During one such raid, General Solo discovered the Imperial plans for post-Endor operations. While most Imperial forces were located and destroyed within a few weeks of the battle, rumors of soldiers hiding out in the forests of Endor refusing to accept the dishonor of surrender circulated for years.

▲ **Imperial Holdouts** Imperial soldiers who had escaped from the main ground battle began to gather at hidden bases across the moon.

The rebels, no longer interested in the Imperial fleet, put distance between themselves and the Death Star before a huge explosion tore the battle station apart. On Endor the detonation was greeted with wild celebrations by the rebels, while surviving Imperial soldiers watched on in horror. Some surrendered. Others violently lashed out in any way they could.

Rebel propaganda teams began to transmit recordings of the Death Star's destruction across the galaxy. News of the Emperor's death provoked spontaneous uprisings on many worlds, including Coruscant. While the Empire would suppress many of these, the war had decisively swung toward the Rebellion. Endor was the Rebel Alliance's greatest success and marked the dawn of the New Republic.

▲ **Under Fire** General Solo led a surprise raid against a hidden and fortified Imperial position on the far side of Endor.

Commanders

▲ **A Final Request** Facing hopeless odds, Lieutenant Bey told Leia she didn't want the princess to have to write a death notification to her next of kin. It was not needed—Bey survived and returned to raise her son, Poe Dameron.

PRINCESS LEIA ORGANA
After traveling to Naboo on a diplomatic mission, Princess Organa took command of the defense of the planet. She, Lieutenant Shara Bey, and Queen Sosha Soruna piloted N-1 starfighters against the Imperial forces. Though heavily outnumbered, they fought until New Republic reinforcements arrived.

CAPTAIN LERR DUVAT
At the order of the late Emperor, Captain Lerr Duvat executed an attack on Naboo. He released a climate disruption array from his Star Destroyer, the *Torment*, but faced unexpected resistance from Naboo starfighters and the New Republic, who dispatched the satellites and destroyed his ship.

▲ **Unknown Assailant** When Naboo's climate went out of control, forming typhoon-strength storms around the planet, the population panicked. Lieutenant Bey determined the Empire were using an orbital array to launch the attack.

Naboo (Theed)

DATE: 23 AFE ▪ **LOCATION:** NABOO, OUTER RIM TERRITORIES ▪
COMBATANTS: EMPIRE VS. NEW REPUBLIC ▪
OUTCOME: NEW REPUBLIC VICTORY

THE CONTINGENCY

Emperor Palpatine planned for the future of the Galactic Empire after his death. He formulated a strategy to tear apart the Empire in order to flush out its weakest elements while his most trusted protege, Gallius Rax, rebuilt the organization from the ground up in the Unknown Regions. Operation: Cinder formed the first part of this "Contingency," for which Palpatine issued the order from beyond the grave using Sentinel droids.

Naboo was an early target. Princess Leia Organa, Lieutenant Shara Bey, and Queen Sosha Soruna confronted the Empire's ruinous satellites in old N-1 starfighters that had survived the Emperor's demilitarization of Naboo—the same craft that Leia's father had once fought in. General Lando Calrissian and Nien Nunb arrived with rebel support in the form of a Mon Calamari cruiser and defeated the Imperial forces in orbit. But not before the Empire deployed a battalion of stormtroopers for a ground invasion.

The Imperials held the advantage. They had more troopers and combat walkers at their disposal. But the Naboo had one hope: an ion pulse weapon. Recognizing the powerful device as the only way to stop the Empire's forces, the rebels engaged the enemy in the streets of Theed until Del Meeko, an Imperial defector, activated the ion pulse. It disabled all Imperial weapons. The victory won the Royal House of Naboo as allies to the emerging New Republic. The Empire attempted three additional invasions of Naboo, but the New Republic Defense Fleet turned them back every time.

OPERATION: CINDER

Before his death, Emperor Palpatine masterminded Operation: Cinder, a vicious campaign designed to punish the galaxy in the event of his demise—he didn't believe the Empire in its current form should survive beyond him. The campaign targeted at least a dozen worlds including Naboo, Vardos, Burnin Konn, Candovant, Abednedo, Commenor, and Nacronis. Utilizing orbital bombardment arrays, Operation: Cinder blasted planets with bolts that devastated their ecological systems or shattered their planetary crusts. The result was widespread loss of life. The New Republic intervened when they learned about targets in time, but several planets were devastated.

▶ **No Defense** Imperial Commander Iden Versio watched helplessly as Operation: Cinder was targeted at her own homeworld, Vardos.

Rebel Starfighter Doctrine

The Rebel Alliance's victory in the Galactic Civil War was built on the back of their effective use of starfighters. For much of the conflict the Alliance did not have access to heavy capital ships and relied on a mix of hit-and-fade missions or anti-blockade operations pioneered by their fighter wings. Whereas the Empire remained rigid in their fighter doctrine, the flexibility and inventiveness of the rebels, coupled with the skill of their pilots and durability of their ships, proved to be a war-winning combination. The all-round ability of rebel craft enabled them to take on enemy TIEs and, where needed, Star Destroyers without significant reorganization in combat.

▲ **Not Obsolete** The Rebel Alliance recognized the potential of Clone Wars-era weaponry and materiel, and launched numerous raids on Imperial facilities to repurpose aging starfighters and press them back into service.

EFFECTIVE ACQUISITION
After the Clone Wars, the newly formed Galactic Empire dismantled the military forces of the Republic as obsolete. The replacement of aging starfighters with new TIE models opened the way for the Rebel Alliance to locate and repurpose starfighters bound for the scrap heap that were still capable of service. The use of stripped-down Y-wings as both bombers and anti-capital-ship fighters became a trademark of the Rebellion, particularly in its earliest years. Though they were vulnerable to TIE fighters, they also allowed rebel pilots to cause

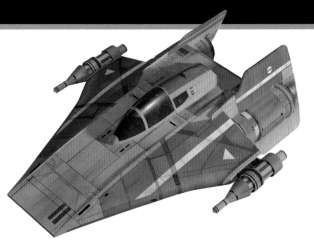

▲ **Rebel Interceptor** While not as durable as the X-wing, the A-wing gave the rebels a fast and formidable weapon for tackling TIE interceptors.

significant damage to military targets and then escape into hyperspace afterward. As a result, Y-wings served in the Alliance and New Republic navies for many years.

SURVIVABILITY AND FLEXIBILITY
While access to, or production of, starfighters was a key concern for the Alliance, their greatest need was for skilled pilots. The rebels could not win a war of attrition against the Galactic Empire, but the use of deflector shields on their starfighters allowed for rebel pilots to survive battle more regularly than their opposition and, more importantly, learn

◀ **Rebel Symbol** The X-wing fighter became synonymous with the Rebel Alliance. Its ability to engage both TIEs and Star Destroyers made it an invaluable weapon.

from mistakes that might otherwise have killed them. In the Alliance's earlier years, squadrons were generally formed of identical fighters, the A-wings of Phoenix Squadron and the X-wings of Yavin being key examples. These ships, with their shields and hyperdrives, could be used in

▲ **Strike Force** Though slow and vulnerable in dogfights the Y-wing had huge value as a fighter-bomber.

a variety of escort or strike missions and operate independently of capital ship support. The increasing regularity with which rebel squadrons fought against Imperial capital ships meant Alliance pilots learned how to survive close-range action against Star Destroyers and other vessels, even if only for the limited time it took to escape. While a direct hit from a heavy turbolaser would still prove fatal to almost any starfighter, shields and hyperdrives increased survivability, maximizing the retention of piloting knowledge. Under the New Republic, fighter squadrons diversified further with

▲ **Greatest Victory** The Rebel Alliance's greatest hour came at Endor as their use of varied starfighters operating from a flexible doctrine helped win the day.

a range of ships operating together to increase mission options in battle, as seen in the actions fought by both Vanguard and Alphabet Squadrons.

KEY INFO

VANGUARD SQUADRON

The New Republic's ability to evolve their starfighter policy was evidenced by the operations undertaken by Vanguard Squadron in the period after the Battle of Endor. The pilots of Vanguard were all capable and qualified in the different starfighters making up the New Republic navy and would often undertake missions using a mix of fighter craft. As a result, depending on mission parameters, Vanguard could tackle multiple objectives within a single combat deployment in a manner that the Empire was often unable to react to. This flexibility ensured that New Republic forces were able to maintain momentum and achieve victory in the war's final battles.

▶ **Skillful Fliers** The highly skilled pilots of Vanguard Squadron could operate any of the New Republic's starfighters to devastating effect.

Zavian Abyss

DATE: 23 AFE ■ **LOCATION:** ZAVIAN ABYSS, EXPANSION REGION ■ **COMBATANTS:** NEW REPUBLIC VS. EMPIRE ■ **OUTCOME:** NEW REPUBLIC VICTORY

STALKING THE *STARHAWK*

When Imperial Intelligence discovered the New Republic's Project Starhawk, they tasked Captain Terisa Kerrill of the Star Destroyer *Overseer* with investigating and annihilating the new weapon. She would stop at nothing to sabotage the ship's construction, which Kerrill believed was still underway. When she intercepted a message from the New Republic about vital supplies en route to the construction site, she jumped at the opportunity to spoil the mission, unaware that the message itself was merely a decoy.

Kerrill's old rival, Commander Lindon Javes of the New Republic, had laid a trap for the *Overseer* deep in the Zavian Abyss. He ordered his Vanguard Squadron into position at a narrow choke point between deadly asteroids. Kerrill walked right into the ambush. Instead of a defenseless supply convoy she found a far more frightening discovery: the *Starhawk* was

FIGHTING IN THE ABYSS

The Zavian Abyss was rarely traveled in times of war or peace. Home to colossal electrically charged asteroids, this foreboding corner of space suffered from limited visibility as well as volatile obstacles. Long before the Galactic Civil War, a *Venator*-class Star Destroyer fell victim to the dangers of the abyss, its wreckage providing an ominous warning for those passing through. The hazardous environment of the Abyss hampered the autopilot of most ships, leaving vessels at the mercy of their biological pilot's skill.

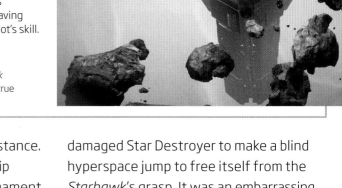

▶ **Armed and Operational** The *Starhawk* prototype emerged from the mist to reveal its true power to the Empire.

operational and within striking distance. The massive New Republic warship activated its most impressive armament, a tractor beam with incredible power. The *Overseer* was helplessly snared in the beam's grasp, pulled against its will into the path of a giant asteroid. With no other options, Kerrill ordered her heavily

damaged Star Destroyer to make a blind hyperspace jump to free itself from the *Starhawk*'s grasp. It was an embarrassing loss for Kerrill and a successful first mission for the New Republic's latest vessel.

▼ **Clearing the Way** Laser cannons helped clear a path for capital ships by targeting the electrical asteroids.

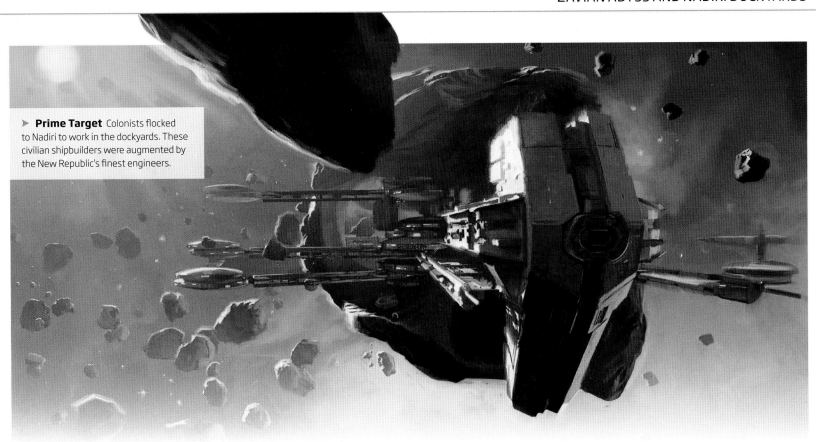

▶ **Prime Target** Colonists flocked to Nadiri to work in the dockyards. These civilian shipbuilders were augmented by the New Republic's finest engineers.

Nadiri Dockyards

DATE: 23 AFE ▪ **LOCATION:** NADIRI DOCKYARDS, CORE WORLDS ▪ **COMBATANTS:** NEW REPUBLIC VS. EMPIRE ▪ **OUTCOME:** IMPERIAL VICTORY

IMPERIAL VENGEANCE

Seeking revenge after the ambush at the Zavian Abyss, the Empire staged a diversionary attack on Mon Cala to draw New Republic forces away from the Nadiri Dockyards. There, the prototype *Starhawk*-class battleship was undergoing its final outfitting. With Vanguard Squadron reinforcing Mon Cala, the Imperial Titan Squadron pounced upon the lightly guarded shipyard with the help of reinforcements provided by Admiral Sloane.

Their first target was the dockyard's network of shield generators. Together, they provided protection from long-range missile attacks, but once they were destroyed by the Imperial starfighters the prototype vessel was left exposed. The squadron ruthlessly hunted the dockworkers' transports as they attempted to evacuate, confident that

victory was at hand. The *Starhawk*'s advanced armor could withstand most Imperial attacks, but by employing baradium-enhanced munitions, the small squadron was able to inflict significant damage to the hulking warship. The vessel's hyperdrive was their primary target, and after they obliterated it the Star Destroyer *Overseer* moved in to strike the final blow.

General Hera Syndulla, commanding at the dockyards, called for reinforcements from nearby New Republic forces. Just as the *Overseer* launched its own baradium payload, Commander Lindon Javes arrived in his flagship, the MC75 star cruiser *Temperance*, and physically shielded the valuable *Starhawk*. The two battered capital ships limped out of the dockyards with the Imperials not far behind.

PROJECT STARHAWK

Looking to speed up the end of the Galactic Civil War, the New Republic devised a new class of battleship to surpass the Empire's own Star Destroyers. From the salvaged hulls of captured destroyers, the shipbuilders at Nadiri fashioned an advanced warship with superior armor, armaments, and shields. The *Starhawk*'s hatchet-shaped bow housed a powerful tractor beam, capable of snaring a fully powered Imperial Star Destroyer. The construction of such a weapon left some wondering if the New Republic had adopted the brutal practices of the Empire they sought to replace.

▲ **Final Touches** With the installation of its massive tractor beam array, the *Starhawk* was ready for early trials.

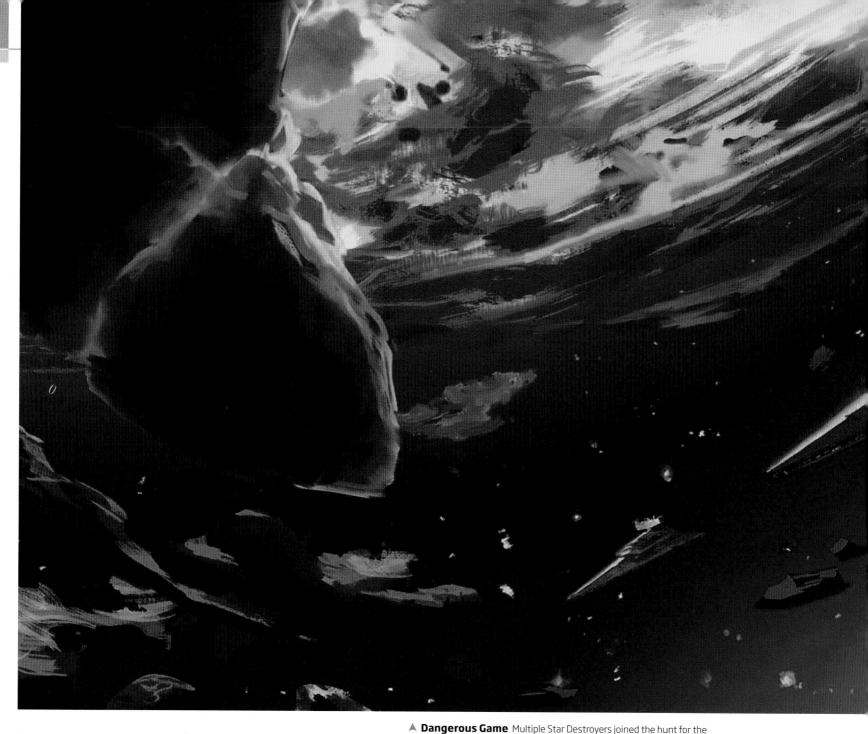

Commanders

▲ **Dangerous Game** Multiple Star Destroyers joined the hunt for the New Republic *Starhawk* prototype. Eager to avenge a string of Imperial losses, their aggression left them exposed to a deadly trap near the unstable moon.

COMMANDER LINDON JAVES
This experienced starfighter pilot joined the battle in his own X-wing fighter. His presence on the battlefield provided enough distraction for General Syndulla to evacuate the *Temperance* and Project Starhawk's civilian engineers and flight crew.

CAPTAIN TERISA KERRILL
From the bridge of her Star Destroyer, Kerrill stayed one step ahead of her New Republic foes. She anticipated their moves and called in reinforcements in advance. Her leadership in hunting down the *Starhawk* was rewarded with a new mission in the Unknown Regions.

▲ **Veteran Commanders** Wedge Antilles and Hera Syndulla, both heroes of the Rebellion, were attached to Project Starhawk. Such a critical military development required the attention of the New Republic's best and brightest.

Galitan

DATE: 23 AFE ▪ **LOCATION:** GALITAN, CORE WORLDS ▪ **COMBATANTS:** EMPIRE VS. NEW REPUBLIC ▪ **OUTCOME:** STRATEGIC NEW REPUBLIC VICTORY

NEW REPUBLIC TRAP

The final showdown between Captain Terisa Kerrill's Imperials and the New Republic's *Starhawk* prototype occurred near Galitan. The battleship was badly damaged at Nadiri and was limping toward safe harbor at Chandrila with the Empire not far behind. The arrival of Anvil Squadron gave the New Republic forces new hope, bolstering the defense provided by Vanguard Squadron and the MC75 star cruiser *Temperance*.

With the *Starhawk* cornered by the Star Destroyer *Overseer*, Admiral Sloane took no chances and committed additional destroyers to the fight. Confident in her superior numbers and strategy, Captain Kerrill ordered Titan Squadron to first clear the way by attacking Anvil Squadron's frigate and then mount a precision strike on the *Starhawk* itself. A hole in the battleship's hull gave a Titan Squadron pilot the opening they needed to fly inside the giant ship and strike at the heart of its tractor beam core. The attack caused a catastrophic explosion within, sealing the *Starhawk*'s fate. Kerrill and her Titan Squadron retreated with their mission now complete, satisfied that their target was irrevocably damaged. The remaining Star Destroyer captains showed less strategic restraint, instead choosing to stay behind to engage the remaining New Republic forces.

Cornered by the Imperials in the shadow of the unstable moon, Hera Syndulla ordered the damaged *Starhawk* to crash into the exposed core of Galitan. The resulting shock wave wiped out every Imperial ship and allowed the New Republic personnel to escape. Most importantly, the survival of these skilled workers meant that Project Starhawk would continue.

KEY LOCATION: MOON DEBRIS

With the *Starhawk* seriously damaged, the New Republic commanders attempted to retreat to their capital of Chandrila in the Bormea sector, but reaching this safe harbor meant that they first had to traverse the turbulent Ringali Nebula. There lay the remains of the shattered moon Galitan, a celestial body pulled apart by the tempestuous forces of the nebula. The explosive event left the fiery core of the moon exposed, and flying too close to the molten debris meant certain destruction.

➤ **Deadly Battlefield** Molten fragments dotted the starscape around the moon, creating a dangerous battlefield for Imperial and New Republic squadrons alike.

Jakku

DATE: 24 AFE ▪ **LOCATION:** JAKKU, INNER RIM ▪ **COMBATANTS:** EMPIRE VS. NEW REPUBLIC ▪ **OUTCOME:** DECISIVE NEW REPUBLIC VICTORY

THE END OF THE WAR

This remote desert planet in the Western Reaches was unremarkable save for the part it played in Emperor Palpatine's long-planned Contingency. Decades before his death, Palpatine identified the planet as the site for a final trap. His commands, to be fulfilled by his servant Gallius Rax, called for the destruction of the entire planet, obliterating the New Republic fleet as well as many of his own forces, whom he blamed for his death.

To lure the New Republic into the fight, the Empire took up defensive positions across the planet, committing nearly every weapon at their disposal to the defense—infantry, armor, starfighters, and capital ships. Rax's commanders believed they were mounting a final stand, but his ultimate aim was to cause maximum casualties. Political squabbling in the Senate delayed the New Republic's assault, leaving the defending Imperial ground troops to struggle on the harsh desert world for some time.

When the attack was finally authorized, the New Republic believed they had cornered the largest remaining Imperial fleet and had the advantage of superior numbers. This was thanks, in part, to the recent completion of three *Starhawk*-class battleships—advanced warships representing the pinnacle of New Republic naval technology. Alongside the bulk of the New Republic's fleet, they prepared for the most sweeping military confrontation of the Galactic Civil War.

Commanders

ADMIRAL GIAL ACKBAR
From his flagship *Home One*, Admiral Ackbar oversaw the New Republic naval action aimed at the Super Star Destroyer *Ravager*. He commanded the most powerful armada ever launched against Imperial forces, but was focused on minimizing losses during the prolonged fight.

COUNSELOR GALLIUS RAX (KILLED IN ACTION)
Personally groomed by the Emperor for this moment, Rax ordered much of the Imperial remnant to Jakku as a trap. There he planned to use Sith artifacts to destroy the planet in the midst of battle, but he failed when fellow Imperial Rae Sloane intervened.

▲ **Ground Forces** The New Republic landed squads of commandos on Jakku's surface by way of U-wing transports. They sought to capture key defensive holdouts and strongpoints in the face of fanatical Imperial resistance.

▲ **Theaters of War** Falling debris was a constant threat as fighting raged across Jakku. The New Republic launched a simultaneous attack in space, in the atmosphere, and on the planet's surface.

▶ **Air Support** As the Imperial defenses crumbled, New Republic starfighters were increasingly able to provide air support for the troops on the ground, further diminishing the exhausted Imperial armies.

Jakku: Map

Jakku saw conflict across every possible theater: in orbit above the planet; in its atmosphere as the fighting intensified; on its surface as rebel landing teams and Imperial outposts fought for key positions; and even underground as fighting entered tunnel networks and bunkers: The sand-covered surface of Jakku offered few natural landmarks to guide the flow of the battle. Much of the engagement played across unremarkable sand dunes, making it difficult for reinforcements to identify where they were needed most. Falling debris from the clash above threatened to change the battlefield at any time, providing new waypoints as well as new dangers for the infantry to navigate. Detonating reactors and chemical spills poisoned the atmosphere and scorched entire regions into glass. Defenders set up in a haphazard fashion in an ill-prepared attempt to fight off attacks that could arrive from any direction, making chaos the defining characteristic of the battle.

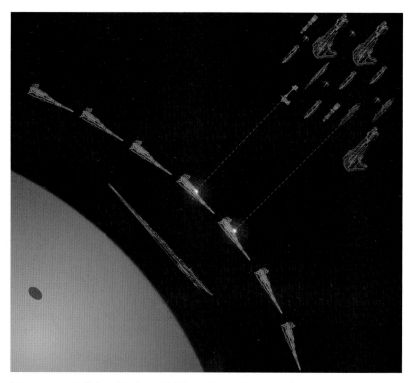

1 Destroyer Defense The Imperial defense above Jakku centered around the Super Star Destroyer *Ravager*, the flagship of Grand Moff Randd. The Imperial fleet formed a nearly perfect defensive perimeter with the *Ravager* at its heart, shielding the Empire's most prized dreadnought from fire.

THE OBSERVATORY

While the battle across Jakku raged, Gallius Rax entered a facility known as the Observatory to carry out the ultimate phase of Palpatine's Contingency. Part research facility, part control center, this secret outpost housed a cache of Sith artifacts to be thrown into the world's core, setting off a cataclysm that would destroy everyone on and around the planet. Yet before he could complete this mission, Rax was stopped by a combined team of Imperial Admiral Rae Sloane and New Republic operatives Norra and Brentin Wexley.

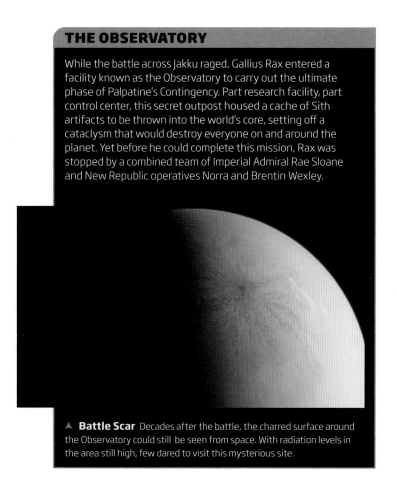

▲ **Battle Scar** Decades after the battle, the charred surface around the Observatory could still be seen from space. With radiation levels in the area still high, few dared to visit this mysterious site.

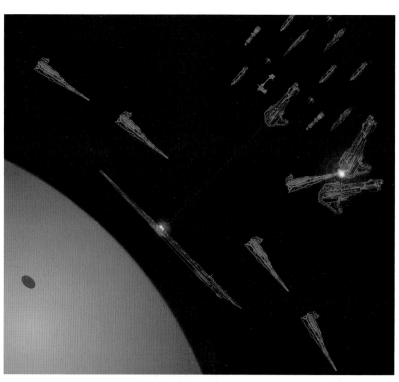

4 Breaking Point The Star Destroyer *Punishment*, under command of Captain Groff, panicked under the assault of the imposing battleships. Groff steered his ship into the *Amity* at full speed, causing debris from both ships to terminally damage the nearby *Concord*.

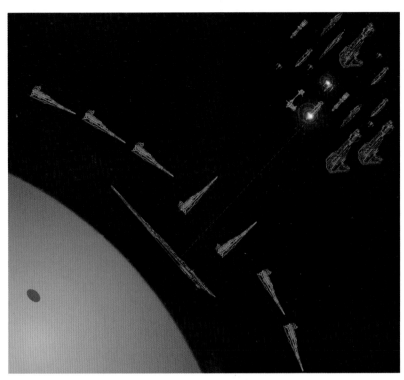

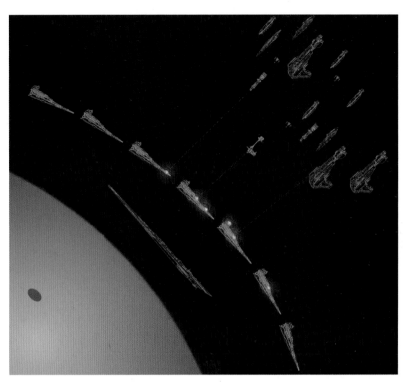

2 Imperial Coordination The Star Destroyers forming a defensive perimeter moved in concert to allow the *Ravager* to fire turbolasers and torpedoes. They then returned to their defensive positions while the dreadnought cycled its weapons to rearm for the next volley.

3 *Starhawk* Assault Three New Republic *Starhawk*-class battleships, *Unity*, *Amity*, and *Concord*, pressed the attack on the Imperial fleet. Though the New Republic outnumbered the Empire, the Imperial defensive net held firm against the barrage as the chaotic battle became more tightly constricted.

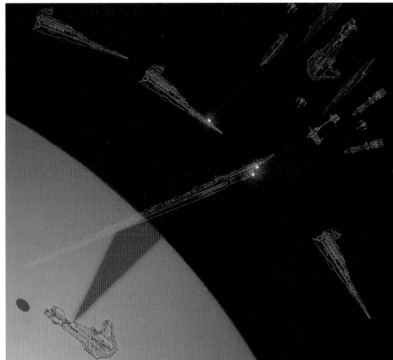

5 Strategic Sacrifice Seeing the gap left by the *Punishment*, Commodore Agate of the *Concord* ordered her crew to abandon ship and closed in for a suicidal strike on the *Ravager*, unleashing her battleship's full arsenal. As her ship fell from orbit, she locked its powerful tractor beam onto the dreadnought.

6 Fall of Titans At Agate's request, Fleet Admiral Ackbar ordered the remaining New Republic ships to focus fire on the *Ravager*'s engines. This allowed the *Concord* to pull the Super Star Destroyer down to the planet, destroying both vessels in the process and allowing the New Republic to emerge victorious.

▲ **Final Plunge** As the *Ravager* plummeted through Jakku's atmosphere, a B-wing piloted by Lieutenant Gina Moonsong of Blade Squadron was caught in the tractor beam pulling the ship toward the surface of the planet.

Jakku: Decisive Moment

Despite being outnumbered, the Imperial fleet gathered at Jakku made a remarkable stand using a coordinated defense strategy centered around their only remaining Super Star Destroyer, the *Ravager*, under the command of Grand Moff Randd. In space above the besieged planet, the dreadnought was protected by ranks of smaller Star Destroyers. In concert, an individual Star Destroyer would maneuver away and allow the *Ravager* to fire a volley of its primary weapons, then return to its defensive position shielding the prized flagship once again.

The New Republic surged forward their finest ships, the *Starhawk*-class battleships *Unity*, *Amity*, and *Concord* in an attempt to drive a wedge through the tight defense. The screen held firm until the captain of the Star Destroyer *Punishment* lost his nerve at the sight of the massive warships and staged a suicidal attack on the *Amity*. Commodore Kyrsta Agate, commanding the *Concord*, was unable to maneuver away from the resulting debris and her ship was fatally damaged. As her vessel began to slip toward the planet below and certain death, Agate pointed the *Concord*'s powerful tractor beam directly at the *Ravager*. She called for nearby New Republic starfighters to simultaneously focus their fire on the dreadnought's engines, leaving Grand Moff Randd helpless as his titanic starship was dragged to the surface by Commodore Agate's sacrificial strategy. Its destruction marked the beginning of the end for the Imperial fleet.

▲ **Falling Flagship** The *Ravager*'s destruction was visible to hundreds of thousands of personnel engaged in combat across and above Jakku. In some places, Imperial forces rapidly surrendered in the face of inevitable defeat. In others, pockets of fanatical resistance continued.

Jakku (continued)

▲ **Reinforcements Arrive** A former Imperial corvette now in the service of the New Republic, The *Corvis* mounted rescue operations for downed New Republic forces and assisted in the infiltration of an Imperial facility near Carbon Ridge.

After a prolonged battle on all fronts, it became increasingly clear that the New Republic would emerge victorious at Jakku. The Super Star Destroyer *Ravager* had fallen, the Contingency had failed, Rax had been killed, and other key members of the Imperial high command were either dead or had disappeared. The New Republic had endured significant losses of their own but clearly held the upper hand. With his military crippled, the highest-remaining Imperial political figure, Grand Vizier Mas Amedda, signaled his willingness to surrender. The treaty, known officially as the Galactic Concordance, meant the end of large-scale offensives. Yet on Jakku, fighting raged on for months as pockets of the Imperial forces there held out until the very end. Even more astonishingly, a few Imperial ships made mysterious

hyperspace jumps into uncharted regions of space.

Although Imperial government was dissolved with the signing of the Galactic Concordance, pockets of Imperial remnants persisted throughout the galaxy for years to come, some out of misdirected loyalty to the old regime and others out of selfish attempts to remain in power, however limited. Complacent in their victory, the New Republic began the process of disarming, limiting their ability to make war. They were unaware that their enemy was not truly vanquished, but now lay in hiding somewhere in the unexplored vastness of the Unknown Regions.

KEY COMBATANT: TEMMIN WEXLEY

The son of a New Republic fighter pilot and among the youngest to serve at the Battle of Jakku, Temmin "Snap" Wexley flew under the command of Wedge Antilles as a member of Phantom Squadron. His X-wing was struck by falling debris from the *Concord*, leaving him stranded on Jakku's sandy surface. He found himself surrounded by chaos as the war entered its dying moments.

▶ **Downed Allies** Wexley joined forces with another downed New Republic pilot, Lieutenant Moonsong. Not all were lucky enough to survive their fall to the surface.

▼ **Sea of Destruction**
Members of the New Republic-aligned Inferno Squad looked upon the wreckage of the Empire they helped to defeat.

KEY LOCATION: GRAVEYARD OF GIANTS

Even before the battle had fully ended, Niima the Hutt began consolidating her wealth by way of scavenging the remains of downed warships. Such was the volume of debris on Jakku that decades later, the practice still continued throughout the wastes now known as the Graveyard of Giants. Scavengers spent their lives exploring the eerie wrecks, surrounded by the bleached bones of their long-dead crews. Junk bosses paid paltry wages for salvaged equipment to be shipped offworld at a profit.

▶ **Faded Glory** The *Ravager* lay half submerged in the sands of Jakku, picked over for its remaining parts.

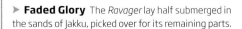

The Imperial Remnants

The Battle of Jakku ended the Galactic Civil War as a military conflict; the Galactic Concordance ended it as a political conflict. The defeated Empire agreed to reduce forces already decimated by the year of campaigns after Endor, remain within their newly defined territories, pay reparations, and surrender Coruscant and their military academies. But the galactic jubilation that followed soon gave way to a feeling of unease. New Republic leaders moved cautiously, determined to create a new government based on shared purpose rather than fear. Some worlds welcomed this new approach, but others yearned for order, lamenting the chaos caused by pirate rings, ambitious warlords, and criminal gangs.

▲ **Post-Imperial Flexibility** Outland TIE fighters—an innovation introduced in the Galactic Civil War's waning days—had folding wings and landing gear, allowing isolated groups of Imperial holdouts to forgo vulnerable docking facilities.

AN UNCERTAIN PATH

The Galactic Concordance granted a new future to Imperial survivors in a swath of space in the Core, Colonies, and Inner Rim. This region included ancient, conservative worlds that had supported Palpatine, among them Commenor, Humbarine, Tinnel, Rendili, and Denon. But the various fragmented successors struggled to turn their domain into a viable state, squabbling over everything from relations with the New Republic to what Imperial legacies deserved preservation.

▲ **New Leaders** At least publicly, most post-Imperial warlords vowed to restore the Empire. But many were more interested in carving fiefdoms out of the regime's wreckage.

UNREST ON THE FRINGES

Far from the Core, New Republic control was theoretical at best, creating a vacuum filled by both credit-hungry criminal enterprises and Imperial loyalists dreaming of renewed glory. A bewildering array of pocket states sprung up in the void: would-be Imperial successors such as Moff Adelhard's territory in the Anoat sector, ambitious regimes including the New Separatist Union and the Confederacy of Corporate Systems, and the pirate state known as the Sovereign Latitudes.

KEY INFO

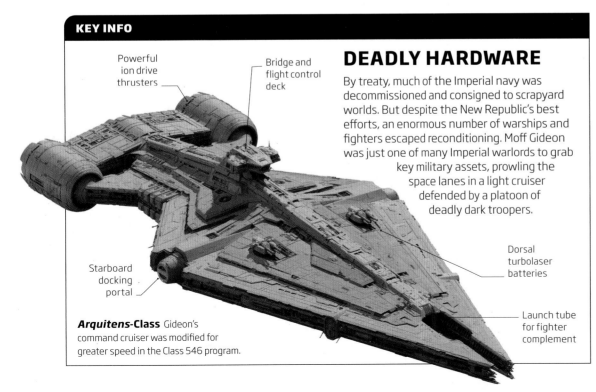

Powerful ion drive thrusters

Bridge and flight control deck

Starboard docking portal

Dorsal turbolaser batteries

Launch tube for fighter complement

***Arquitens*-Class** Gideon's command cruiser was modified for greater speed in the Class 546 program.

DEADLY HARDWARE

By treaty, much of the Imperial navy was decommissioned and consigned to scrapyard worlds. But despite the New Republic's best efforts, an enormous number of warships and fighters escaped reconditioning. Moff Gideon was just one of many Imperial warlords to grab key military assets, prowling the space lanes in a light cruiser defended by a platoon of deadly dark troopers.

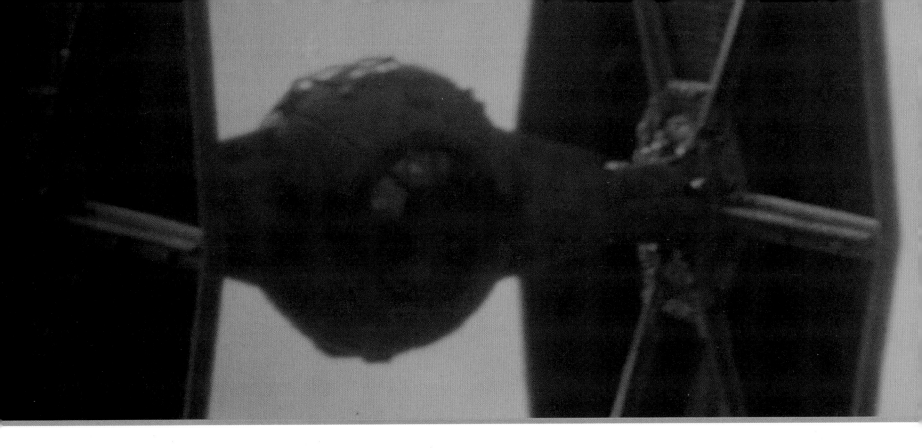

▲ **No Peace** The Imperial remnants had to survive skirmishes with not only the New Republic but also pirate gangs, avaricious guilds, and hired guns seeking their own path.

UNCERTAIN FUTURES

Many Imperial veterans took advantage of New Republic amnesties, renounced the Empire they had served, and lived quietly. But others either remained devoted to the cause or feared they would face retribution if they admitted their former allegiance. Some of these former Imperials fled their homeworlds and assumed new identities, wandering the galaxy in search of a new sense of purpose or just a way to survive. Former stormtroopers were particularly prized as mercenaries, enforcers, and thugs, adding to galactic instability.

▶ **Remnant Garrisons** Intact Imperial bases such as the ones on Morak and Nevarro were valuable prizes for those warlords seeking firepower to match their ambitions, offering valuable weapons and equipment.

THE IMPERIAL LEGACY

The inner systems' Imperial remnant soon disintegrated, but several of its key worlds became leaders of the new Centrist faction in the New Republic. The Centrists pushed for a stronger central government and military, while secretly supporting the rise of the First Order.

A NEW ORDER RISES

The true successor to the Empire would arise in the Outer Rim, around a string of industrialized worlds that stretched in an arc from Yaga Minor to Bastion. Most New Republic leaders advocated leaving the First Order alone, seeing it as a backwater hermit state that posed little threat to the difficult work of galactic reconstruction. But others in the New Republic warned that the First Order was not what it seemed. They cited intelligence that the regime was harassing and intimidating neighboring systems, openly breaking the terms of the Galactic Concordance, and expanding its activities into the Unknown Regions, where its actions were worrisomely difficult to monitor.

FIRST ORDER—RESISTANCE WAR

- **TUANUL**
  First Order Massacre

- **TAKODANA**
  A Long-Awaited Fight

- **STARKILLER BASE**
  Destroyer of Worlds

- **CASTILON**
  Freeing the *Colossus*

- **D'QAR**
  Covering the Evacuation

- **OETCHI**
  Decapitation Strike

- **CRAIT**
  Last Stand

- **BARABESH**
  Unified Resistance

- **EXEGOL**
  Against All Odds

CHAPTER 4

First Order–Resistance War: Introduction

GALAXY MAP

War Renewed While relatively short in duration, the war between the First Order and Resistance was fought with an intensity that rivaled even that of the Galactic Civil War. The destruction of the New Republic's capital showed that even the most well-protected systems were not safe from the First Order or the sinister machinations of the reborn Emperor Palpatine.

KEY
1 Tuanul
2 Takodana
3 Starkiller Base
4 Castilon
5 D'Qar
6 Oetchi
7 Crait
8 Barabesh
9 Exegol

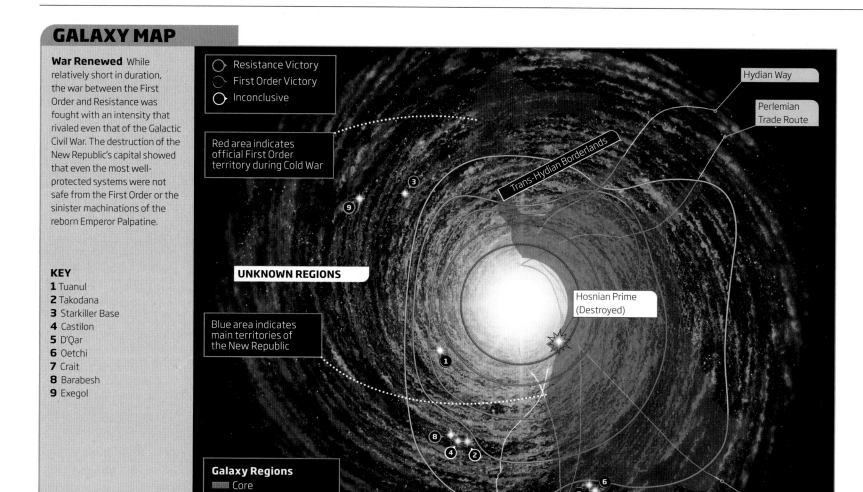

- Resistance Victory
- First Order Victory
- Inconclusive

Red area indicates official First Order territory during Cold War

UNKNOWN REGIONS

Blue area indicates main territories of the New Republic

Trans-Hydian Borderlands

Hydian Way

Perlemian Trade Route

Hosnian Prime (Destroyed)

Corellian Run

Corellian Trade Spine

Rimma Trade Route

OUTER RIM

Galaxy Regions
- Core
- Colonies
- Inner Rim
- Expansion Region
- Mid Rim

TIMELINE

1 Tuanul
The First Order raided a Jakku village to secure a map to the lost Jedi Luke Skywalker. The Resistance droid BB-8 fled with the map.

3 Starkiller Base
The Resistance infiltrated Starkiller Base and sent squadrons of X-wings to destroy the superweapon before it could fire again.

53 AFE

2 Takodana
The First Order tracked BB-8 to Takodana, battling Resistance X-wings–a major clash that followed years of quiet conflict.

4 Castilon
The First Order had occupied the *Colossus* to use as a refueling hub, but the mobile station's people resisted and the *Colossus* escaped.

After Palpatine's death at Endor, the Empire disintegrated with stunning speed. But that was by design: Palpatine had engineered the Contingency to purge all but the most ruthless Imperials, who retreated into the Unknown Regions to create a successor state. There they forged the First Order, which secretly accumulated military power, decapitated the New Republic, then sought to wipe out Leia Organa's Resistance to claim dominion over the galaxy. But neither the First Order nor the Resistance knew of Palpatine's ultimate design: a new Sith empire, the Final Order, meant to sweep all pretenders aside once the former galactic ruler returned from death.

Rise of the First Order

Security in the New Republic depended on sector defense forces bolstered by a small, centralized Defense Fleet—a policy championed by Mon Mothma, who rejected the legacy of Imperial militarization and wanted a state that would succeed through ideals and not compulsion. That appealed to an exhausted galaxy and worlds that favored neutrality, but Leia Organa warned that the First Order were plotting to restore Imperial power. Her entreaties went unheard, particularly after her bid to lead the New Republic was wrecked by the revelation of her parentage. Giving up on the New Republic, Organa founded the Resistance to counter the First Order, supported in secret by former allies and sympathetic senators. Most politicians derided her warnings as a relic's paranoid warmongering, but she was right: the First Order had inherited Palpatine's secret Imperial shipyards and fleets in the Unknown Regions and built a massive war machine in violation of all treaties. Disaster was coming, and the New Republic was utterly unprepared for it.

Galactic Revolutions

The war arrived with a lightning strike: the First Order unveiled the Starkiller superweapon by destroying the New Republic capital, decapitating the Senate's leadership and leaving the Defense Fleet in ruins. A Resistance raid destroyed Starkiller Base, but left Organa's group vulnerable. They barely evacuated their stronghold on D'Qar ahead of a First Order counterstrike, and were pursued to Crait and all but destroyed there. Over the next year Organa patiently rebuilt her forces, but lacked the strength to openly oppose Kylo Ren's regime. Then everything changed: Palpatine returned from death, vowing that the day of revenge was at hand and readying a vast fleet of warships—each armed with a superlaser—at Exegol, deep in the Unknown Regions. Rey, the "last Jedi," and Ren, who'd returned to the light and reclaimed the name Ben Solo, confronted the Emperor on Exegol, with Rey broadcasting the planet's location to the Resistance. A sprawling "Citizens' Fleet" joined the Resistance forces to strike the Sith armada before it could launch. Sidious and his fleet were destroyed and the galaxy rose up against the First Order, ushering in a new era free from the shadows of the Empire and Sith.

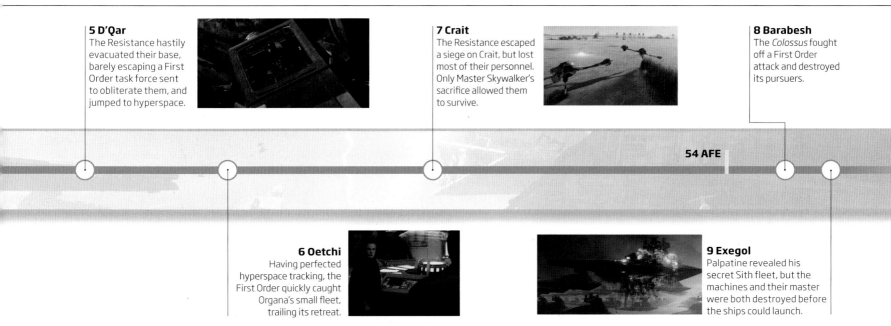

5 D'Qar
The Resistance hastily evacuated their base, barely escaping a First Order task force sent to obliterate them, and jumped to hyperspace.

7 Crait
The Resistance escaped a siege on Crait, but lost most of their personnel. Only Master Skywalker's sacrifice allowed them to survive.

8 Barabesh
The *Colossus* fought off a First Order attack and destroyed its pursuers.

54 AFE

6 Oetchi
Having perfected hyperspace tracking, the First Order quickly caught Organa's small fleet, trailing its retreat.

9 Exegol
Palpatine revealed his secret Sith fleet, but the machines and their master were both destroyed before the ships could launch.

❝ The map to Skywalker. We know you've found it, and now you're going to give it to the First Order. ❞

KYLO REN, MASTER OF THE KNIGHTS OF REN

▲ **Rapid Assault** Captain Phasma directed her stormtroopers to suppress the Tuanul villagers' resistance while Kylo Ren focused on his objective. Though the villagers were armed, their homemade weapons were no match for the stormtroopers' blaster rifles, and the attack became a massacre.

Commanders

COMMANDER POE DAMERON (CAPTURED)

Commander Poe Dameron, a hotshot Resistance pilot, was the only military combatant among the defenders. When the First Order arrived just after him, Poe fought back and killed a number of stormtroopers, but was swiftly overpowered by Kylo Ren.

CAPTAIN PHASMA

As the leader of the First Order's stormtrooper forces, Captain Phasma brooked no disobedience from her soldiers and closely monitored their performance. She gave the command for the stormtroopers to execute the Tuanul villagers, and noted that FN-2187 didn't fire as ordered.

Tuanul

DATE: 53 AFE ▪ **LOCATION:** JAKKU, INNER RIM ▪ **COMBATANTS:** FIRST ORDER VS. RESISTANCE/CHURCH OF THE FORCE ▪ **OUTCOME:** FIRST ORDER VICTORY

▼ **The Village Burns** The First Order flexed their power, superior numbers, and weaponry to threaten the defeated Tuanul villagers after setting their homes on fire.

FIRST ORDER MASSACRE

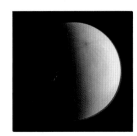

More of a skirmish than a battle, the events at Tuanul were nonetheless critical for the Resistance and First Order. Believing that Lor San Tekka held valuable information that could save the Resistance, General Leia Organa sent Commander Poe Dameron to Jakku to seek out the legendary traveler and Resistance ally. Poe found what he was looking for in the peaceful village of Tuanul, and was given a map to Luke Skywalker's location. San Tekka willingly gave the data to Dameron to assist the Resistance. But as they completed the hand-off, Captain Phasma and a company of First Order stormtroopers attacked the village.

The shock troops fanned out from their transports, firing their blasters to suppress any counterattack. Flametroopers followed, using their incendiary weapons to ignite any structures and force their defenders into the open. Their humble homes aflame, the villagers used homemade weapons–maces, axes, and blaster pistols–to defend themselves. They were no match; the First Order had the advantage in power, training, and numbers. The stormtroopers cut off Poe Dameron's escape by blowing up his X-wing, forcing the pilot to give the map to his astromech droid, BB-8, who escaped. In the midst of the battle, Kylo Ren's personal shuttle arrived.

Ren interrogated Lor San Tekka about the map, then executed the old adventurer with his lightsaber. Dameron tried to intervene, but the darkside warrior used the Force to immobilize him. Ren then ordered Captain Phasma to eliminate the villagers. Phasma commanded her troopers to open fire, and all complied but one: a soldier designated FN-2187.

KEY CASUALTY: LOR SAN TEKKA

One-time explorer Lor San Tekka proved himself loyal to the New Republic and the Resistance. He retired to a quieter life on Jakku, practicing the Church of the Force's faith–something that was perhaps inspired by his admiration for the Jedi Order. Before his retirement, San Tekka assisted Luke Skywalker in uncovering Jedi history that Emperor Palpatine had tried to erase. He believed it important to preserve lore from the past for Skywalker and the future Jedi that he would train. It was during these excursions that he got to know a youthful Ben Solo–at that time one of Luke's students–before he fell to the dark side.

▶ **Former Allies** Years earlier, Ben Solo and Lor San Tekka had both joined Luke Skywalker on his expedition to the lost Jedi outpost on Elphrona.

Takodana

DATE: 53 AFE ▪ **LOCATION:** TAKODANA, MID RIM ▪
COMBATANTS: FIRST ORDER VS. RESISTANCE ▪
OUTCOME: INCONCLUSIVE

A LONG-AWAITED FIGHT

The First Order and Leia Organa's Resistance were enemies before meeting on Takodana, having fought a number of skirmishes. But both sides had avoided all-out war: Organa still believed she could awaken the New Republic to the threat posed by the First Order, while the First Order needed more time to build up their fleet and finalize testing of the Starkiller superweapon, which they believed would allow them to sweep the New Republic aside with a single devastating strike.

That strike came at Hosnian Prime, incinerated by Starkiller Base along with the New Republic Senate and much of its starfleet. As word of the cataclysm spread, the First Order and the Resistance faced each other in battle for the first time on the frontier world Takodana. Both sides sought a map to Luke Skywalker encoded into the memory of Resistance astromech BB-8. The First Order arrived first, leveling Maz Kanata's castle and hunting for the fugitive droid. But the Resistance were close behind, sending an X-wing squadron led by Poe Dameron. Kylo Ren quickly ordered First Order troops to withdraw: BB-8 escaped them, but Rey, a Jakku scavenger of mysterious origins, had seen the elusive map. Ren took Rey captive, vowing to use his Force powers to pry Skywalker's location from her mind. With the last Jedi destroyed, the First Order would be unstoppable.

Commanders

COMMANDER POE DAMERON
Poe Dameron barely survived a crash landing on Jakku, trekking across the planet's deserts in search of transport offworld and a chance to return to the Resistance. After the near-disaster of his hunt for Lor San Tekka, he was relieved to find himself in an X-wing cockpit once again.

KYLO REN
A mysterious servant of Supreme Leader Snoke, Kylo Ren had no formal role in the First Order hierarchy, much to the annoyance of his rival, General Hux. He acted as Snoke's agent, and the stormtroopers on Takodana hurried to obey his every command, eager to avoid his infamous wrath.

▲ **Strike Force** The Resistance scrambled 11 T-70 X-wings, led by Poe's *Black One*. Dameron's pilots were eager to finally engage their First Order tormenters in open warfare.

◄ **"Innocent" Bystanders** The First Order sweep netted Han Solo, Chewbacca, and the deserter FN-2187, now know as Finn, who'd been trying to return BB-8 to the Resistance.

▲ **Ancient Refuge** Galactic rivals had long accepted, or at least tolerated, the eccentric Maz Kanata and her sprawling castle, treating it as neutral ground. The First Order attack marked a shocking break with a centuries-old tradition.

KEY COMBATANT: STORMTROOPERS

After driving Maz Kanata's guests from her castle with a barrage of firepower, the First Order landed stormtroopers to sweep up the escapees and locate BB-8. Troops fanned out with blasters and nonlethal weapons suitable for crowd control and subduing dissenters. The First Order trained troopers from childhood, an effort that built on Kamino's program to create a clone army. Stormtrooper cadets grew up hardened by endless exercises, making them skilled with blasters, hand weapons, and fists. On Takodana, FN-2199 spotted a batchmate, FN-2187, who'd deserted on Jakku. The two former colleagues faced off in a decidedly unconventional duel: riot-control baton against lightsaber.

▶ **New Skills** Finn had never wielded a lightsaber, but years of close-combat drills let him hold his own. Things went less well on Starkiller Base, where he fought Kylo Ren.

Neo-Imperialism

The Galactic Empire's defeat did not see an end to the ideology that had been nurtured and propagated by Palpatine's "New Order." The signing of the Galactic Concordance seemed to bring an end to Imperialism, but the survival of key figures such as Grand Admiral Rae Sloane and Commandant Brendol Hux ensured that the new regime they helped create was built on Imperial lines. Their determination to rebuild the Empire without making the same errors set the First Order on a path toward radical Neo-Imperialism based on fanatical devotion to totalitarian notions of "order" and violent disdain for the Republic and democracy.

▲ **Supreme Leader** The First Order had all the qualities of an Empire without an Emperor. Snoke filled this gap for the next generation of First Order officers. None realized he was merely a tool of Palpatine.

REBUILDING THE EMPIRE
As part of his contingency plan in the event of his death, Emperor Palpatine had selected his most fanatical followers to secretly rebuild the Empire in the Unknown Regions. In the aftermath of the Battle of Jakku these figures secretly escaped the known galaxy to begin the construction of what would become the First Order. In the absence of Palpatine himself, command was to fall to Gallius Rax, but Rax's death at Jakku left Grand Admiral Rae Sloane as the ranking officer. Her initial plan was to ensure that the First Order would be built in the image of Palpatine and the Imperial ideology he had used to rule the galaxy.

THE FIRST ORDER
The security of the Unknown Regions allowed the former Imperial state to grow over time. Indoctrination programs that espoused Neo-Imperial policy became a stable of education policy in the First Order and the children of those who had served Palpatine were rapidly radicalized. To construct an armed force, the First Order also began a campaign of kidnapping and enslaving children from nearby settlements, and they too were subject to reprogramming to ensure absolute loyalty and dedication. Control of the First Order also fluctuated over time. Grand Admiral Sloane ruled in the aftermath of Jakku but the emergence of Snoke, himself a puppet of Palpatine, provided the First Order with a Force-wielding figurehead behind which to rally themselves. As a result, Snoke eliminated or sidelined the other leaders who stood in his way. Memory of and allegiance to the Empire had not died out in the known galaxy. Many "Centrist" politicians in the

KEY INFO

GRAND ADMIRAL RAE SLOANE

Grand Admiral Sloane had saved the Imperial fleet at Endor and saw the opportunity to rebuild a stronger Galactic Empire as too tempting to reject. Sloane helped preserve the Imperial ideology that would become the First Order's foundation. However, though Sloane was a highly capable figure, she did not provide a focal point in the way that Palpatine had. The emergence of Snoke as a figure who could utilize the Force led to Sloane's eventual downfall.

◄ **Imperial Leader** Sloane, perhaps more than anyone else, was responsible for the survival of the Galactic Empire and its ideology after Jakku.

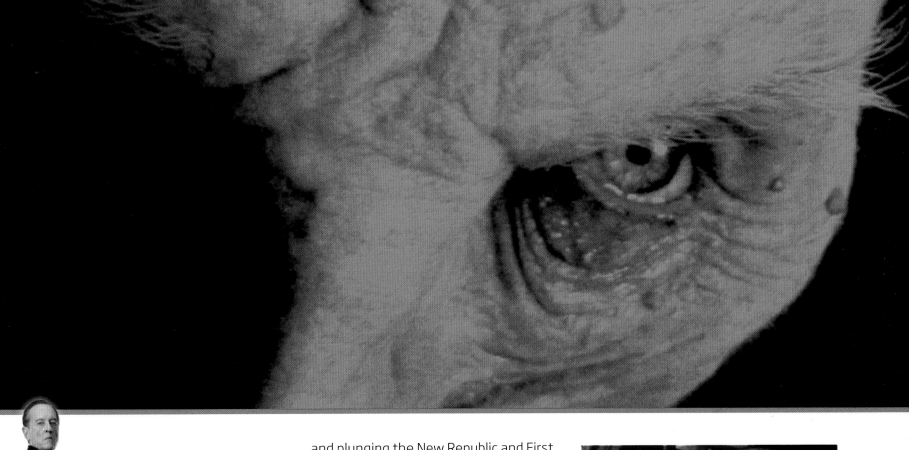

◀ **Allegiant General** Enric Pryde had served in the Galactic Empire and was truly loyal to the Emperor. When Palpatine returned, Pryde moved to follow him.

Galactic Senate were secretly loyalists aiming to disrupt the New Republic's attempts to govern and therefore pave the way for the First Order's rise. This they achieved in 47 AFE when the Centrist-aligned systems of the New Republic finally seceded and joined the First Order, giving the Neo-Imperials territory within the borders of the known galaxy

and plunging the New Republic and First Order into a Cold War that lasted several years. This period finally ended with the First Order's devastating attack on the New Republic capital and the destruction of the Galactic Senate and Defense Fleet.

GENERATIONAL SCHISM

Over time, a divide opened between those who had served Palpatine and those raised in the First Order. Armitage Hux rose to the rank of general after assassinating his own father and, while Snoke lived, was loyal to the First Order but had no strong feelings toward the fallen Galactic Empire. Emperor Palpatine's

▲ **New Leaders** Together, General Hux and Captain Phasma organized the First Order's armed forces and orchestrated the indoctrination that secured their loyalty.

return did not move many of the younger First Order officers, whereas older officers, those like Allegiant General Enric Pryde, were quick to fall in behind him when the opportunity arose.

▼ **Starkiller Base** The First Order utilized Imperial symbols and weaponry to conquer the galaxy. General Hux's speech on Starkiller Base was effectively a Neo-Imperial manifesto.

▲ **Prime Target** As Starkiller Base's shields came down, the Resistance squadrons made a diving attack on the thermal oscillator facility. However, unlike the Death Star, the Starkiller's weak point was so heavily armored it was virtually invulnerable.

Starkiller Base

DATE: 53 AFE ▪ **LOCATION:** STARKILLER BASE (ILUM), UNKNOWN REGIONS ▪ **COMBATANTS:** FIRST ORDER VS. RESISTANCE ▪ **OUTCOME:** RESISTANCE VICTORY

DESTROYER OF WORLDS

Deep in the Unknown Regions of the galaxy, the First Order turned the planet Ilum into a terrifying superweapon. This small, frigid world, once known as a sacred site for the Jedi Order, was transformed into a weapon that dwarfed the destructive power of the Death Stars that came before–a weapon that could win a war with a single shot.

After decades spent assembling their fleet and Starkiller in secret, the First Order was finally ready to reveal their true nature to the galaxy by launching a devastating strike on the heart of the New Republic. They believed their attack was justified as the New Republic had been secretly supplying the Resistance–long a thorn in the First Order's side–despite public denials. For these successors of the bygone Galactic Empire, the Starkiller's strike would bring order to a poorly governed galaxy as they swept in to establish their rule in the New Republic's wake.

Their first target was the Hosnian system, then home to the New Republic Senate and most of its defensive fleet. As the blast surged across the galaxy on the way to its targets, the

▲ **Plan of Attack** Using intelligence provided by Captain Wexley and a First Order defector named Finn, Resistance leaders devised a multi-phased attack plan: a small team would infiltrate the base prior to a strike aimed at destabilizing the weapon.

galaxy looked on in terror. The first test of the Starkiller was a chilling success, killing billions of innocents, decapitating the New Republic's political institutions, and leaving few challengers to fight back against the First Order's might. From their base on D'Qar, the Resistance launched a reconnaissance flight to gain an understanding of the enemy before them, only to discover a weapon built on an astonishing scale with formidable defenses. Worse yet, the Resistance base was the station's next target.

KEY WEAPON: THE STARKILLER

Ilum was extensively mined by the Empire in the search for kyber crystals for the Death Stars' superlasers; its deeply scarred surface and hollowed-out crust made it a perfect candidate for conversion into a superweapon. Charging the Starkiller's dark-energy cannon required it to consume the energy of an entire star, which was then stored in the planet's crystalline interior, regulated by a thermal oscillator until ready to fire.

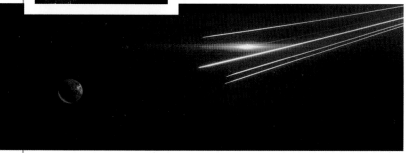

▲ **Hosnian Cataclysm** The Starkiller's blast splintered off to strike multiple targets simultaneously, wiping out the entire Hosnian system and the New Republic Home Fleet.

Commanders

COMMANDER POE DAMERON
The former New Republic pilot personally led the Resistance's squadrons at the Battle of Starkiller Base. His ability to improvise in the heat of battle was a vital asset when leading such a small force against a secretive enemy, making him well suited to adapt to the changing situation.

GENERAL ARMITAGE HUX
Hux gave a rousing speech to his soldiers on Starkiller Base, rallying them for the all-out war that was to come. Though Hux gave the order to fire the weapon, he himself answered to a much more sinister master—Supreme Leader Snoke, who preferred to lead the First Order from the shadows.

Starkiller Base (continued)

The daring Resistance plan first required a small strike team to infiltrate Starkiller Base to lower the station's formidable planetary shield. If they could bring down this barrier, it would allow the Resistance fighter squadrons to carry out the next phase of the plan, an assault on the thermal oscillator that regulated the massive energy contained within the station as it charged. This mission fell to Han Solo, who had helped destroy both the Empire's Death Star battle stations, joined by his copilot Chewbacca and a former stormtrooper, Finn. The veteran of so many unlikely missions, the elder captain's experience as a smuggler made him particularly well suited for an infiltration mission with so many unknowns. Solo's first challenge was to penetrate the planetary shield he sought to disable, a feat that

required him to fly his freighter, the *Millennium Falcon*, through the shield at lightspeed and then rapidly decelerate before smashing into the surface.

Though the planet was regularly patrolled by armored vehicles, sentry droids, and speeder craft, such a small strike team was able to move unnoticed to infiltrate the base by way of a flooding tunnel on the snowy surface. Once inside, they took First Order commander Captain Phasma hostage and forced her to disable the shield at gunpoint. With this first phase complete, the Resistance ordered their squadrons to exit hyperspace and begin their attack. Solo then turned his attention to rescuing a Resistance-aligned prisoner, Rey, and finally improvised an attempt to sabotage the thermal oscillator from the inside.

▼ **Ungraceful Entry** Upon entering the planet's atmosphere at lightspeed, pilot Han Solo flew the *Millennium Falcon* below tree level to avoid detection by First Order scanners. His subsequent crash landing was not graceful, but marked a successful infiltration.

▲ **Into Position** Han Solo, Chewbacca, and Finn made their way on foot to the infiltration site equipped with little more than their personal blasters and a satchel of explosives.

THE DEATH OF HAN SOLO

Han Solo confronted his son, now known by his chosen name of Kylo Ren, believing he could convince the First Order leader to return to his parents' side. Solo underestimated his son's loyalty to Snoke and his desire to destroy his own past. In a moment of embrace, Ren struck down his father, ending the life of one of the galaxy's most famous war heroes with a single stab of his lightsaber.

▲ **Attempt at Salvation** Inside the oscillator, Han Solo diverted from his sabotage mission to confront his son, leaving Chewbacca to finish the task alone.

▶ **Too Far Gone** Ren came from a line of legendary heroes, but was too corrupted for Han to save.

Starkiller Base: Decisive Moment

Even without its planetary shields engaged, Starkiller Base was heavily defended against capital ship and bomber attacks, meaning only maneuverable starfighters could carry out the second phase of the attack plan. Leading the charge was Commander Poe Dameron, who ordered Red and Blue Squadrons out of hyperspace within close proximity of the surface. This tactic allowed Dameron's fighters to find their target before the First Order could launch their own TIE fighters in response.

The Resistance X-wings' first volleys of torpedoes could not damage the well-protected exterior of the thermal oscillator. It would take multiple attack runs to penetrate its armor, requiring time the pilots simply did not have.

Ground fire from heavy laser cannons and missile launchers dealt substantial casualties to the Resistance squadrons, destroying half of their number after just five minutes of fighting. But when Dameron saw the destruction caused by Han Solo's sabotage on the ground, it gave him the opening he needed to attempt a finishing blow.

Through the newly blown hole in the armored exterior, Dameron narrowly piloted his way inside the oscillator, pummeling the assembly's weak points with volley after volley of proton torpedoes. This feat of flying and precision caused fatal damage to the oscillator, and Starkiller Base began to collapse as the energy confined inside could no longer be contained.

▲ **Fighting Heritage** Resistance pilots studied battles from the earlier Galactic Civil War. Training maneuvers that simulated attack strategies seen at the Battles of Yavin and Endor helped prepare them for this moment.

▶ **Diving Attack** The Resistance fielded New Republic surplus model T-70 X-wings. They quickly realized that their proton torpedoes were ineffective against the oscillator's thick armor.

▲ **Black Leader** As commander of both Blue and Red Squadrons, Poe Dameron flew as Black Leader, choosing to style his personal call sign after his uniquely equipped fighter, *Black One*.

▲ **Maximum Firepower** From inside the thermal oscillator, Dameron bracketed multiple weak points in the structure with successive torpedo attacks, maximizing the damage.

Starkiller Base (continued)

With the thermal oscillator irrevocably damaged by Dameron's torpedoes, a series of explosions and ground quakes erupted as the planet fell apart from the inside. When the fuel cells ruptured, Supreme Leader Snoke ordered his senior leaders to retreat and other First Order troops scrambled to save themselves. The base's cascading collapse gave key First Order personnel enough time to evacuate, unlike the instantaneous explosion that consumed the first Death Star decades before. The imploding superweapon finally erupted in spectacular fashion as the energy contained inside consumed all that remained of the base, replacing it with a miniature star.

Upon the Resistance's return to their headquarters on D'Qar, the celebration was bittersweet. The victory at Starkiller Base ensured the insurgent organization's immediate survival but left many doubts about how it might continue to fight. The Resistance stood alone, no longer able to count on the New Republic for vital supplies or funding. The death of Han Solo meant the loss of an inspirational hero at a time when he was needed most. Moreover, the Starkiller Incident, at it came to be known, revealed the First Order to be far more powerful than previously imagined. If Supreme Leader Snoke's armies could construct a planet-sized superweapon in secret, Snoke could easily have been hiding more ominous secrets in the furthest reaches of the galaxy. The First Order's invasion was just beginning.

▲ **Mission Accomplished** The crust of the planet that housed Starkiller Base began to crumble from the inside out. Explosions on the surface heralded the catastrophic eruption to come as Resistance X-wings withdrew to a safe distance far outside the planet's orbit.

CASUALTIES

RESISTANCE: With more than half of Red and Blue Squadrons' fighters lost in combat, the Resistance would be underequipped and staffed for future battles. Only Han Solo perished in the ground infiltration.
FIRST ORDER: While losses during the ground and air battles were modest in comparison, the chaotic and poorly led evacuation of Starkiller Base left many thousands of First Order troops unable to escape before it exploded.

▲ **Deadly Skies** The Resistance ground team looked on as the fighter squadrons attacking the oscillator took devastating losses from TIE fighters and ground-based missile batteries.

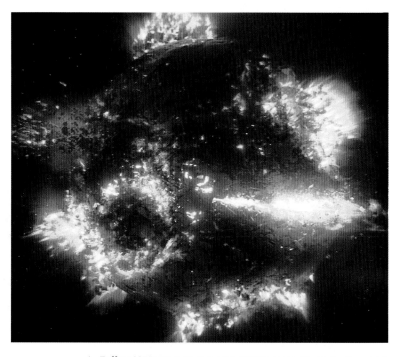

▲ **Fallen Heroes** Ilum, once prized for its connection to the Force and its concentration of kyber crystals, imploded as the energy of a captive sun burst through the planet's crystalline crust. In its place stood a micro-star later known as Solo in honor of the fallen rebel.

◄ ▲ **Chilling Confrontation** After killing Han Solo, Kylo Ren turned his attention to Finn and Rey. In a series of lightsaber duels, he incapacitated the former but failed to defeat the latter. The untrained scavenger shocked Ren with her abilities, leaving him seriously injured. Rey then rescued Finn and they escaped aboard the *Millennium Falcon*.

Castilon

DATE: 53 AFE ▪ **LOCATION:** CASTILON, MID RIM ▪
COMBATANTS: FIRST ORDER VS. RESISTANCE ▪
OUTCOME: INCONCLUSIVE

FREEING THE *COLOSSUS*

The Resistance had to allocate their scant resources carefully. In the case of the *Colossus* station on Castilon, they needed to monitor the First Order's activity but without any agents to spare, they recruited Kazuda Xiono, a pilot in the New Republic Defense Fleet. Xiono was to infiltrate the platform, spy on the enemy, and report his observations to the Resistance. The First Order attempted to press the platform's owner, Captain Imanuel Doza, to permit their occupation as a security force. They slowly increased their numbers until they achieved their goal and fully occupied the *Colossus*. The situation turned to conflict when the First Order applied too much pressure while searching for the Resistance spy.

The attack on Castilon unfolded with only limited Resistance involvement. Xiono gathered forces from the platform's Ace Squadron, a team of racing pilots, and its civilians to expel the First Order's occupation forces. The Aces flew their own motley ships, capitalizing on their speed and skills they had gained from countless races above the *Colossus*. They successfully freed the *Colossus*, which then fled into hyperspace.

While seemingly inconclusive, Castilon would later prove pivotal to the Resistance. Although the *Colossus* didn't arrive on D'Qar as planned, the delay meant the ship avoided the First Order attack on the Resistance base and would later arrive to assist the Resistance in the climactic battle at Exegol.

▲ **Resistance Spy** Xiono's confidence grew with his time on the *Colossus*, and after the First Order arrested Doza he took action and led an offensive against the First Order's occupation.

Commanders

KAZUDA XIONO
After freeing his allies Yeager and Doza from First Order captivity, Xiono worked with them to liberate the *Colossus*. Following the destruction of Hosnian Prime, his home, Xiono united the Aces and *Colossus*' citizens to stand against the First Order as the ship navigated off Castilon.

MAJOR ELRIK VONREG (KILLED IN ACTION)
Failing to secure the *Colossus* for the First Order, Vonreg turned to eliminating Xiono and his cohorts. Vonreg led his pilots in his scarlet TIE interceptor as they attacked the platform; he focused his fire on Yeager before Xiono destroyed Vonreg and his starfighter.

▲ **Back in Action** Jarek Yeager had put his rebel pilot days behind him, but he joined the battle to cover the *Colossus*' escape from Castilon. Yeager eliminated multiple TIE fighters and drew Major Vonreg away from the fleeing ship.

KEY LOCATION: THE *COLOSSUS*

The *Colossus'* stationary position in the oceans of Castilon belied its true nature. Seemingly an aircraft refueling platform, the *Colossus* served those traveling through the Mid Rim and into nearby Wild Space. A community of racers formed on the platform; known as the Ace Squadron, they also defended the *Colossus* from pirate attacks. The station eventually attracted the First Order; they planned to leverage the *Colossus* as a base for the war against the Resistance. Tensions on the platform rose following the destruction of Hosnian Prime, and during the Battle of Castilon it was revealed that the *Colossus* was actually a giant starship.

▶ **Rough Takeoff** The *Colossus'* flight systems and hyperdrive had been inactive for 20 years, but the ship successfully escaped from Castilon.

D'Qar

DATE: 53 AFE ▪ **LOCATION:** D'QAR, OUTER RIM TERRITORIES ▪
COMBATANTS: FIRST ORDER VS. RESISTANCE ▪
OUTCOME: RESISTANCE VICTORY

COVERING THE EVACUATION

The Resistance claimed victory at Starkiller Base, but their celebration was short-lived. The First Order had tracked the Resistance reconnaissance ships that provided intelligence on the icy stronghold and narrowed in on the Resistance position at D'Qar. Knowing reprisals were forthcoming, the Resistance had already started to prepare for the First Order's arrival by organizing mass evacuation. Abandoning bases once they were discovered by the enemy was something the organization was more than used to executing. They were adept at quickly establishing and dismantling their outposts, and as such, had evacuation protocols readily available.

Lieutenant Kaydel Connix led the D'Qar evacuation from the ground. Having a single ultimate authority directing the retreat was of the utmost importance as it streamlined the operation. Though the command structure of the Resistance was notably flexible, they followed emergency plans with military discipline. Mi'ala Frenoc was promoted into Connix's vacant operations controller role and assisted the lieutenant in directing the Resistance high command to their vessels: an assortment of frigates and star cruisers. Together they split the Resistance leadership between the *Vigil*, the *Anodyne*, the *Ninka*, and the *Raddus* in hopes of keeping at least one commanding officer safe

▼ **Formation Flying** The heavy bombers of Cobalt and Crimson Squadrons took aim at the *Fulminatrix*. Carefully trained, the bomber crews flew in tight formation to maximize their defensive fire.

Commanders

COMMANDER POE DAMERON
When the First Order arrived at D'Qar, Commander Dameron distracted them by flying his X-wing into combat while the Resistance evacuated. However he disobeyed General Organa's orders and pressed the attack on the dreadnought, at the cost of numerous Resistance lives.

**CAPTAIN MODEN CANADY
(KILLED IN ACTION)**
Moden Canady commanded the *Fulminatrix*, a First Order Siege Dreadnought. He unleashed the dreadnought's firepower on the Resistance base, but Dameron's counterattack caught Canady's crew off guard and all perished when the vast warship exploded.

▲ **A-wing Escorts** Lieutenant Tallissan "Tallie" Lintra piloted her A-wing in defense of the escaping Resistance fleet and as an escort to the heavy bombers.

in the event of a successful First Order attack. The *Raddus*, General Organa's flagship, formed the heart of the Resistance fleet. It was stationed at the rear where it could use its powerful experimental shields to protect other craft from long-range fire.

The First Order were confident they would eliminate the Resistance forces. They arrived with three *Resurgent*-class Star Destroyers and one *Mandator IV*-class Siege Dreadnought, the *Fulminatrix*. The dreadnought alone could have devastated most rebellious worlds. Though the First Order did not have the element of surprise, they did not delay their attack.

KEY WEAPON: FIRST ORDER DREADNOUGHT

Commander Dameron called the First Order's *Mandator IV*-class Siege Dreadnought a fleet-killer. With more firepower than a dozen Star Destroyers, the formidable dreadnoughts were flexible in their assault functions. Large orbital-bombardment autocannons allowed the ship to punch through planetary shields, while multiple turbolasers and tractor beam projectors allowed it to capture and eliminate enemy ships in space battles. Dreadnoughts were crafted for utter destruction.

▲ **Resistance Target** The *Fulminatrix* should have been able to easily wipe out the Resistance.

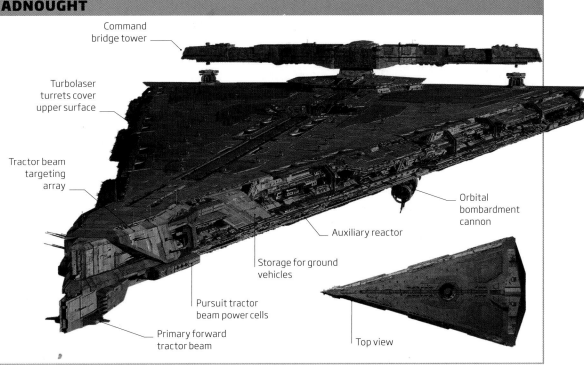

Command bridge tower

Turbolaser turrets cover upper surface

Tractor beam targeting array

Orbital bombardment cannon

Auxiliary reactor

Storage for ground vehicles

Pursuit tractor beam power cells

Primary forward tractor beam

Top view

D'Qar (continued)

The Resistance were already off the planet by the time the First Order started their bombardment of the surface. Fleet crews quickly processed personnel across the four capital ships and reassigned soldiers of every rank into new key roles. The organization's lean numbers meant no one could sit idle while they waited to jump into the safety of hyperspace.

In order to keep the First Order's focus off the ships entering orbit above D'Qar, Commander Dameron, a pilot with a reputation for being a hotshot, volunteered a plan to distract them. General Organa approved, and Dameron undertook the mission single-handedly. He effectively kept the dreadnought from pointing its cannons toward the disappearing Resistance, but rather than rejoining the Resistance fleet, Dameron insisted on removing the dreadnought from the field. Ignoring Organa's

KEY WEAPON: RESISTANCE BOMBER

When the Resistance needed to penetrate heavily armored targets, they deployed MG-100 StarFortress bombers. Each ship was crewed by a pilot; a flight engineer; a bombardier; and two gunners, and carried a full magazine clip of proton bombs (1,048 weapons). When the craft weren't in battle, the Resistance used them as transports, carrying supplies to blockaded systems.

Armored flight deck

Forward laser cannon

Proton bomb magazine

Targeting and tracking array

▶ **Slow Target** The bombers required more nimble escorts for protection from enemy attacks.

▲ **TIE Retaliation** TIE fighters that had scrambled too late to stop Dameron were in prime position to target the ungainly heavy bombers and their escorts. The heavy crossfire and debris from exploding ships destroyed multiple bombers in a chain reaction–but one got through.

orders, Dameron brought the Cobalt and Crimson bomber squadrons into the fray. They believed the orders came from Organa via the proper chain of command, so they flew into position while escort fighters surrounded them to defend them from First Order starfighters.

Captain Canady, commander of the *Fulminatrix*, witnessed the bombers moving in for their attack run and redirected the TIE fighters toward them. General Organa monitored the doomed attack from her position aboard the *Raddus*. The situation was too volatile for the lumbering bombers and all but one were shot down. The final bomber destroyed the *Fulminatrix*, but the loss of pilots was painful, and, from Organa's viewpoint, unnecessary. The evacuation and ensuing battle dealt a severe blow to the already ragtag Resistance's numbers and resources.

▶ **Last Act** As the last survivor of the *Cobalt Hammer*, Paige Tico released the ship's proton bombs onto the *Fulminatrix*. She died in the ensuing explosion.

▲ **Dreadnought Carnage** Only a single bomber dropped its payload, but that was enough to tear the First Order dreadnought apart. As explosions ripped through the *Fulminatrix*'s hull, more than 200,000 of its crew were killed, including Captain Canady, who accepted his fate and did not try to escape.

AFTERMATH

The loss of the base on D'Qar was a blow to the Resistance's operations. They suffered immense casualties in both lives and ships, including their irreplaceable bomber squadrons. General Organa demoted Commander Dameron to captain for flouting her orders in the battle. The fleet escaped, but the First Order used new technology to track the fleeing Resistance ships through hyperspace. The crew of the *Colossus*, believing the Resistance base to still be present and functional, traveled to D'Qar for supplies—particularly hyperdrive fuel. After they learned the base had been wiped out, they saw the opportunity to obtain coaxium from the *Fulminatrix*'s wreckage. Resistance spy Kaz Xiono succeeded with the help of a contingent of pirates who had gotten stuck on the *Colossus* when it fled Castilon.

▲ **Debris Field** The *Colossus* arrived above D'Qar to find all that remained was the battered wreckage of the Resistance and First Order fleets.

Oetchi

DATE: 53 AFE ▪ **LOCATION:** OETCHI, OUTER RIM TERRITORIES ▪
COMBATANTS: FIRST ORDER VS. RESISTANCE ▪
OUTCOME: FIRST ORDER VICTORY

DECAPITATION STRIKE

The Resistance suffered a devastating series of losses at the Battle
of Oetchi, a brief but disastrous engagement that underscored the vast
technological disparity between it and the First Order. After their
evacuation of D'Qar, the Resistance fleet was searching for a new base with
enough power to transmit their call for help to any allies in the Outer Rim.
Upon coming out of hyperspace in the Oetchi system the Resistance faced
a stunning revelation: the First Order had the ability to track their fleet
through hyperspace. Armed with aging surplus equipment and just four
warships, the Resistance was now in a race to evade an entire squadron
of state-of-the-art Star Destroyers and the First Order's city-sized flagship,
the mighty Star Dreadnought *Supremacy*.

First Order fighters seized upon the element of surprise by launching
an attack that wiped out the Resistance fighter squadrons in their hangar
aboard the *Raddus*, then landed a devastating blow to the cruiser's
command bridge. The Resistance's most experienced naval commander,
Admiral Ackbar, was killed and the movement's principal leader, General
Organa, was incapacitated. With their leadership now depleted, the
outgunned, outnumbered, and aging Resistance fleet could neither outrun
their opponents nor spare the fuel for a futile jump to hyperspace. Their
only hope of survival was to use their speed to maneuver out of range of
the First Order's heavy guns until they could reach safe harbor.

▲ **Relentless Assault** As the Resistance starfighter squadrons
prepared to scramble to defend the fleet, a precision missile strike on
their hangar annihilated the entire force before they could launch.

Commanders

**GENERAL LEIA ORGANA
(INCAPACITATED)**
With years of wartime leadership
experience, General Organa
instantly realized the dire
situation. She called for her fleet
to fall back, forcing the attacking
TIEs to retreat to the safety of
their capital ships, but not before
they landed a strike that left her
severely wounded.

KYLO REN
The son of General Organa, Kylo
Ren directly led the starfighter
strike that severely damaged the
Resistance flagship. The attack
was strategically important to
the First Order as they sought to
finish what little remained of the
Resistance fleet, but also deeply
personal for Ren as he faced an
enemy force led by his mother.

▲ **Fighter Superiority** Strafing attacks by First Order TIE fighters did
significant damage before they were recalled to their carriers.

▲ **Mounting Losses** Captain Poe Dameron, having recently been demoted for his brash actions at D'Qar, lost his entire fighter wing at Oetchi. He narrowly escaped the attack with his life, but afterward found himself frustratingly sidelined.

KEY WEAPON: THE *RADDUS*

This decommissioned New Republic star cruiser found a new life in service of General Organa's Resistance. It was renamed in honor of Alliance hero Admiral Raddus, who decades earlier had led the rebel fleet into action at the Battle of Scarif. Though outclassed by contemporary Star Destroyers, its experimental shield technology allowed it to repel long-range barrages.

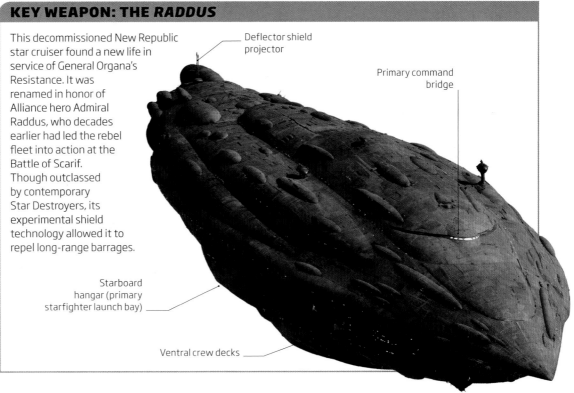

Deflector shield projector

Primary command bridge

Starboard hangar (primary starfighter launch bay)

Ventral crew decks

New Republic Disarmament

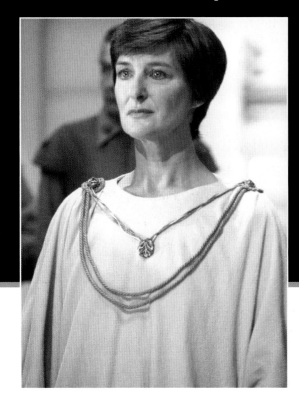

After years of struggle to defeat the Empire, the Alliance followed its victory at Endor with the declaration of the New Republic. This restored democracy continued to grow in strength, both politically and militarily, in the months following the Emperor's death, and victory at the Battle of Jakku saw an end to large-scale fighting. With the establishment of the Galactic Concordance, New Republic Chancellor Mon Mothma proposed a policy of demilitarization, in part fearing that the new government might transform into the militaristic regime it had replaced. The Military Disarmament Act not only transformed the makeup of the burgeoning New Republic, it would have consequences for decades to come.

▲ **Principled Position** As the first elected Chancellor of the New Republic after years of rebellion, Mon Mothma sought to set aside her military responsibilities and reassume her role as a democratic political leader.

A NEW DOCTRINE

The reduction of the New Republic's military became law after the Senate passed the Military Disarmament Act. The widely supported legislation called for the reduction of the New Republic military by 90 percent, a move that limited the centralized power in a time of newfound peace and ushered many

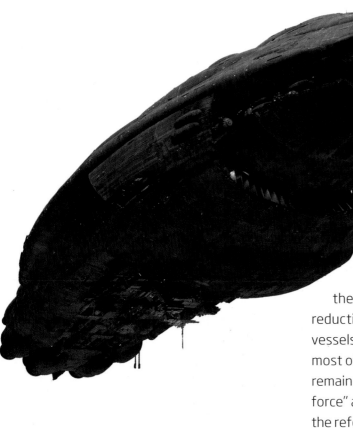

◄ **Dawn of Tranquility** This highly automated star cruiser favored shields over offensive firepower.

Alliance heroes into early retirement. So too went most of the New Republic fleet, as such a large reduction meant even newly completed vessels saw early decommissioning. With most of the fleet in mothballs, what little remained was designated a "defense force" as attention turned to protecting the reformed Senate and the host planet that served as New Republic capital.

➤ **Automated Sentries** New Republic security droids filled roles previously held by organic guards.

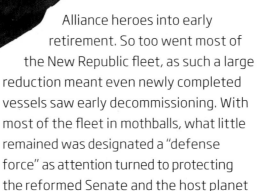

PEACETIME EVOLUTION

Over time, the New Republic Defense Force evolved to operate under its restrictive charter. To function with such limited personnel, the force was designed around increased automation to augment the skeleton crews that remained behind. In some cases full automation was the goal, as cargo shipping and even prisoner transports were designed to be operated without any organic crew members. This approach also saw the more widespread return of droid security forces in place of living beings, a practice that both the Empire and the Rebel Alliance had only minimally employed.

LOSING ITS GRIP

Unlike their heavy-handed predecessor, the New Republic did not put an emphasis on expansion, and did not force any star system into membership. Parts of the galaxy that had bowed to Palpatine's rule

returned to their pre-Empire independence, leaving local governments, monarchs, cartels, or warlords to fill the power vacuum. Without the Jedi Order to maintain peace, enforcing New Republic laws in the more lawless reaches fell to local defense forces, rangers, or marshals. While this approach helped avoid the appearance of military authoritarianism, some corners of the galaxy saw major upticks in crime. Illicit activities tolerated by the Empire were pushed out of the Core Worlds where the New Republic had more influence, but they soon found a home in the overlooked outlying regions.

Even pockets of Imperialism, technically illegal, continued in places where the New Republic had little presence.

UNPREPARED FOR WAR
Though they were aware of the First Order's existence, the New Republic were unwilling to face this successor to the Empire. Some, such as Leia Organa, warned of the danger posed by allowing this enemy to grow unchecked, but her pleas for action merely saw her Resistance branded as extremists and warmongers. Sympathetic senators secretly supplied the Resistance with

▲ **Off Limits** New Republic pilots were expressly prohibited from engaging in combat with First Order forces, even in self-defense.

surplus equipment but it was never enough to match the First Order head on, and merely stoked the enemy's belief that the New Republic was being deceitful and encouraging chaos across the galaxy.

KEY INFO

THE HOSNIAN CATACLYSM

The First Order's initial salvo against the New Republic was a crushing blow. The Starkiller superweapon annihilated the New Republic capital on Hosnian Prime and most of the Defense Fleet with a single blast. The policy of conflict avoidance and non-intervention had allowed the First Order to build their secret superweapon, fleet, and armies virtually unchecked. Most New Republic leaders perished before ever learning the truth.

◄ **Warnings Unheeded** Up until the final moment, Commander Korr Sella tried to convince the Senate to take action. But it was too late.

► **First Strike** As well as the Senate, the Starkiller wiped out the Republic's top military commanders.

Commanders

GENERAL LEIA ORGANA
After Holdo's plan to evacuate the *Raddus'* crew failed, Leia Organa found her movement trapped, and put all her hopes on a desperate appeal for aid sent out into the galaxy. That call would be answered in stunning, heartbreaking fashion.

SUPREME LEADER KYLO REN
Though master of the First Order, Kylo Ren seethed over Rey's refusal to join him in ruling the galaxy. He followed his mother down to Crait's surface, determined to destroy her and all she had built. The galaxy would then find peace—and perhaps Kylo might find it as well.

▶ **Under Siege** Leia Organa had faced long odds before, but the spark of freedom had never felt closer to being extinguished.

▼ **Monstrous Parade** Kylo Ren's shuttle hovered above a line of First Order walkers, poised to crush the lone redoubt standing between his regime and galactic domination.

Crait

DATE: 53 AFE ▪ **LOCATION:** CRAIT, OUTER RIM TERRITORIES ▪ **COMBATANTS:** FIRST ORDER VS. RESISTANCE ▪ **OUTCOME:** TACTICAL FIRST ORDER VICTORY

LAST STAND

After the Resistance fleet was ambushed at Oetchi, its three surviving ships traveled through space at sublight speeds, unable to escape because of a lack of fuel and the First Order's hyperspace tracking technology. But Vice Admiral Amilyn Holdo had a plan: transfer all personnel to the *Raddus*, and then evacuate all hands to U-55 loadlifters outfitted with experimental "bafflers" designed to foil scans. The *Raddus* would be sacrificed, but 400 Resistance fighters would escape to the salt planet Crait, lying low until they could contact allies of General Leia Organa. Disturbed by a wave of desertions via escape pods, Holdo decided to share her plan with only a handful of loyalists: if the First Order learned of it from a deserter, the transports would be easy to detect and destroy.

Her plan was undone by a security breach: Poe Dameron had sent Finn and Rose Tico to find a way to disrupt the First Order tracking system, and they had unwittingly revealed the scheme to the slicer DJ, who tipped off the First Order to save his own skin. Twenty-four of the 30 transports were destroyed, with Holdo only saving the others by sacrificing herself, using the *Raddus* as a hyperspace missile that carved through the First Order flagship and its escorts. But the "Holdo maneuver" seemed merely a stay of execution: the Resistance survivors were trapped in an old rebel base on Crait, with no prospect of rescue and the First Order—led by a vengeful Kylo Ren—on their doorstep.

DESTRUCTION OF THE *SUPREMACY*

Alone on the *Raddus*' bridge, an anguished Vice Admiral Amilyn Holdo shut down the fail-safes on her flagship's hyperdrive and jumped to lightspeed. The vessel remained intact for only a split second, but that was long enough for it to rip through the *Supremacy* and the First Order fleet.

▼ **Unexpected Luck**
The "Holdo maneuver" used hyperspace coordinates that Poe Dameron had already programmed into the *Raddus* but had not been able to execute.

Crait (continued)

▼ **Red Tails** The speeders' stabilizing mono-skis carved through Crait's thin crust of salt, revealing the rhodochrosite soil underneath and sending gaudy crimson plumes skyward in their wakes.

The Resistance managed to power up the former rebel base's shield generator as protection against orbital bombardment. But Supreme Leader Ren ordered a superlaser siege cannon—an experimental weapon salvaged from the *Supremacy*—deployed to burn through the base's armored blast door. A formidable array of AT-M6s and other First Order armor escorted the cannon to defend against a Resistance breakout.

Hopelessly outgunned, the Resistance sent out a desperate plea for help, while crewing the old rebel turrets and trenchworks and scrambling 13 pilots in flimsy ski speeders to try and neutralize the cannon before it came within firing range. Several speeders were ripped apart by devastating fire from the walkers and TIE fighters, and the craft's laser cannons proved unable to sever the tough cables connecting the siege cannon to the AT-HH tugs hauling it across Crait's salt plains. Rey's arrival in the *Millennium Falcon* drew away the escorting TIE fighters, but it

KEY WEAPON: SKI SPEEDER

Ski speeders were no one's weapon of choice: they were civilian sports craft dating back to a brief galactic fad for asteroid slalom, converted by the Rebel Alliance as a last resort. The rickety relics were difficult to control, relying on their ventral mono-skis to ensure they didn't become airborne. Surveying these unlikely craft, a dismayed Dameron called them "B-wings that can't fly."

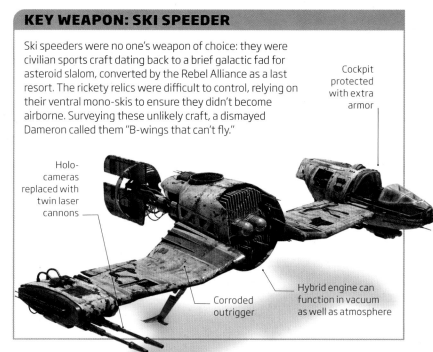

Cockpit protected with extra armor

Holo-cameras replaced with twin laser cannons

Corroded outrigger

Hybrid engine can function in vacuum as well as atmosphere

▲ **An Opportunity Lost** General Hux and Kylo Ren monitored the First Order advance from an *Upsilon*-class shuttle above the line of walkers. But Hux's anticipation turned to frustration when Luke Skywalker entered the fray: Obsessed with his former teacher, Ren broke off the attack on the Resistance to settle an old score.

was not enough. Rather than send his remaining pilots to their doom, Dameron ordered the attack broken off–a command Finn disobeyed, surviving only after Tico smashed her ski speeder into his, knocking him off course. But salvation came from an unlikely source: Luke Skywalker returned to confront Ren and the First Order.

The odds seemed impossible: one man with a lightsaber facing down the entire First Order. But Skywalker's intervention lured Ren into confronting him, buying the Resistance crucial time. Realizing the Jedi was stalling, Dameron led his troops deeper into the caverns in search of a way out. The exit he found was blocked, but Rey used the Force to clear it of debris from the outside. The survivors escaped aboard the *Millennium Falcon*, their numbers so reduced that the freighter could carry all of them. Their cause seemed hopeless, but Organa assured Rey they had everything they needed to prevail. The First Order had failed to extinguish freedom's embers, and Skywalker's last stand would become a rallying cry against tyranny echoing across the galaxy.

▲ **For the Cause** Now fully committed to the cause of the Resistance, Finn refused Dameron's order to break off the attack, braving the fires of the siege cannon's tracer beam in a desperate effort to keep the dreaded weapon from firing.

KEY WEAPON: SUPERLASER

The First Order's siege cannon was miniaturized Death Star technology, a 200-meter-long superlaser able to chew through a planetary mantle. While a devastating addition to the First Order's arsenal, the cannon was still experimental technology: it needed considerable time to recharge, had to be positioned by tug walkers, and was largely defenseless, requiring a large escort to protect it.

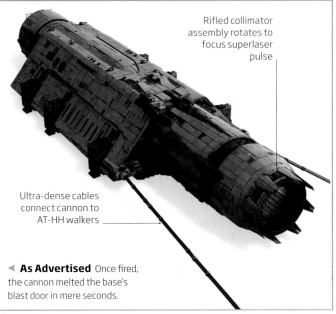

Rifled collimator assembly rotates to focus superlaser pulse

Ultra-dense cables connect cannon to AT-HH walkers

◀ **As Advertised** Once fired, the cannon melted the base's blast door in mere seconds.

Crait: Map

The Crait outpost was first established by Bail Organa and visited by Leia when she was just a teenager. The Alliance began fortifying Crait as a base after the Battle of Yavin, but rejected it after a skirmish there with Imperial forces. Organa chose not to share its location with the New Republic, one of several bases she held back in case they might be needed one day. Crait's defenses included a shield generator, blast doors, and artillery batteries. The shield's activation forced the invading First Order army to deploy beyond the protective perimeter and advance overland to engage the enemy, just as the Empire had done decades earlier on Hoth. But Kylo Ren's forces had something in their arsenal that Darth Vader had lacked—a "battering ram" cannon packing experimental superlaser technology. The Resistance launched rickety ski speeders in a desperate attempt to destroy the cannon before it could be towed into firing range.

IN THE TRENCHES

The Crait base was protected by two lines of trenches dug into the planet's rhodochrosite soil; pathways that connected Spiezoc v-120 and v-232 artillery emplacements left behind by the Alliance. To slow down the First Order advance, Poe Dameron sent crews to the batteries and ground troops into the trenches to thwart a possible advance by snowtroopers and soften up the enemy's line of walkers. But the batteries proved ineffective against the walkers, and Ren kept his infantry in reserve for the final assault, deploying TIE fighters to strafe the trenches and the helpless troops.

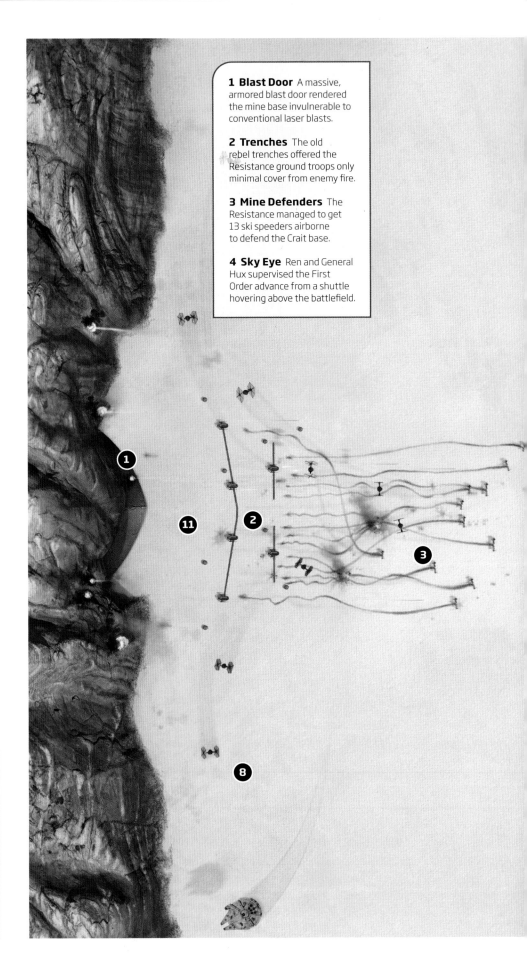

1 **Blast Door** A massive, armored blast door rendered the mine base invulnerable to conventional laser blasts.

2 **Trenches** The old rebel trenches offered the Resistance ground troops only minimal cover from enemy fire.

3 **Mine Defenders** The Resistance managed to get 13 ski speeders airborne to defend the Crait base.

4 **Sky Eye** Ren and General Hux supervised the First Order advance from a shuttle hovering above the battlefield.

▲ **Tough Tech** The Resistance troops found the Spiezoc batteries' controls caked with rhodochrosite and encrusted with salt, but the fire-control systems remained functional despite disuse.

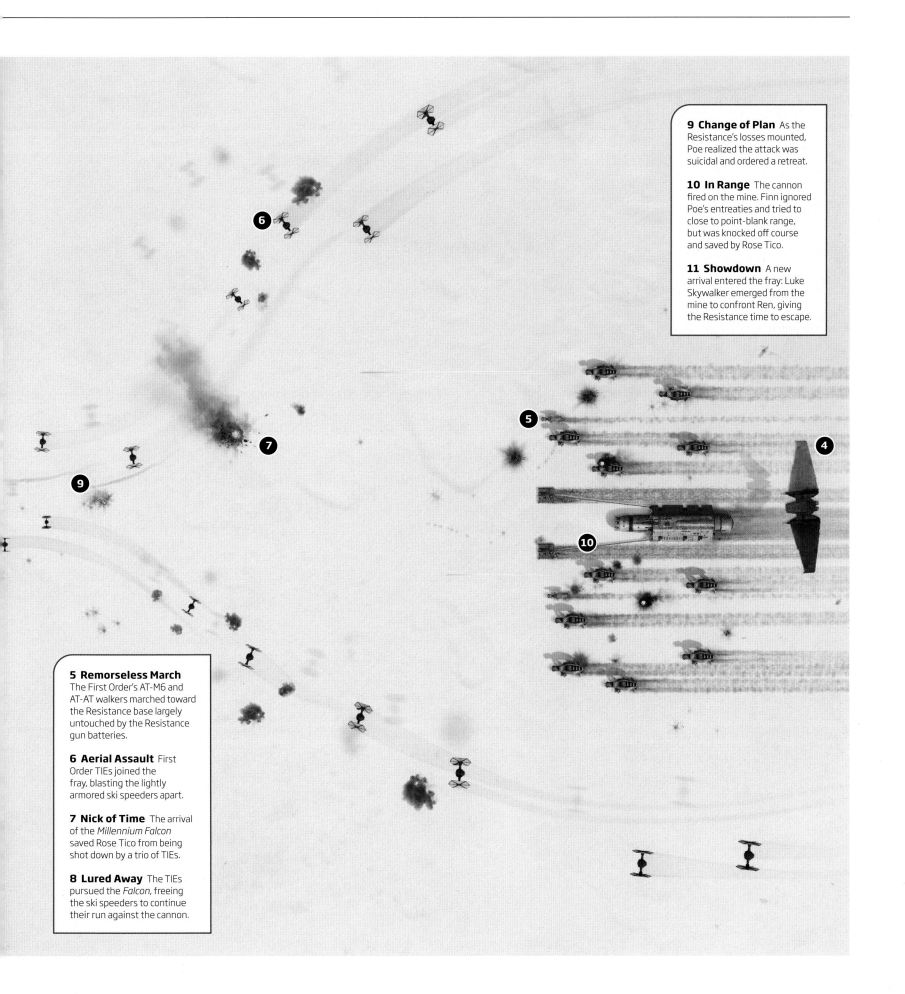

9 Change of Plan As the Resistance's losses mounted, Poe realized the attack was suicidal and ordered a retreat.

10 In Range The cannon fired on the mine. Finn ignored Poe's entreaties and tried to close to point-blank range, but was knocked off course and saved by Rose Tico.

11 Showdown A new arrival entered the fray: Luke Skywalker emerged from the mine to confront Ren, giving the Resistance time to escape.

5 Remorseless March The First Order's AT-M6 and AT-AT walkers marched toward the Resistance base largely untouched by the Resistance gun batteries.

6 Aerial Assault First Order TIEs joined the fray, blasting the lightly armored ski speeders apart.

7 Nick of Time The arrival of the *Millennium Falcon* saved Rose Tico from being shot down by a trio of TIEs.

8 Lured Away The TIEs pursued the *Falcon*, freeing the ski speeders to continue their run against the cannon.

Crait: Decisive Moment

▲ **A Skywalker Reunion** Leia Organa was astonished to see her brother after so many years. When Luke kissed her forehead and pressed Han Solo's dice into her palm, Leia's Force connection with her sibling let her sense the true nature of this most unexpected visitor to Crait.

When Luke Skywalker walked out onto the shattered surface of Crait, Kylo Ren ordered every First Order gun to target him—only to have the smoke clear and reveal his old master unhurt and unruffled. Ren then descended from his shuttle to spar—verbally and physically—with the legendary Jedi Master. It was only at the end, after his saber jabs and thrusts somehow missed, that Ren realized he'd been fooled. His saber's glowing blade passed right through Skywalker, who offered his nephew an at once sad and barbed farewell—"see you around, kid"—and then faded away. Luke had been using an ancient Jedi technique commonly known as Force projection, in which a Force user creates a simulacrum that can see, hear, and interact with others even at a distance of many light-years. For true masters, the illusion is so convincing that droids and mechanical sensors are fooled, other organic beings can touch and be touched by the simulacrum, and conjured objects may remain corporeal for a time.

Force projection was immensely taxing, needing a Force user to pour their essence into the cosmic energy field and surrender completely to it. The effort of maintaining the illusion required all of Luke's strength; when he broke the link with his projection and returned to his body on Ahch-To, he was utterly spent. The Jedi Master lingered for a moment, exhausted, before letting go and becoming one with the Force.

◄ **Thirst for Vengeance** Kylo Ren burned to tear down the galaxy's entire old order: Empire and Republic, Jedi and Sith, and the Skywalker legacy that had been his burden since birth. But his greatest obsession was to cast down Luke Skywalker, the Jedi Master who once stood over a sleeping Ben Solo with an ignited lightsaber in his hand and the terrible knowledge of his apprentice's future in his mind.

▲ **Living Legend** For the officers of the First Order, a lone man in plain and worn robes should have barely registered as a nuisance, let alone a threat. Those aboard the command shuttle wondered why their newly anointed Supreme Leader had grown pale at seeing a slight, older man alone on the battlefield. What could frighten Kylo Ren?

▶ **Blinded by Hate** Undone by his anger at the sight of his old master, Kylo Ren never wondered why Luke seemed scarcely aged since their last, long-ago meeting, or why he carried the blue-bladed lightsaber he'd lost battling Kylo's grandfather, Darth Vader. Those aspects were part of Luke's Force projection, designed to play on his nephew's deepest fears.

Crait (continued)

▲ **Missing Critters** Poe Dameron told the Resistance survivors to follow the vulptices who'd made the Crait base into a den, reasoning they might lead them to an undiscovered exit.

▼ **White as... Salt** The salt coating and crystalline structure of Crait had enough in common with subzero environments–intense surface glare and low skid resistance–that the First Order deployed its snowtrooper forces as infantry.

After escaping Crait, the Resistance gathered their few remaining assets, such as Inferno Squad's agents and Black Squadron's ace pilots. Organa found temporary refuge with Resistance sympathizers on Ryloth, and discovered why her plea from Crait had gone unheeded: the First Order had not only blocked communications but also targeted those who might have responded–former soldiers, pilots, and strategists, old rebels and Imperials alike–assassinating some and imprisoning others.

Organa and Dameron moved swiftly to recruit former Alliance fighters such as Carlist Rieekan, Wedge Antilles, Norra Wexley, and Yendor, as well as ex-Imperials such as Teza Nasz. Inferno Squad's Shriv Suurgav led a mission to Bracca to steal X-wings destined for the smelter, while Dameron and Finn joined a mission to Corellia that freed high-value detainees, bringing them to a safe house on Helmaxa maintained by the anti-authoritarian group known as the Collective. Through patient work the Resistance was reborn over the next year, with Organa's freedom fighters founding a new base on the jungle world Ajan Kloss. No one dreamed that an old enemy had returned from death and was hiding in the Unknown Regions, gathering his forces and plotting his revenge.

▲ **A Useful Skill** On Ahch-To, Master Skywalker scoffed at Rey when she stammered that the Force's uses included lifting rocks. Her time on the ancient Jedi island gave Rey an ecstatic vision of the Force's unity with all things—an entity so much bigger than anything she could have imagined. But on Crait, she found that the simple act of lifting rocks was exactly what the desperate survivors of the siege needed.

CASUALTIES

FIRST ORDER: The First Order's casualties on Crait were minimal: a few TIE pilots killed battling the *Millennium Falcon* in aerial duels. Far more serious was the opportunity lost when the Resistance escaped Kylo Ren's trap.
RESISTANCE: The Resistance hoped to land 400 fighters on Crait to await rescue, a number reflecting losses at D'Qar and Oetchi that it could barely afford. But only a few dozen reached Crait alive, and the survivors of the siege were able to fit aboard the *Falcon* without feeling unduly crowded.

▲ **Starting Over** When Rey saw what the Resistance had been reduced to, her first impulse was despair. But she took heart from the spirit of the survivors.

Barabesh

DATE: 54 AFE ▪ **LOCATION:** BARABESH, OUTER RIM ▪ **COMBATANTS:** FIRST ORDER VS. RESISTANCE ▪ **OUTCOME:** RESISTANCE VICTORY

UNIFIED RESISTANCE

The First Order waged an unrelenting hunt for all pockets of resistance throughout the star systems, remaining steadfast in their mission to crush all who opposed their bid to control the entire galaxy. After the First Order conducted an orbital bombardment of Aeos in retaliation for the population's role in assisting the *Colossus*, the supertanker itself was finally discovered hiding in the Barabesh system.

The *Colossus*, aside from its own defensive armament, was protected by the Resistance pilots of Jade Squadron under the command of Venisa Doza, wife of Captain Imanuel Doza.

They were joined by the station's private starfighter squadron, the Aces, at the controls of high-performance racing fighters. Even a former pirate, Synara San, flew in support of the squadrons in an attempt to defend the station against the overwhelming might of the *Resurgent*-class Star Destroyer *Thunderer*.

The ragtag squadron's first target was the vessel's engines, using ion bombs at close range. The strike initially failed to penetrate the capital ship's shields, but the tables turned when several Resistance operatives held captive by the First Order managed to escape and disarm the ship's defenses from inside.

▼ **False Confidence** The *Thunderer* unleashed its full complement of TIE fighters against the *Colossus* and its Aces. The First Order soon found that the station's reputation as home to some of the galaxy's best pilots was well earned.

This exposed the Star Destroyer to fighter attacks and the *Colossus*' bombardment, which both inflicted significant damage.

The First Order mounted a boarding action on the *Colossus* and quickly overran the defensive positions in the station's hangar, but they faced stiff resistance from the station's inhabitants, who used creative tactics and took advantage of narrow corridors to hold off the assault until the Star Destroyer was defeated. Barabesh was a small battle, but this uprising by a band of misfits foreshadowed the larger conflict ahead for both the First Order and those who would rally together to fight them.

Commanders

CAPTAIN IMANUEL DOZA
Though it endangered their lives, the station's civilian occupants chose to stay for the fight rather than back down from tyranny. As chief officer of the *Colossus*, Doza committed everything his station had to the battle knowing that defeat would bring deadly reprisals to all on board.

**COMMANDER PYRE
(KILLED IN ACTION)**
Pyre's security forces failed to secure key prisoners during the battle, allowing them to sabotage the Star Destroyer. He personally confronted them but was outmaneuvered and subdued. The prisoners escaped but Pyre was killed when the ship exploded.

▲ **Inside Job** A trio of escaped prisoners, Kazuda Xiono, Tamara Ryvora, and Jarek Yeager, infiltrated the Star Destroyer's engineering section and sent a message to the *Colossus*, warning the station of the impending attack and allowing them to prepare hasty defenses.

▶ **Colossal Victory** As Captain Doza looked on from the bridge of the *Colossus*, precision ion bomb strikes against the Star Destroyer's thrusters set off a chain reaction that obliterated the vessel from within, killing all on board.

Military Uniforms

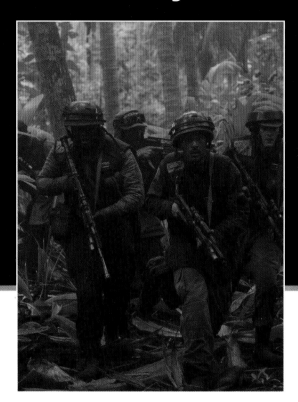

Throughout the Galactic Civil War and the First Order-Resistance War, military uniform styles evolved only slightly on both sides. The Galactic Empire favored homogeneity and crisp lines for its various ranks; their superior resources meant they could allocate more funds to the manufacturing of identical uniforms. The Rebel Alliance, however, had looser regulations for its soldiers. Certain designations, such as pilots, had more consistent appearances, while many ranks donned practical clothing for their specific tasks. The First Order and Resistance later followed these outfitting trends. The stark differences in military uniforms made it simple to identify enemies and fellow soldiers with a quick glance.

IMPERIAL ERA

When Emperor Palpatine reorganized the Galactic Republic into the Galactic Empire, many uniform designs transferred into the new regime. Within a couple of years, the basic cut of Republic uniforms was upgraded to emphasize practical usage and performance. The uniforms of officers and technicians were made from tough gaberwool, with various hues denoting particular roles, while plastoid composite protected stormtroopers and pilots. Specialized accessories could be added to all uniforms to suit different environments and climates. The Rebel Alliance, by way of contrast, formed from loosely connected but still disparate cells, and initially did not have cohesive uniforms for its personnel. When the organization's numbers grew, it formalized basic and functional looks for its soldiers that it could support with limited funds. That evolved into different uniforms for various roles and environments, with the Alliance closely guarding the secret of where its uniforms were manufactured.

GALACTIC EMPIRE

Precise Lines Imperial soldiers of all ranks were responsible for ensuring their uniforms fit properly. Sloppiness or non-conformity were severely punished.

◄ **Technician**

Officer ►

◄ **Pilot**

Infantry ►

REBEL ALLIANCE

Flexible Fit Rebel soldiers made whatever components were available work for their needs. That approach gave the organization a rougher appearance.

◄ **Technician**

Officer ►

◄ **Pilot**

Infantry ►

FIRST ORDER

Modern Adjustments
The First Order optimized Imperial uniforms with more modern modifications. Alterations were rooted in efficiency rather than comfort.

◄ **Technician**

Officer ►

◄ **Pilot**

Infantry ►

RESISTANCE

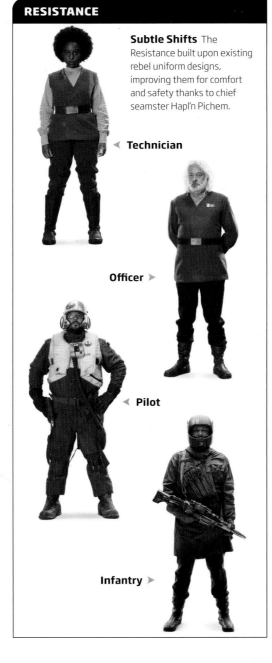

Subtle Shifts The Resistance built upon existing rebel uniform designs, improving them for comfort and safety thanks to chief seamster Hapl'n Pichem.

◄ **Technician**

Officer ►

◄ **Pilot**

Infantry ►

FIRST ORDER ERA

The ideals of the Galactic Empire influenced the First Order in every area, from doctrine, to procedures, to uniforms. As the First Order expanded in the Unknown Regions, the organization gradually increased the manufacturing of uniforms to meet its needs, focusing on how to elevate different aspects to allow soldiers to achieve optimal results. For example, the First Order altered the standard stormtrooper armor with an updated joint design to enhance flexibility, and installed trackers on each set of armor in order to monitor troopers' activities at all times. Uniforms for officers and technicians became more streamlined compared to the Imperial ensembles, and the First Order removed the rank insignia plaques, instead denoting rank with braid cuffs sewn on the left sleeves. The Resistance, operating separately from the New Republic and its financial support, simply repurposed designs from the Rebel Alliance. The uniforms prioritized utility above all else, featuring thick, durable material that could withstand a Resistance soldier's scrappy existence. The Resistance introduced new rank badge designs denoting whether an individual was army or navy personnel.

Exegol

DATE: 54 AFE ▪ **LOCATION:** EXEGOL, UNKNOWN REGIONS ▪
COMBATANTS: FIRST ORDER/SITH ETERNAL VS. RESISTANCE ▪
OUTCOME: DECISIVE RESISTANCE VICTORY

AGAINST ALL ODDS

The Battle of Exegol was the final engagement in a conflict that had divided the galaxy for decades. The return of Emperor Palpatine and the launch of the Final Order fleet by the Sith Eternal threatened to fill the vacuum left by the destruction of the New Republic and, in alliance with the First Order, subjugate the galaxy. Under Supreme Leader Snoke, the First Order had long been contributing to Palpatine's return by siphoning off crew and resources, without even its own military commanders realizing.

The Resistance responded to this new threat with a two-stage plan. All available ships would engage Palpatine's fleet at Exegol to prevent the armada from launching, while General Lando Calrissian took the *Millennium Falcon* to the Core Worlds in a bid to rally reinforcements.

The journey to Exegol was convoluted and dangerous, requiring a flight into the depths of the Unknown Regions, but the Resistance fleet was able to follow a flight path provided to them by the Jedi trainee Rey. The Final Order fleet also faced difficulties ahead of the battle. To deploy into orbit, the closely packed Star Destroyers had to be guided out of Exegol's atmosphere by a navigational signal and could not activate their

▶ **Final Battle** Upon arriving at Exegol the Resistance came face to face with Palpatine's vast fleet. The Resistance fighters used their size to their advantage, threading between the capital ships to nullify their firepower.

Commanders

GENERAL POE DAMERON
After the death of General Organa, Dameron took command of the Resistance military. Firmly trusting that the galaxy would rise up against the Emperor, Dameron led the Resistance forces to Exegol in a bid to delay the Emperor's fleet from deploying. He orchestrated the battle from his X-wing's cockpit.

EMPEROR PALPATINE (KILLED IN ACTION)
The Emperor had always been a superior political strategist, but his overconfidence often forced his military commanders into impossible situations. His determination to lay a trap for Rey and the Resistance meant he delayed the deployment of his fleet, to disastrous effect.

▲ **Dangerous Journey** The route to Exegol was complicated by gravity wells, solar winds, and magnetic crossfields. A wrong turn would be disastrous. The Resistance were only able to make the journey by following the route of the Jedi Rey.

shields until they were clear. If the Resistance could destroy the beacon on the planet's surface, then the fleet would be left helpless.

The sudden arrival of the Resistance triggered the engagement but also highlighted that neither the First Order nor the Sith Eternal had adequately learned the lessons of the Battle of Endor regarding anti-starfighter operations in close-proximity fleet battles. The *Xyston*-class Star Destroyers could only use their ion cannons for fear of hitting each other. Similarly, while there were enough TIE daggers available to crush the Resistance threat, they too were reluctant to overwhelm the opposition in case they damaged the vulnerable capital ships in the process.

As a result the Resistance ships were able to survive the enemy's first defensive barrages, passing between the ranks of Star Destroyers to close in on the planet's navigational beacon.

KEY WEAPON: *XYSTON*-CLASS STAR DESTROYER

The Final Order fleet comprised more than a thousand *Xyston*-class Star Destroyers. Based around the venerable design of the *Imperial I*-class ships of the Galactic Empire, these vessels were slightly larger than their forebears and armed with an axial superlaser capable of destroying entire worlds. A full fighter complement of 72 TIE daggers could also be deployed into battle.

Enhanced communications array

Shield generator dome

Point-defense laser cannons with automated targeting

Red markings of the Sith Eternal

Heavily reinforced hull armor

Superlaser cannon mounted beneath hull

Exegol (continued)

Recognizing the Resistance's plan, Allegiant General Pryde deactivated the planetary navigation beacon in favor of one on his flagship, the *Steadfast*. In response the Resistance altered their plan to stage a landing directly onto the Star Destroyer's hull.

This landing comprised a company of Resistance infantry and defectors from the First Order riding orbaks, led by General Finn and his comrade Jannah. As former stormtroopers, both knew that First Order doctrine, similar to that of the Empire at Endor, would not cope well against such a low-tech approach.

The deployment of Sith troopers onto the *Steadfast*'s upper hull initially countered the Resistance advance, but Resistance fighters were able to strafe the enemy positions, damaging the ship in a manner that made the TIE dagger pilots reluctant to

follow suit. The arrival of the Citizens' Fleet then drew the fighters further away. Despite this the Sith troopers still held a significant numerical advantage over the Resistance, and Sith jet troopers from the Final Order fleet were able to land directly on the *Steadfast*'s hull and join the battle.

General Finn and Jannah were able to bypass the majority of the enemy soldiers and utilized explosives to destroy the beacon. However, realizing that this would only be a temporary reprieve, Finn ordered the Resistance forces to retreat while he and Jannah rewired a nearby laser battery to target the *Steadfast*'s bridge. The resulting attack killed General Pryde and his entire command crew. The ship lost power and began to descend toward Exegol's surface.

▲ **Cavalry Charge** Knowing that the First Order would expect any landing to be speeder based, Finn and Jannah led their attack on orbaks. The confusion caused by this approach bought them valuable time to close on the *Steadfast*'s navigation beacon.

KEY COMBATANT: SITH TROOPERS

The foot soldiers of the Sith Eternal were fanatically loyal to the Sith and the Emperor in particular. As the children of the cultists of Exegol, they had been subjected to flash-imprinting and loyalty conditioning techniques based on Kaminoan cloning. Thus primed for service to the Emperor, they had been trained for combat their entire lives and were devoted to ensuring that Palpatine would reconquer the galaxy. However, their military training was based on ex-Imperial doctrine that had not evolved significantly since Endor and they expected opposition to break and retreat before them. As a result, they were outmaneuvered while fighting on the *Steadfast*'s hull and were eventually defeated.

▶ **Elite Soldiers** Sith troopers had trained all their lives to fight for the resurrected Emperor.

▲ **Counterattack** With Resistance forces deployed onto the hull of the *Steadfast*, Sith jet troopers arrived from the nearby Star Destroyers in an attempt to dislodge them. Armed with heavy blaster cannons, they were a formidable foe.

▲ **Decapitated** Though the *Steadfast*'s navigation beacon was damaged, Finn knew it would not be enough. He and Jannah turned the ship's own weapons upon its command bridge, to devastating effect.

Exegol: Map

The main fighting at Exegol was concentrated in the planet's atmosphere. The Final Order Star Destroyers had previously broken out of the subterranean shipyards where they had been built, smashing through the thin crust of the planet's surface. Now holding in their launch positions, many of the Star Destroyers were directly above the Sith Citadel, while the *Steadfast* held position among them.

The navigational beacon designed to guide the fleet into orbit was located on the surface near the Citadel and this was the initial target of the Resistance fleet, who broke through the lines of Star Destroyers to reach it before doubling back toward the *Steadfast*.

PALPATINE'S FINAL ACT

Palpatine was likely one of the most powerful Force users in history. At the height of the battle, he channeled the dark-side energies of the Sith temple into a Force lightning attack that disabled the Resistance and Citizens' Fleets. With final victory in reach, Palpatine once again allowed himself to be distracted by a Jedi. He broke off his Force attack to engage Rey in combat and the Resistance regrouped.

▲ **Unlimited Power** Palpatine drew deeply on the dark side to unleash a Force lightning attack that paralyzed his enemies in the skies above the Citadel.

1 Launch Damage The Star Destroyers of the Sith Eternal had been constructed in shipyards beneath Exegol's surface. Their launch left huge holes across the planet.

2 Rey's X-wing Arriving before the Resistance fleet, Rey broadcast the route to Exegol to her comrades, then landed her X-wing fighter in order to confront Palpatine.

3 Resistance Fleet Although the Resistance were dwarfed by the Sith Eternal fleet, General Dameron committed his force to battle in the hope that reinforcements would come.

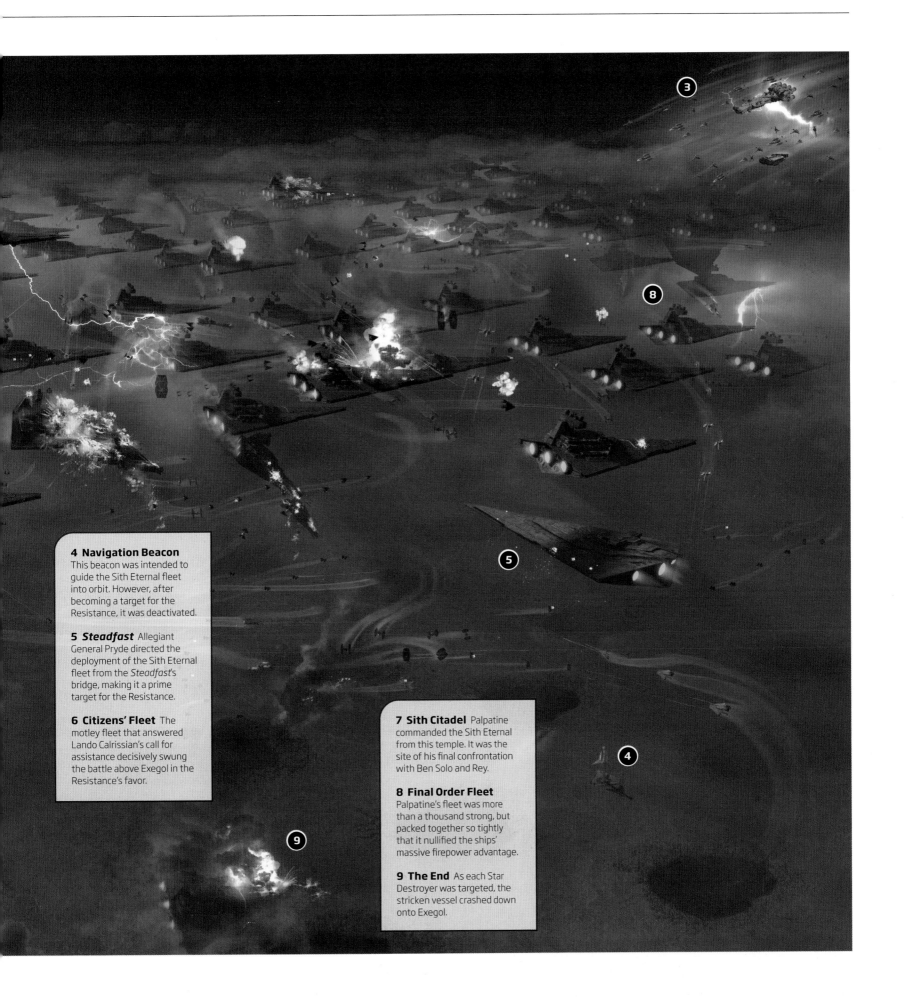

4 Navigation Beacon
This beacon was intended to guide the Sith Eternal fleet into orbit. However, after becoming a target for the Resistance, it was deactivated.

5 *Steadfast* Allegiant General Pryde directed the deployment of the Sith Eternal fleet from the *Steadfast*'s bridge, making it a prime target for the Resistance.

6 Citizens' Fleet The motley fleet that answered Lando Calrissian's call for assistance decisively swung the battle above Exegol in the Resistance's favor.

7 Sith Citadel Palpatine commanded the Sith Eternal from this temple. It was the site of his final confrontation with Ben Solo and Rey.

8 Final Order Fleet Palpatine's fleet was more than a thousand strong, but packed together so tightly that it nullified the ships' massive firepower advantage.

9 The End As each Star Destroyer was targeted, the stricken vessel crashed down onto Exegol.

Exegol: Decisive Moment

Emperor Palpatine had believed that fear and the absence of hope could quell the galaxy into subjugation. Palpatine's broadcast in the lead-up to the Battle of Exegol announcing the "Final Order" had been designed to terrorize people into submission. Not for the first time, he had miscalculated.

The fear of a return to totalitarian rule under the resurrected Emperor acted as a motivator to the people of the galaxy to rise up and secure their freedom. When General Calrissian broadcast a message to the Core Worlds offering them the chance to fight and end Palpatine's tyranny forever, the citizens of the galaxy answered.

The fleet that Calrissian led to Exegol was a highly irregular one. Some people came in single-seater starfighters, others in armed freighters. Some worlds, like Mon Cala,

▲ **Citizens' Fleet** Hearing General Calrissian's call to arms, the people of the galaxy rose for their freedom. A mix of small fighters, freighters, and heavy Mon Calamari capital ships combined into the largest single fleet the galaxy had ever seen.

▼ **Millennium Falcon** General Calrissian's impassioned message to the Core Worlds swung the battle and the war in favor of the Resistance. Having rallied an enormous armada, the *Falcon* was fast enough to lead them all to Exegol.

◀ **Rebel Hero** Wedge Antilles was one of the Rebellion's greatest heroes. He answered Calrissian's call and journeyed to Exegol to fight the Final Order, serving as a gunner on the *Millennium Falcon*–the same ship that had helped him destroy the second Death Star at Endor. Sadly, he arrived too late to save the life of his stepson, Temmin Wexley.

mobilized their heaviest capital ships. On the *Steadfast*, the officers of the First Order were left astounded at the scale of the force that was now arrayed against them. The subsequent destruction of that ship left the Final Order fleet effectively leaderless. For the Resistance, Generals Dameron and Calrissian were able to coordinate their forces to begin destroying enemy capital ships one by one. The smaller vessels fell upon the Final Order's TIEs, who found themselves heavily outnumbered and with little room for maneuver. The fighters and smaller craft passed between Final Order vessels to destroy their superlasers, while the heaviest capital ships opened fire on the Star Destroyers' vulnerable engines.

▼ **Enemy Engaged** The Citizens' Fleet overwhelmed the TIE daggers of the Final Order and began to attack the Star Destroyers. Unable to maneuver, activate their shields, or fire freely, the Final Order fleet was helpless.

Exegol (continued)

▼ **The *Steadfast* Falls** With the bridge of the First Order flagship obliterated and General Pryde dead, the Resistance succeeded in trapping the Final Order fleet at Exegol.

The *Steadfast*'s destruction left the Final Order fleet helpless in the face of thousands of reinforcements from across the galaxy. Under the orders of General Dameron, Resistance fighters targeted the superlaser cannons housed within the Star Destroyers' ventral hangar bays. The first ship the Resistance targeted was the *Sutta*, commanded by Captain Strok. The damage done to the superlaser tore that ship apart. Flying alongside General Dameron, the smuggler Zorii Bliss transmitted targeting data to the rest of the Citizens' Fleet who began to attack other Star Destroyers.

Coordination within the Final Order fleet began to completely break down. Without the guiding oversight of the *Steadfast* the fleet could not deploy, and instead of joining forces individual ships began recalling their fighters to protect themselves.

▲ **Vulnerability** The Star Destroyers' superlasers were tied to the ships' reactors. Destroying one destroyed them both.

Within the Sith Citadel, Palpatine channeled Force lightning into the atmosphere to disable the Citizens' Fleet, almost robbing it of victory at the last moment, but could not maintain the effort while also fighting the Jedi Rey. By concentrating his efforts on her he granted his enemies a reprieve. His subsequent death in combat with Rey destroyed the Sith Citadel.

DEATH OF THE EMPEROR

The Emperor had planned and prepared for immortality through the powers of the dark side. Having lured his granddaughter Rey to Exegol he initially intended to transfer his spirit into her body. Instead, the Force connection between Rey and Ben Solo restored him to his former glory. But for all his power the Emperor was consistently arrogant and over-confident. Split between crushing the Resistance and destroying Rey he achieved neither. She reflected his own Force lightning back upon him and he could not withstand the power he had unleashed upon himself. The resulting blast destroyed his body and spirit.

◀ **Final Justice** The Emperor never wavered from his faith in the dark side of the Force, right up until the moment it destroyed him.

Exegol (continued)

With Palpatine dead the Resistance could not be stopped. The Final Order fleet fell into disarray as the Resistance systematically destroyed each Star Destroyer. As the fleet's numbers thinned the crews of the remaining vessels began to abandon ship rather than face inevitable death aboard their doomed warships.

Disabled Star Destroyers fell from the sky, crashing into Exegol. Many pierced the surface completely, causing irreparable damage to the vast subterranean infrastructure that had previously been used by the Sith Eternal to build the fleet. The damage that Palpatine's demise inflicted on the Sith Citadel meant that the dark-side energies within it no longer disrupted Exegol's atmosphere. The clouds began to part and for the first time in centuries the sun shone on the world.

CASUALTIES

RESISTANCE: Many of the Resistance's best pilots died at Exegol before reinforcements arrived. Among them was Temmin "Snap" Wexley, who was swarmed by TIE daggers and shot down.
SITH ETERNAL: The resurrected Emperor Palpatine and the entirety of the Sith Eternal cult were wiped out in the battle. Alongside them, General Pryde and the crew of the *Steadfast* all perished.

▶ **Heavy Blow** The death of "Snap" Wexley was a morale-sapping blow for the rest of the Resistance.

▲ **Fallen Order** The dying Star Destroyers of the Final Order fleet crashed onto the surface of Exegol. While far more isolated than Jakku, it remained to be seen whether Exegol would similarly attract those seeking wealth or Sith mysteries among the wreckage.

▲ **Resistance Triumphant** Returning to Ajan Kloss the victorious pilots of the Resistance celebrated, but also grieved for their fallen friends.

As the battle began to wind down, word reached the Resistance that ships across the galaxy had also begun to launch attacks on First Order Star Destroyers and positions. Robbed of their leadership or reinforcements, these First Order vessels were isolated and easy prey to determined attack.

Upon arriving back at their base on Ajan Kloss, it was clear to the Resistance that revolution had begun across the galaxy. Much as had been the case with the Empire at the end of the Galactic Civil War, the last vestiges of the First Order would take time to hunt down and destroy. But once again hope had proven a far more powerful weapon than fear or oppression.

EVENTS IN THE REST OF THE GALAXY

While hearing the call to arms from General Calrissian, not every willing ship could get to Exegol in time. Instead, many of the galaxy's citizens began to revolt against the First Order forces subjugating their worlds. Lacking any coherent orders these First Order capital ships were left vulnerable against forces who would no longer be oppressed. As the Sith Eternal fell on Exegol so too did the armada of the First Order across the galaxy.

▲ **Holdo Maneuver** Above the Forest Moon of Endor a *Resurgent*-class Star Destroyer was split in two by a heavy freighter entering hyperspace on a collision course.

Index

Page numbers in **bold** refer to main entries

Index continued

Penguin Random House

SENIOR EDITOR David Fentiman
PROJECT ART EDITOR Jon Hall
PRODUCTION EDITOR Marc Staples
SENIOR PRODUCTION CONTROLLER Mary Slater
MANAGING EDITOR Sarah Harland
MANAGING ART EDITOR Vicky Short
PUBLISHING DIRECTOR Mark Searle

DESIGNED BY Robert Perry
MAP ARTWORKS BY Richard Chasemore

FOR LUCASFILM
SENIOR EDITOR Brett Rector
CREATIVE DIRECTOR OF PUBLISHING Michael Siglain
ART DIRECTOR Troy Alders
ART DEPARTMENT Phil Szostak
STORY GROUP Leland Chee, Pablo Hidalgo, Matt Martin,
Emily Shkoukani, and James Waugh
ASSET MANAGEMENT Chris Argyropoulos, Jackey Cabrera,
Gabrielle Levenson, Bryce Pinkos, Erik Sanchez, Jason Schultz,
and Sarah Williams

First American Edition, 2021
Published in the United States by DK Publishing
1450 Broadway, Suite 801, New York, NY 10018

Page design copyright © 2021 Dorling Kindersley Limited
DK, a Division of Penguin Random House LLC
21 22 23 24 25 10 9 8 7 6 5 4 3 2 1
001–317007–Oct/2021

© & TM 2021 Lucasfilm LTD.

ACKNOWLEDGMENTS

DK Publishing: We would like to thank Chelsea Alon at Disney;
Brett Rector, Robert Simpson, Michael Siglain, and Troy Alders
at Lucasfilm; Julia March for proofreading; and Vanessa Bird
for the index.

Lucasfilm Publishing: We would like to thank Amanda Gonzalez
and Riley O'Keefe at Lucasfilm Games; Kate Izquierdo
at Lucasfilm; Joseph Hochstein at Marvel Comics;
Jonathan Wilkins at Titan.

This paper is made from
Forest Stewardship Council™
certified paper—one small
step in DK's commitment to
a sustainable future.